Cinema and Evil

Cinema and Evil:
Moral Complexities and the "Dangerous" Film

By

Dara Waldron

**CAMBRIDGE
SCHOLARS**

P U B L I S H I N G

Cinema and Evil: Moral Complexities and the "Dangerous" Film,
by Dara Waldron

This book first published 2013

Cambridge Scholars Publishing

12 Back Chapman Street, Newcastle upon Tyne, NE6 2XX, UK

British Library Cataloguing in Publication Data
A catalogue record for this book is available from the British Library

ISBN (10): 1-4438-4342-3, ISBN (13): 978-1-4438-4342-3

For Ylva, Anton and Karl.

TABLE OF CONTENTS

ACKNOWLEDGEMENTS

It is difficult to begin an acknowedgements when so many people have been of support. I extend a particular word of thanks to Professor Keith Reader for the criticism that helped, in many ways, shape the book as it currently stands. Constructive criticism can be, as I have learned, the bread of life. My publishers, *Cambridge Scholars Publishing*, have allowed me time to get on with things, yet have offered crucial support when needed. Soucin Yip-Sou has been instrumental in bringing the finer–often most pertinent–elements together. I would also like to thank Karina Gechtman-Harroch at *Independent Film Company* for the ultra-professionalism she showed in all our dealings. I am particularly grateful to Lynne Ramsay and Nicole Rivelli. Not only did they supply great images to work with but responded in kind to my interest and research concerns with haste. It's refreshing to know that those working within the industry at such a high level maintain such close control over their work.

I extend thanks to my father John, for the years of support and encouragement. My mother Mary has been immense through waves of worry and struggle. That she once sat up all night compiling a bibliography of mine, from fragments and notes, is a testament to the debt I owe. My sister Kate has been at the coldface of the proofing process, offering much needed comments. To have someone to talk about what I talk about with was a real bonus. My sister Sheila and brother-in-law Alberto have been partners in crime; without whom something very different would have emerged. The nights in Donnybrook with Conal and Sue (and the raucous yet inspiring 'debates' with Anto) were breaks from the silent stare of the computer; cogs in the machinery of what you now hold. My Uncle Tony and Aunt Lye came to my rescue at a time in my life when I really needed it, helping generate the belief to persevere in what I do. I now have an official platform on which to say 'thank you.' My friends and family in Sweden, who gave me sanctuary over the years, when ideas for this book silently and not so silently surfaced, deserve their own special recognition: Steffan, Eva, Malin, Kerstin, Mattias, Göran, Magnus, Karen, Joakim and Anna-Lena: tack så mycket!

Many of the colleagues I have had the pleasure of working with have contributed immensely. Brian Coates has been an immeasurable friend and support since I arrived in Limerick, an intellectual father figure to so many young aspiring academics. I extend gratitude to Brian and his wife, Eileen. Mícheál O'Haodha helped me to believe in the project again, and I extend a particular note of gratitude his way. In addition, Andrew O'Shea, Jack Anderson and Rashmi Sawhney were the main beacons of support during the postgrad years, when the wheels of production were set in motion; a time remembered with fondness. I have been fortunate enough to have Michael Kelly to discuss the stages in getting a book to where it is at now, and Michael's generosity has been very much appreciated. I also want to thank my colleagues in LSAD, in particular Martin Healy and Kieran Cashell. In addition, thanks to the LSAD library staff for their help in sourcing films and texts. Finally, and no less importantly, Séan Molloy and Bob Lacey unknowingly helped me rediscover 'where I was at.' I returned from a weekly sojourn in Lublin–heavy on 'craic'–with the newfound confidence to write this book. I dedicate what I have written, however, to my partner Ylva, and our children, Anton and Karl. Ylva's support for what I do has been unquantifiable; I invest this 'thank you' with all my love.

This was his world, he said to himself, the sad, oppressive world that God had provided for him, and he was responsible to it,
—Gabriel García Márquez, *Love in the Time of Cholera.*

INTRODUCTION

"To articulate the past historically does not mean to recognise it 'the way it really was' (Ranke). It means to seize hold of a memory as it flashes up at the moment of danger…the danger affects both the content of the tradition and its receivers,"
—Walter Benjamin, *Theses on the Philosophy of History*.

When the words 'film' and 'evil' appear together, opinion is forthcoming. Such is the appeal of film and the understanding of 'evil.' Asked to consider the instrinsic bond between evil and film, even the most indifferent will declare 'Hitchcock,' 'The Omen,' 'Lord of the Rings,' or something of the sort. This kind of spontaneous reaction, no doubt, is testimony to the fact that, to paraphrase Ernesto Laclau's thoughts on democracy, evil is a floating signifier (Laclau in Docherty (ed): 1993; 242). Everybody has his or her tuppence to offer, and so worth devalues. In Laclau's terms, signifiers float. But they float when attachment to a signified ceases. And so, because any attempt to account for what evil actually signifies within certain fields is a complex endeavour, this study is an attempt to assess this endeavour as it pertains to film. Or more precisely, evil–that oldest of moral problems–and its filmic treatment.

The reasons are many for undertaking this. The project developed–and the name testifies to this–from a curious fascination with *Literature and Evil* (1973), a book by French theoretician and general *enfant terrible* Georges Bataille. Bataille's Evil takes its cue from canonical texts (canonised for rather different reasons), and the critical evaluation of these, but the very fact that Evil is underscored with a big 'E' gives a rather salubrious significance to it; somewhat out of kilter with what I, with a Catholic education like Bataille, believed it to be. Bataille's undertaking is as subtle as it is hard-edged. Each chapter focuses on a writer; each is a close reading of a text. Critical assessment of de Sade and the Brontës, to name but a few of the writers sourced in the text, is outrageously *straightforward* in its method. In today's academic climate, Evil, which can act as a byword for many things, can seem outmoded when evaluating actions. If it has a literary mystique it has a similar one in film. For if a lack of research on literature's evil is striking, it is more so in film. Characters like Neff (Fred McMurray) in Billy Wilder's masterpiece *Double Indemnity* (Wilder, 1942), or for that matter, Hannibal Lector (Antony Hopkins) in *The Silence of the Lambs* (Demme, 1991), capture the ethical imagination either because they are evil or because they are caught in its spell. Neff is a victim of evil, Lector a likeable cannibal.

Having envisaged a not dissimilar study of film and its curious use of evil, for it to grow wings, selection was needed. Yet because selection is an exercise in taste, and taste is an aesthetic process, the project needed to be developed in a way similar to that of Bataille. I felt compelled to look at canonical filmmakers who made what I (somewhat loosely) call 'dangerous' films (which we come to shortly). I had an intuition that these artists would benefit from an exploration of evil, when considered as not solely the preserve of the auteur (as each filmmaker discussed in the book can be referred to in this way) who deals with morally contentious issues, but the preserve of films in which morally contentious issues are intrinsically dangerous in *affect*.

The question then is why choose certain films above others. Why choose one film and indeed the films of one filmmaker over another? The answer is threefold. Firstly, my interest lay in the problematic treatment of evil in film, something filmmakers addressed in this capacity. Because there is a distinct difference between evil understood in the common vernacular, and evil as it is understood as an ethical problem, the research kept coming back to films that responded to evil as problematic. For example, Steven Spielberg's *Schindler's List* (1993) is an intriguing response to the evil of the Holocaust. However, I didn't intuit it a film dangerous as I come to designate the 'dangerous' film theoretically (more of this to come later). Oliver C. Speck echoes my feelings here. Speck believes that *Schindler's List* addresses a viewer with no ethical stake in viewing the film, given that it, "represents the Holocaust (the term is in itself a representation) as an abstract event of a confrontation of good and evil, as well as something that is safely sealed away in the past" (Speck: 2010; 12). Spielberg's *Minority Report* (2002) is more expedient; if, that is, the crime in the film bore more directly on the problem of evil; the ethical rather than metaphysical in such a high-octane thriller. Secondly, and personally, my interest in the filmic treatment of evil is an interest in film methods used to confront evil.

Hence, an analysis of certain innovative strategies, used to engage the topic of evil as a problem, is at the forefront of the films discussed in the book. It is for this reason that the book spans a century of filmmaking, with many genres and styles. As the century expands, the filmmaking process takes new directions. Whether the ethical import of the long take used by Van Sant, or the close-up used by Pasolini to dangerously engage the spectator, filmic strategies are used to engage the longstanding problem of evil. It is for this reason Fernando Meirelles's *Cidade de Deus* (City of God (2002)), which, because it makes reference to St. Augustine's famous text, would seem ready-made for such a study, (particularly as it deals with evil in children), didn't make the cut. It is not that Meirelles's film isn't a film about evil. It's rather that, as a formal exercise, it didn't fit the constraints of the dangerous film, as it would come to be elucidated in the book.

Thirdly, the films discussed in this book, albeit, significantly different, have been controversial. Many have been banned. In many cases, the filmic confrontation with evil, and the investigation into its problematic nature has been deemed too unsavoury for public consumption. A number of the films' subject matter have had an equally unsavoury impact on the public register–films dealing with the Moors Murders and the Columbine Massacre are just two examples–by using film to consider the ethical implications of such events. The Dardenne Brothers' *Le fils* (The Son (2002)), discussed at intervals in this book, is an example. The Brothers state that the film responds to the death of James Bulger. Explored in much greater depth in later chapters, suffice to say that in form and content *Le fils* raises significant concerns about how we should respond to evil. The use of handheld cameras realistically framing the action, making us feel as if we are following a real event, accompanies a simple plot about a man who meets his child's child killer. That children have the capacity for evil, perhaps the moral issue of concern in the film, is important. But the decision to tackle such raw subject matter, as well as the way this subject matter is tackled is fascinating. The film comments–formally *and* morally–on evil.

Filmic modes of inquiry need assessment, in conjunction with evil as a concept used to address both form and content. I chose to limit the study of evil required for such an assessment to that bequeathed (to us) from Christianity onwards, beginning with St. Augustine. I took this decision in the knowledge that–in the main–Augustine saw evil as a problem; not necessarily that which could be resolved but one to be responded to. As I was interested in how, like Augustine, filmmakers responded to evil, I turned to Augustine as my first port of call. In order to explore the response given by various filmmakers, it was necessary to unpack evil as a concept first.

The institutionalisation of religion in the West gathered force from Augustine onwards, with the influence of his writings looming over the topic of evil since. Evil, as Rowlands states in *The Philosopher at the End of the Universe* (2005),

> "Was appropriated by the Roman neoplatonist Plotinus (*c.* AD 204-270), and then worked its way down to a guy called Augustine–St Augustine of Hippo (AD 354-430). And Augustine incorporated the idea of a non-physical reality into Christian metaphysics. Everything after can be read as a response to Augustine" (Rowlands: 2005; 220).

Rowlands is correct about the unique contribution Augustine made to the problem of evil. Equally, as Mark Larrimore states in *The Problem of Evil: A Reader,*

> "While experiences of pain, guilt, loss, disappointment, disharmony and senselessness are surely among those experiences all religions help people face, seeing these as constituting a single "problem of evil" is the historical exception. Even in the West, engagement with a single "problem of evil" is intermittent at best. Understanding the "problem of evil" as primarily philosophical–a problem for thought–is rarer yet" (Larrimore (ed): 2001; xviii).

Larrimore emphasises the key concepts which come to contribute to an emerging problematic. Evil is confronted as a problem, one which is most specifically rendered from Augustine onwards. The first chapter traces this in anchor points, around concepts such as the moral and responsibility. It then reads these points through the lens of significant *cultural loci*: the Cathars, Milton, etc. as those influenced by the looming shadow of the Bishop. From this, two methodological strains–somewhat antithetical–come together as the methodology of the book. The first is the struggle with evil in Augustine. Subjects such as the Law, desire, language, excess, and the will are central to this discussion. These are subject areas pioneered in a huge outlay of texts; over a significant period of time. Those influenced by these texts constitute the second methodological strain; Augustine's legacy found in commentaries by Aquinas *et al* as well as considerably less orthodox subject areas. The first chapter begins with these.

The second strain includes the widening exposition of ethics in Lacanian psychoanalysis; in particular the way in which the ethical writings of Lacan–friend and colleague of Bataille–bear on the concept of evil. It also addresses the relationship between Kant and Lacan. Many recent Lacanian scholars, from the Slovenian school spearheaded by the mercurial Slavoj Žižek, to Joan Copjec stateside, have been instrumental in developing Lacanian ethics in the context of the philosophical tradition. While I draw on these thinkers in various instances, particularly in relation to Augustine and his consideration of evil, the contentious, indeed rather absurd claim–in this way inverting cause and effect–that Augustine is the first Lacanian is made, such is the emphasis on the Law in Augustine as it works itself out in Lacan. Of course, this is a wild assertion. It has little 'logical' sense. But given the terrain on which each theoretical work is deployed, and the insignificant differences, there is a sense that evil as a problem is to be confronted in each precise case and in each case precisely.

For Augustine, "reason looks for the truth as it is revealed to enlightened intelligence: desire has an eye for what allures by the promise of sensual enjoyment" (Augustine: 1984; 447). Now for Lacan, reason and desire interests the ethicist in relation to evil. For while Law is rational, based on communal needs and wants, its underside may well be the desire it solicits to transgress. And Augustine knew this only too well. Known to enjoy his 'sin' too much, here is a serial transgressor all too aware of the paradoxes of the Law; that is, attempts to abolish evil having the adverse affect, soliciting desire to transgress. Hence with its quasi-repressive capacity to solicit the desire it appears to relinquish, the Law assumes a dark invasive side for Lacan. To trangress, when considered as crossing the Law itself, is paradoxically considered an effect of the Law. Indeed, the great defender of the Law, and possibly the most influential modern philosopher on evil, Immanuel Kant, is the target at whom both Lacan and Augustine (*sic*) point their arrows. For Kant, the *quo sin non* of modern ethics, has a distinction worth noting: it dispenses with God as origin. There is no G-O-D, big Other of concern, when Kant is on the scene.

Bearing this in mind, and the first chapter is an attempt to bring these strains together as *a* methodology, clarity is needed. Emphasis on the will, as I argue, follows a trajectory from Augustine to Aquinas to Kant. While Kant rejects natural inclinations as the source of evil, he nonetheless engages evil in its precise relation to volition. For Kant, as typically enlightened philosopher, the idea that man is predisposed to evil is–of course–misguided. Man is responsible for choosing good and evil maxims. As Kant matures, as I also discuss, he distinguishes between good and evil maxims as the 'two extremes' of human volition. Delving into this distinction coincides with the later realisation that evil maxims can *appear* otherwise: appear as the moral law. What appears good, the law and the rights it upholds, is evil.

That we are morally predisposed, or hardwired to do good, in Kantian ethics, is, of course, a fallacy. It is rather that we choose between good or evil maxims. Now, with *radical evil*, a major concept in Kant's later thought, an altogether more disturbing evil is taken to task. If the will had been given priority in choosing good or evil maxims, Kant now deliberates on evil, referred to as *radical evil*, which corrupts the will itself. The sensuousness, or the 'self-love' involved in early ideas of wickedness, as discussed by Augustine, is replaced; in this case by an evil which takes the appearance of good. Hence Kantian 'duty' is utterly corrupted by it. For this reason a key consideration is *radical evil*.

The infamous Eichmann case, which I discuss in relation to *radical evil* in this first chapter and also throughout this book, refers first of all to the crimes of Adolf Eichmann. Eichmann was a high-profile Nazi involved in the higher ranks of the organisation. He played an integral role in the genocidal Nazi regime; signing off on the death of millions. Yet the Eichmann trial, which took place in Israel in the 1960s, is morally significant also in relation to the significant commentaries around it; and indeed, most famously by the great Jewish German émigré philosopher Hannah Arendt. Arendt, a survivor of the Nazi regime and its terrors, and one of the great writers on totalitarianism (as 20th century problem), reported on the trial for an American newspaper. Her reference to the 'banality of evil' regarding Eichmann's behaviour led to her being ostracised and attacked from Jewish-American circles on return; accused of betraying her people. Arendt was accused of downplaying the monstrosity of evil. Arendt never denied Eichmann was responsible for the death of millions, yet she did confront his perception of himself as an 'army man,' doing 'the duty' required of him. If an example of an utterly corrupted will was needed, in a man believing the evil he chose a manifestation of its opposite, this was it. For Arendt, Eichmann commited the most horrendous evil while "conscience free."

The important point, and this is pertinent to the following discussion, is not that Eichmann was a robot-army man, unable to stand up to his superiors, but that the law had corrupted the will which enabled him to so readily choose evil, while at the same equating the law with good. Although we will return to this discussion in Chapter One, Richard Bernstein's following analysis helps consider the difficulty involved,

> "Ever since Kant used the expression "radical evil" (*radikal Böse*) in *Die Religion inerhalb der Grenzen der blossen Vernuft*, it has been a source of fascination, because it has struck many of his readers (including Arendt) that Kant was dimly aware of the type of evil that exceeds our traditional concepts of evil; perplexity, because it is not clear precisely what Kant means by "radical evil," or how it fits (or does not) with his moral philosophy" (Bernstein: 2002; 12).

Bernstein points to the difficulties of Kantian morality in its later guise; the fact that Kant's mature thought hints at, if not nessarily outlines, the radical nature of certain types of evil. *Radical evil* is not easily unpacked. Recent studies–the specifics of which are considered in the first and final chapter of the book (in an analysis of Michael Haneke's *Das weisse Band* (The White Ribbon (2009))–have been precise in their consideration of *radical evil*, particularly in the aftermath of Eichmann and the Holocaust, and this discussion is central to the methodological strains of the book. Key researchers, Joan Copjec, Peter Dew and Marcus G. Singer, have been instrumental in resurrecting *radical evil* (as versing a radical form of evil) as a problem; helping form the methodology as such. In Kant, the type of evil that dominates the twentieth century is found, and this is central to the methodology developed here.

But, of course, it would be wrong to say that the modern debate ends here. For in recent years the will to violate and 'dehumanise,' once the preserve of philosophy and theology, has been rethought in criminal psychopathology. This is a huge area, and is touched upon at various points. Suffice it to say, research around 'personality' types has gathered momentum in recent years and has many overlaps with the main points of discussion. If an Augustinian-Lacanian axis is forged in the first chapter of this book, viewing the subject as moral agent, while also looking at evil within a wider structural field of motivations, concepts used to explain evil are of particular benefit for behavioural studies. Autonomy is one concern. But so too is the denigration of ""humanistic" philosophy and psychology that treat man as an actor who wills his action and instead sees man as a submitting object of processes that transcend him" (Turkle: 1979; 49-50). That which escapes autonomy as the limit of rational approbation is explored in the first chapter; but this is not to say the will and its bearing on 'personality' or character isn't also at the heart of the discussion.

From this a third methodological strain (one which may well have arisen against the grain of authorial intent) emerges, from which psychopathology, a focal point of films about evil, is brought to bear. As much as we might like to avoid thinking evildoers (as personalities) are naturally formed, neurologically impelled to hurt and dehumanise others, recent studies have returned to 'evil' when faced with this possibility. Linking these studies to earlier writings on evil is of interest. If the following book aims at bringing diverse strains of criticism to bear on evil and cinema, using tools that have had little academic focus, it is in the hope future research will develop these tools. For as much as evil has changed in focus over time, so too has the means for studying it.

If these diverse strains form an eclectic methodology, this is an added bonus. For we live in an age when eclecticism is something we are able to practice. But the main reason I advocate this eclecticism in this book (beginning in the first chapter) is to engage film around moral concerns about a truly global issue: evil. This, I believe is important. For now more than ever, globalisation has changed the dynamic of how we think. Now, more than ever, film needs to be explored outside of national boundaries.

So, having examined evil without any clear application of the methodological framework to wide-ranging case studies in this (first) chapter, the following book may appear strange in its outlay. As reference to film is minimal in the early stages of the text a degree of explanation is needed. Suffice it to say that the dominant Film Studies approach is one I tried to minimise. Why? Well, for one I felt it was necessary to explore evil and its related concepts before immediately channelling them into some kind of 'dangerous' textual expression. For the study of film is a complex negotiation of the verbal and visual, a multi-sensory form of visual art and media, and its content is often the exposition of a particular text. But because evil is complex as a text in itself, well worn as a concept, I felt it necessary to immerse ourselves in its terrain. I felt it important to work through the concept, before seeking to understand its treatment in ethical terms. As Marcus G. Singer notes, the research around extreme evil–outside the domain of theological debate–is relatively thin (Singer: 2004). Therefore, the first part of the study is spent addressing the legacy of the concept.

From Lang to Haneke: the 'Dangerous' Film

Following the theoretical exploration of evil, the genealogy of evil, film can be explored with the tools necessary for engaging with it. Research in present day Film Studies is largely made up of three formats. The first is the monographic study. In this approach a line of development (around a series of concerns) is traced in the work of a particular director. More often than not, the chosen filmic subject is canonised or in the process of canonisation. The 'progress' or high points in a burgeoning career are assessed in this type of analysis; thematic and formal features in variable forms of filmic representation. One could point to many monographs around filmmakers such as Orson Welles as an example; some invariably more challenging than others. A second approach diverges from this method, turning to the director as a subject whose films express the concerns of a particular nation state. The way in which films constitute a National Cinema is the issue; hence concerns with the nation state, the ethico-political community, self/other or other theoretical concepts dominate. Even today, National Cinematic studies remains attractive to the cynically-attuned critic; bent, not just on canonising the directorial celebrity, but on elevating certain films–irrespective of who produced them–to the status of National Cinema.

Thirdly then is the theoretical study. With emphasis given to genre, gender, politics etc., a particular theoretical impetus is explored. But the concept is rarely just ethical. What is bad, immoral or simply evil is rarely broached in film *per se*. Perhaps this book will instigate change. That these fields include many of the most significant ways of researching film means exceptions are not uncommon; even if Film Studies texts whose line of inquiry lies outside these fields are rare. Genre criticism, so important to understanding film, has–to many extents and purposes–stagnated. The study of morality in film has been restricted to those looking at film as a text, working out moral problems on a narrative level, to those who analyse film as itself constitutive of the moral life. While, "the workings of the ethical environment in which we live can be strangely invisible, so too can the workings of cinema" (Wheatley: 2009; 3). For some, the functional use of cinema is itself ripe for moral analysis.

In an interview about his 1994 film, *Benny's Video,* the Austrian director Michael Haneke made reference to 'dangerous fiction.' He used the term 'dangerous' as a descriptor for narrative texts. In the standard, 'dangerous' film, spectators are 'masters of the situation.' The audience confronts 'danger' in the knowledge that they don't have to deal with its consequences. Film is like a carnival ride: danger is a precursor to the relief on escaping it. However, the concept of danger raises other issues. What if danger makes us feel anything but masters of the situation? And instead of feeling removed and therefore above the situation, our immersion makes our moral evaluation all the more necessary. Haneke's comment is therefore a cue, one necessary for examining reproachable moral themes (such as murder, insanity, sexual transgression as well as child homicide) that have been versed in the filmic capacity to unsettle. Indeed, the paedophiliac murderer in Fritz Lang's *M* (Lang, 1931), discussed in the second chapter, serves as a prod from which a discourse on evil can then emerge, the point of which is to instigate a confrontation in us with good and evil; particularly when 'evil' is presented as anything but one-dimensional. Indeed danger sets this challenge for us. In one sense, a spell is cast over the soon to be christened talkie: the problem of evil. In another the murderer–Beckert (Peter Lorre)–can be confronted as a *victim* of evil. If the ethico-scientific, and indeed legally sanctioned injunction against looking at the human subject as evil is dangerous, *M* is an important place to begin.

That humanistic and anti-humanistic approaches yield equally satisfying results makes *M* an interesting film. Applying a strictly anti-humanistic model enhances the powerful aesthetic elements of the film, as they bring forth the central ethical problem; consisting of the intentional murder of children. But this problem extends to the issue of whether an answer can be found in the confessional plea given by this murderer, as passionately delivered by the man himself? If not, is there something beyond Beckert we should look for, something of 'darkness' battling 'light' that had so entranced the makers of expressionist film, which impacts upon him now? And if so, should we look to the silences instrinsic to psychology to come to an understanding of what is meant by something 'beyond,' 'outside' and so on?

In one sense, it might well be common currency to think of killing as the most derisory act imaginable, certainly of an evil expressed in the wilful destruction of the other as other. And in such murder clear agency exists. Indeed, Beckert is a deviant and manipulative killer. In another sense, Beckert says he doesn't want to kill, doesn't murder children because he wills it. Rather, he says that something other to him motivates him to perform the act in question. Whether this 'something' other, from the perspective of humanist philosophies, is a 'personality:' a disposition of the subject in question; or, alternatively, a force impacting on the will like some kind of infectious plague is central to the film. Much of the aesthetic qualities of noir (to which we then turn), I argue, consist of amplifying this central ethical problematic.

Of course, *M* is important in other ways. It is, for the large part, a film noir before film noir; a classic serial killer film before serial killer films; a film about evil before Evil. That it is frequently cited as the greatest German film of all time is testament to its danger. Danger lies in dwelling on child murder, against the backdrop of a perpetrator feeling an evil is forcing its will upon him. Hence evil–remembering the film was released in post-Weimar Germany–may well be cosmically destined to infect those unable to withstand its measures. Claiming that the most brutal criminals deserve to be heard, the film maintains a remarkably modern stance, subtly dangerous. For in *M,* as Andrew Spicer claims,

> "Franz Beckert (Peter Lorre) is a tortured outsider caught between rival forces of police and organised crime. Beckert is painfully aware of his condition, that the desires that dictate his actions are beyond his rational control" (Spicer: 2002: 12).

What Kaes inadvertently celebrates is the film's deliberation on evil. He can therefore ask, "why this fascination, this obsession with carnage, murder and mayhem?" before offering the following response,

> "Lang's *M* is implicated in these current questions but responds to them by suggesting through its very form that something else entirely might be negotiated through these films–something that has to do with our lives, our communities, our cultures" (Kaes: 2008; 8).

Kaes is referring to something that transcends culture: Evil.

From here the book detours through the Americana border territory bequeathed to us from that most European of American auteurs, Orson Welles. Far from the obvious custodian of *noir*, Welles, for many, is *the* great auteur. However, the contribution he makes to the 'style,' genre, or whatever term is most suitable as a descriptor for noir, is of major scholarly concern. Not only is Welles central to a niche of noir scholarship, but–in recent years at least–has been theoretically appraised as a filmmaker who navigates the liminal spaces between the Hollywood studio, the independent film, and the art film well before his time. Welles is particularly unique, in part because, as Joan Copjec says, "*film noir* now appears, fifty years after the first films were made, to be a less local phenomenon" (Copjec (ed): 1996; x). As the provenance of noir advanced into less 'local,' more universal waters, the mercurial Welles followed. This is not least because *Touch of Evil* (Welles, 1958), Welles most insistent study of evil and the film this next chapter takes as its focal point, is a stylistic noir classic. Its classic status lies in its international dimension; the way it explores moral duty. Using the first chapter, particularly the discussion of Kant, as a guide, duty is critically broached regarding immoral acts used to do good. Performing the moral using a particular form of vice is explored regarding Welles's response to a kind of administrative *radical evil*. The danger elicited by *Touch of Evil*, I argue, lies in the clichés it uses to elicit truth. The truth: for Welles, is that immorality otherwise known as a touch of evil sustains moral order. And this truth qualifies as one of the great truths of film noir itself. What makes this film so compelling, this chapter argues, is not so much a corrupt detective with redeemable features, but one who is good only when corrupt.

The middle section turns to evil with reference to the legacy of fascism in Italian film. Looking at those who came to prominence in the 1960s; notably Pier Paolo Pasolini and Liliana Cavani (after the global success of neorealism), the films themselves are–put simply–those that caused most offence. As art films became global 'products' and Italian filmmakers became international stars, the Italian cinema set new parameters for what could and couldn't be shown. My interest, however, derives from cognisance of how Pasolini and Cavani, in films such as *Salò* (Pasolini, 1975) and *The Night Porter* (Cavani, 1973) explore fascism; but fascism, when it concerns not just men and women performing particularly evil deeds against their victims, but a sexual impulse pertaining to life in general. Pasolini and Cavani respond to this. In doing so they focus on what Michel Foucault, in prefacing *Anti-Oedipus: Capitalism and Schizophrenia Vol. 1* refers to as, "varieties of fascism, from the enormous ones that surround and crush us to the petty ones that constitute the tyrannical bitterness of everyday life" (Foucault in Deleuze and Guattari: 1984; xi- xiv). As film texts, these are significant tests of decency. I maintain, however, that moral decency is confronted, not for the sake of it, but so that issues that would come to bear on the aesthetics of violence (as well as violent aesthetics), would become topics of examination. In other words, how the power of fascism is resisted is central. As Gary Indiana says of *Salò*,

> "*Salò* resists ordinary synopsis. Every scene is a kind of crowd scene, the whole cast is almost always present, there are no 'dramatic developments'

between monadic protagonists, but rather a generalised, malignant energy field generated between oppressors and victims; the little threads of characterological continuity add up to nothing resembling a series of subplots; the victims are at one minute like children playing a game without a clue to its meaning" (Indiana: 2000; 69).

Like the earlier *Trilogy of Life*, *Salò* quickly attained cult status. Pasolini's brutal murder after the film's release gave sustenance to this. The blending of Sade and Fascism, with its dark comic undertone, is compounded by one of film's most shocking endings: the torture unto death of those who 'broke the rules.' Similarly contentious in its ending, *The Night Porter* would elicit cries of outrage; classified as a 'kinky turn on' masquerading as art. Roger Ebert of *The Chicago Sun Times* went as far as to say, "'The Night Porter' is as nasty as it is lubricious, a despicable attempt to titillate by exploiting memories of persecution and suffering. It is (I know how obscene this sounds), Nazi chic" (Ebert; 1975). Ebert's assessment has a certain truth to it. On one level, Cavani's film can be viewed as morally questionable–committing to a Nazi fashionability that impacted on transgressive S&M advocates. But on a more pertinent level, the film examines guilt. "If virtue consists (in part) in taking pleasure in the right and not in the wrong things," Mary Devereaux asks, "then what is my character now such that I can take pleasure in these things" (Devereaux in Levinson (ed): 1998; 242). Devereaux's point (albeit stressed in a different context to the one employed here) helps in confronting Ebert's response to the film as a moral one. For if the film concerns a victimhood more complex in its formulation than the vanguards of a therapy obsessed society admit, not everybody might want to be a victim in a prescribed sense: what is exploitative isn't as clear-cut as Ebert might think. Masochism, and the film is about masochism (not sado-masochism), requires a contract between oppressor and victim. Performance is part of a contract used to expiate guilt. It is necessary to illustrate how evil performed 'tragically' can serve as the means for confronting evil.

In turning to the present in the final third of the book, three recent films, and the work of internationally acclaimed Austrian filmmaker Michael Haneke is considered. Haneke is perhaps the most important living director, in Europe at least. His films have been received as probing inquiries into sensitive subject areas, from the Holocaust, to 9/11, to War on Terror, to sado-masochism, in a uniquely personal mode of filmmaking; utilising film as a unique mode of inquiry. Probing or prodding of the spectator (of classical realist cinema) untroubled by their entertainment, is just one of the features of Haneke's films. Ethics, where evil has a central place, is present in a not so obvious guise. Early theatrical releases, from *Der siebente Kontinent* (The Seventh Continent (1989)) to *71 Fragmente einer Chronologie des Zufalls* (71 Fragments of a Chronology of Chance (1994)) can be viewed as films about evil, as can the centrepiece of this trilogy, *Benny's Video* (Haneke, 1994). The trilogy is set within a domain Keith Reader calls a, "cinema of alienated non-communication" (Reader in Quandt (ed): 2011; 377). In this particular domain of cinema, psychological explanation is rarely given. Hence no intent, no psychological reason is given. Because it's the most disturbing instance of this type of film, I have chosen to focus intitally on *Benny's Video*; using it as a springboard into later Haneke films. The film's protagonist and killer, Benny, and his failure to justify the horrible acts he commits is a reason for why the film disturbs: another is the use of the off-screen as a method of representation. *Benny's Video* is, not to mince words, a disturbing account of killing. Yet rather than unpack Haneke's complete oeuvre, as one of the most comprehensive contributions to the cinema of non-justifiable acts of evil in recent years, I explore the shifting concerns with evil that characterise his output in specific terms. I hope a comprehensive study of Haneke and evil will appear. But this is not it.

From *Benny's Video* then to the multiple awards-winning *Das weisse Band* (The White Ribbon (2009)), evil operates on three levels. The first concerns a subject who acts unperturbed by his actions; whose intentions are questionably *unclear*. In the second, a collaborative evil is performed, as intention and the acknowledgment of it become central. There is no doubt that collaboration in evil has a certain fascination in its theorisation. And of course, *Funny Games* (Haneke, 1997 and 2007) seems the most incisive in this regard. As a filmic treatment of an evil based around the actions of two 'posh' adolescent killers, *Funny Games* challenges its spectators to reflect upon their own moral position relating to the types of behaviour they watch on screen. It is, as Oliver C. Speck rightly points out, a "scandalous film" (Speck: 2010; 85). It is, also, close in its aesthetic and ethical aims to Pasolini's *Salò*; more so than other Haneke films from the same period; so I decided to refer to the film(s) without making it (or them) a major anchor point. On the last level, the collaborative turns into the systematic: Haneke now turning to evil consitutive of the *system* of law. Hence the final chapter turns to *radical evil*, and looks to the way in which institutions can shield their members from the responsiblity they hold; particularly as it pertains to *Das weisse Band*.

From the the drowning (and shooting) of up to 200 Algerian protestors in the Seine during a peaceful protest by pro-FLN Algerians in the Parisian 60s, under the orders of the head of police Maurice Papon, to the James Bulger Case in which two-year old Bulger was brutally murdered after his abduction by two ten years old boys in Liverpool in 1993, to the Eichmann trial (in particular Hannah Arendt's report on the event), serious questions are put to the morally attuned Haneke spectator. In this analytical phase the argument that later preoccupations in Haneke films are linked to those present in earlier ones is made: *Caché* (Hidden (2007)) is, for example, *Benny's Video* reworked from a more mature vantage point. For evil, I argue, has an equally fascinating allure in the later 'more mature' Haneke. And yet, even so, and apart from his films displaying a curious attention to evil, arrows pointed at oft-overlooked social considerations are also important to evaluate. Television is just one of these. For Haneke, television fills 'time,' consumes it. And it does this, as Mary-Anne Doane suggests,

> "By ensuring that something happens–it organises itself around the event. There is often a certain slippage between the notion that television covers important events in order to validate itself as a medium and the idea that because an event is covered by television–because it is, in effect, deemed televisual–it is important" (Doane in Mellencamp (ed): 1990; 222).

Doane's approach is of considerable value when accounting for characters like Benny and indeed their need for the 'events' they instigate in normal everyday reality to parallel the virtual recording of them; Benny (Arno Frisch) feels the girl he befriends is 'important' precisely when televisually recording her death. When Benny's father, Georg (Ulrich Mühe), peers over his son's shoulder, at the film he has made, his son appears obviously enamoured by the formal matters on screen, the process of filming the horror relegating the 'real' to an altogether different realm. Not unlike this, Majid's (Maurice Bénichou) suicide in *Caché* is followed by Georges (Daniel Auteuil) returning home to find a recording of the event. In both cases, horrific violence assumes video and 'mediated' form; an evil need to represent death.

In light of this, the secularising of catastrophe on TV, emphasised by the gaze of the newsreader–(frightening if it wasn't so regular a feature of mediatised societies)–finds an echo in the reduction of horror to humdrum banality as found in Haneke films. From 9/11 to the Tsunami disaster, what we see is catastrophism competing on an increasingly global stage. It would be wrong to overlook the importance of this competition, and/or the discussion to Hanekean scholarship, but I believe it masks often-overlooked moral concerns in Haneke films. That Haneke films concern events such as the James Bulger affair is–of course–one thing of note, the manner in which these are complicated and debated another. With this level of complication in mind, I argue that Haneke confronts us morally. Haneke's world is one in which those who acquiesce with power unquestionably, may well be the considered avatars of a cosmic Evil.

CHAPTER ONE

'TRYING TO SEE DARKNESS': A GENEALOGY OF EVIL FROM MANICHEANISM TO BATAILLE

> "Why should I seek for love or study it?
> It is of God and passes human wit;
> I study hatred with great diligence
> For that's a passion within my own control
> A sort of bosom that can clear the soul
> Of everything that is not mind or sense,"
> —W.B. Yeats, *Supernatural Songs.*

In taking the verse of my countryman as inspiration for the journey that follows it might be a way to begin by asking if evil is of the 'mind'? Or of the 'real'? The first thinker to dwell on evil in monotheistic theology, St. Augustine, begins in asking this question. Is evil something we know? Something we sense? Or is it simply something we confront? Can we resist evil in the same way that we resist desire? Posing questions like these in relation to an intractable dualism, influencing the Neo-Platonist and religious phases in Augustine–and his writings on evil–will begin this chapter. Augustinian concepts such as privation and perversion are addressed in a considerably more 'general' way. After introducing Augustine, the analysis will expand to include that of the Cathar heresy from the 12th and 13th centuries. I say 'generally' because any such orthodox reading of Augustine, as interpreted by thinkers like Thomas Aquinas, is set against responses to Augustinian theology in the later sections, examining John Milton's *Paradise Lost* (1667), and ethics from Kant to Bataille. After Kant, an interlude is taken, discussing Tom Hooper's *Longford* (2006), the Coen Brothers' *No Country for Old Men* (2007) and Florian Henkel von Donnersmarck's *The Lives of Others* (2006).

Augustine and Theology

For English theologian John Hick, the theology of Augustine is the "fountainhead" of the Judeo-Christian tradition (Hick: 1977; xi). In the course of his writing Hick develops an Augustinian position, for want of a better word, based around two explicit conflicts, the first with the Manicheans, and the second with the Pelagians. For Hick, it is lines such as, "I have known my soul and the body that lies upon it, and they have been enemies since the creation" which give an interesting glimpse into the dictates and inspiration for the Manichean movement. That the Self originates in 'darkness' and 'light' is central to this. It is a seductive position for early Augustine. For darkness is associated with the body, while light, by extension, with the soul. The structure of this opposition can be felt in the Manichean creed,

> "We know (1) what is said to have been before there was earth and heaven; we know (2) why God and Satan fought, how Light and Darkness mingled, and who is said to have created; we know (3) why eventually earth and heaven shall pass away, and what shall happen thereafter" (Jonas: 1970; 209).

In the Creed, human life is shown to be the product of "darkness" and "light." In a cosmos such as this, the converging body and soul require processes in which both entities are purified. The verse tells how heaven and earth will converge when this occurs. Put simply, Manicheanism is a moderate form of dualism, downplaying 'free choice,' on which moralism is necessarily founded. It emphasises cosmic determinants in day-to-day life. Augustine's attraction to Manicheanism (as described in the *Confessions*) lay in its simplicity as a creed; in which any discussion of the will is frequented. For as Thomas Aquinas notes, "if there is nothing free in us, but we are moved to will necessarily.......praise and blame, in which moral philosophy consists are swept away" (Aquinas: 1998; 556). Aquinas points to a dualist cosmology where morality lacks foundation, when 'necessity' impinges on free choice. Hence Augustine's assertion,

> "For you have right on your side, O Lord, but we are sinners that have wronged and forsaken you; all is amiss with us. We are bowed down by your chastisement. In justice we have been delivered to the author of sin, the prince of death, because he has coaxed us to make our wills conform with his" (Augustine: 1961; 56).

Sees turning away from God as that which makes evil actions occur; considered, equally, as the demands of a "dark prince" (Augustine: 1961; 56). The evildoer rebels against divine authority. Satan, opening up the pathway to evil, as Augustine suggests, coaxes the subject into conformity with his will; all of which is a considered punishment from the Fall. The author of sin is man, but the seductress of the will is Satan. Myth dramatises evil. Without free choice and responsibility given a fully theoretical explanation, evil remains a crucially unresolved problem for the young Augustine. Only as he matures in his thinking on evil–and its associated problems in morality–is another Augustine confronted by the Manichees. It is from this theoretical vantage point, as Forsyth notes, a "coherent Christian system" emerges (Forsyth: 1986; 403). To think the 'lack' in evil requires rejecting its substantialist 'nature.' If substance is the considered origin of Being, then the conceptual evocation of evil must be shown to lack the substantiality on which its own nebulous expression is found.

Augustine will develop his own 'non-substantial' theory of evil. In the aftermath of his Neo-Platonist phase the theory of 'privation' begins to unfold. Now, in order for this theory to be developed in the way he wants, evil must be shown to have no ontological status,

> "One should not try to find an efficient cause for a wrong choice. It is not a matter of efficiency, but of deficiency: the evil will is not effective but defective. For to begin to have an evil will, is to defect from he who is the Supreme existence, to something of less reality. To try to discover the causes of such defections–deficient, not efficient causes–*is like trying to see darkness*, or hear silence" (Augustine: 1984; 479-80).

Evil is synonymous with "trying to see darkness" (Augustine: 1984; 479-80). In a significant attempt to break with the indicative nature of Manicheanism, Augustine would consider evil as a deficiency in a thoroughly good creation (Augustine: 1984; 79). The rejection of Manicheanism thus requires the expedient retention of the 'free will' as a concept. For if a groundbreaking exposition of morality and the associated will to transgress serves as reposte to the Manichees, concepts need to be developed for this. By making the will and its companion concept, responsibility, central to things, Augustine's God can appear to be absolutely 'good' in all areas of intervention. Notably less optimistic in its deployment of good and evil, this brand of Neo-Platonism (in the anti-Pelagian tracts) maintains the concept of 'free will' in its consolidation of volition as choice, even if in doing so Augustine must then demonstrate how any battle between good and evil, perceived from a distance, is illusionary; the subject fights the battle. God, by contrast, is perfect. In the by a considerable distance darker *City of God*–Augustine, particularly in sections like 'Why absolution from sin does not entail deliverance from death, sin's punishment?'–can then assume a less lenient position on sin,

> "But as it is, the punishment of sin has been turned by the great and wonderful grace of our saviour to a good use, to the promotion of righteousness. It was then said to man, 'You will die if you sin.' Now it is said to the Martyr, 'Die rather than sin.' ...So by the ineffable mercy of God even the penalty of man's offence is turned into an instrument of virtue" (Augustine: 1984; 513-14).

Considering, as Augustine does, "even the penalty of man's offence is turned into an instrument of virtue" (Augustine: 1984; 514) means, to jump one step ahead, that the sinner is necessary if the perfect Goodness in God is to be maintained. For the Manichean, 'Man' lacks responsibility. But, contrastingly, Augustine deliberates on sin. He does so in more deliberate consideration of the sinner, as Charles T. Mathewes notes, as the affect of perversion (Mathewes: 2001; 231). For the important point is that in perversion the sinner promotes 'righteousness.' A discordant monotheism emerges. In challenging the Manichees we find a certain shift, one whereby the will is by default good, even if not surprisingly, at this theoretical point, a significant breakthrough is accredited to Augustine, "the evil action is not an act in the sense of "actualization" at all, but rather an annihilation, an ontological defection" (Mathewes: 2001; 78).

For Mathewes, it is paradoxical–in light of evil acts–to consider an evildoer in any way good: that is, the evildoer as simply corrupt (in the eyes of Augustine at least). Contextualising evil as a kind of defect, the horror, for the victim at least, of the evil act is itself significantly undermined. Consider, as an example, a father who rapes and abuses his children while maintaining his day-to-day activities, as was the case with Josef Fritzl, in the notorious Austrian incest and imprisonment case. Fritzl's dungeon of horror, in which he imprisoned his eldest daughter Elizabeth and then raped and abused her over a period of twenty years, while fathering seven incestuous children, is almost beyond thought. Yet is it preposterous to think Fritzl in his own twisted way was striving to protect his daughter and therefore do good? Yet Fritzl actually claimed this in his defence. "I know she was unhappy at home, but we only ever had her best interests at heart" he is said to have said about the daughter he imprisoned for twenty four years. Indeed, the horrifying image of what Fritzl did bears all the hallmarks of (a base) intractable evil (he was apprehended on bringing one of his daughters to hospital); even if his 'basement' family, imprisoned for years, materialised from the perverse belief he was protecting their mother. On reprimand, Fritzl spoke about believing his daughter, imprisoned for twenty-five years, would become a drug addict, or worse still, a runaway, had he not sought to protect her in his own way.

Fritzl is a raw example of the evildoer claiming his believed in good as the *true* good. In an Augustinian sense, Fritzl has been perverted from the true good. By claiming the Nazi occupation of Austria formed his personality, Fritzl sought to alleviate responsibility for the crimes he committed.

Now the question such consideration, of course, brings is if evil is a lack of good? In one sense, Augustine argues, "sin for man is a disorder and perversion; that is an aversion from the most holly Creator and a conversion towards the inferior things that he has created" (Augustine; 1993). In investing in or in willing this, a lesser good is invested in by the sinner. Yet in keeping to a primordially human essence, 'perversion' as a rationale is used to account for a failure to simply will the true good. Turning to the concept of 'self-love' to explain this failure–which means turning towards pleasurable forms of self-gratification before turning towards God (Augustine: 1961; 55), helps to account for sin as a perversion of the will's natural inclinations towards good. Perversion, however, goes deeper. For Augustine, man's perversion is a consequence of the catastrophic Fall. Hence the event from which 'humanity' emerges as imperfect is contextualised around two issues; the Fall and God's Goodness,

> "The Nature of God is unchangeable and completely incorruptible, and nothing can do it harm; and they held (the Manichees) according to sound Christian teaching, that the soul, which could change for the worse through free choice, and could be corrupted by sin, is not a part of God, nor of the same nature of God, but is created by him and far inferior to its creator" (Augustine: 1984; 454).

Augustine's longstanding deliberation on sin (as a perversion) and evil (as privation) fuels the ensuing theological debate (Augustine: 1984; 454). Man is conditioned by the Fall. When, in the context of the catastrophic Fall, evil is considered afresh, the will is not, for Augustine, directed towards evil alone; just a lesser good. Most important, the soul is pure, even if the will is thoroughly corrupt. Sinning doesn't make man an evil being *tout court*; it makes him a merely corrupt one. It may be that Augustine offsets, and allows others, his own guilt when theorising in this way. In doing so, evil actions are made to comply with good motives. It is also possible that evil is a wrong path, and evildoers such as Fritzl's idea of the good at variance with the Good. But around this, Augustine will state,

> "Even the wicked will is a strong proof of the goodness of (the devil's) nature. But God, as he is the supremely good Creator of good natures, so is he of evil will the most just ruler; so that, while they make an evil use of good natures, He makes a good use even of evil wills. Accordingly, He caused the devil (good by God's creation, wicked by his own will) to be cast down from his high position, and to become the mockery of his angels" (Augustine: 1984; 17).

Now, the question is whether evil is a means to find the good? Or, as Mathewes notes, whether evil is necessary. For Mathewes, theorising evil as necessary, with causality, whether aiming to, minimises the way acts such as Fritzl's are viewed (Mathewes: 2001; 92). For theorising evil as a cause, for Augustine, lessens the responsibility of the agent (as an evildoer). In addition, a victim status is given to those who commit horrifying evil. Yet at the same time, Mathewes questions Augustine on this point. To conclude then, Augustine's contribution to Christianity is most directly felt in the dual concepts of privation and perversion; both of which work against the idea there is a 'cause' to evil. There is no disputing this fact. Without these two concepts, monotheism would lack its theoretical foundation. Dualism, as Augustine shows, would threaten Christianity. Now defeating Manicheanism reduces the level of this threat, shaping Augustine's views on morality in more ways than one; 'free will' shaping responsibility for sin. But there is no doubt that in doing so Augustine flits between the Manichees and the Pelagians. Challenging both focuses the debate, without which, it may not be tested. Recent analysis has, however, reopened this debate. The following takes issue with this.

Responsibility

Interpretations of Augustinian evil are quick to find discontinuities in Augustine's thought. Jones Irwin has pointed to the discontinuous nature of the early and late Augustinian position; with the early 'humanist' texts considering 'free will' and 'moral autonomy' as constituent of the good with the later works moving away from this position (Irwin: 2002; 164). The 'humanism' developed in the anti-Pelagian *On Free Choice of the Will* and *Refractions* (1860) is refuted in the later and darker *City of God*.

Mathewes, in addition, attributes a ""monarchic" and "asymmetrical" ontology and "axiology"" (Mathewes: 2001; 76) to the mature Augustinian position, so that doubt as to whether the orthodox stands for the opposition between good and evil emerges. If privation as a position works asymmetrically, as Irwin notes, goodness can remain intact when the 'asymmetrical' model remains intact. But the evil act is countered by a good which Irwin identifies in Augustine as grace. Of course, grace is a problematic term, and it is particularly so when action is autonomous: we cannot be determined to act. Paradox notwithstanding, the autonomous subject and the problems pertaining to this morally in Augustine's thought are given a significant address by Irwin. Irwin begins by addressing Augustine's opposition–*quo* his analysis–to the determinists (Irwin: 2002; 162). Indeed, the following is an indication of this opposition,

> "We undertook this discussion because of those who deny that evil is due to free choice of will and who maintain that God, if this is so, deserves blame as the creator of every kind of thing. Thus they wish in their wicked error–they are the Manichees–to introduce a being, evil in nature, which is unchangeable and coeternal with God" (Augustine; 1844-64).

As Irwin points outs, there is significant cause to suggest Augustine comes to reject this. Yet when he sets upon exploring the causes of evil outside a realm considered 'natural,' he begins to look closer at what he calls the temporal law. As his theology matures he audaciously claims that, "prohibition causes the desire to commit the unlawful act" (Augustine: 1984; 514). In this instance, the age-old problem of transgression, of which the philosophical tradition will find both its enemy and friend, is encountered. Now: Augustine is clear on one thing. Regarding the origins of the law, he maintains the will is free. Yet the humanism evident in the Pelagian dialogues is in some ways countered, certainly in terms of pessimism, with the less humanist *City of God*. When the 'humanist' interpretation is given precedence (in early texts), God watches over a system thought to be derived, as the Pelagians argue, from human activities (Irwin: 2002; 166). *City of God* is less forthcoming in this regard. The main issue now is, 'why does man choose to sin?,' coupled with 'why does man choose sin ahead of virtue?' As Carol Harrison has argued,

"It is possible for man to will the good which he knows but to find that he is incapable of acting upon it. This is a universal human experience and one which Augustine's understanding of the will, in contrast to ancient and post-Enlightenment thinking, goes a long way to explaining" (Harrison: 2002; 91).

A certain Neo-Platonic resonance is evident in this position, with the will considered a "universal human condition" (Harrison: 2002; 91). Irwin and Harrison discuss the will in different capacities. For Irwin, the will finds itself impacted on by the conceptual distinction of grace, bearing heavily on Augustine's discussion of good and evil, particularly as it relates to volition. Because intervention takes the form of grace, the will–considered as volition–assumes a central importance for Augustine. Incorporating the idea of externality into a theory of the will, without accrediting evil to divine sources, makes man's responsibility for evil even more central. For Irwin, there are two important points to make around this. Firstly, autonomy relies on an autonomous subject. Otherwise, moral acts are impossible; the moral act is unimaginable without such a subject. Secondly, in a move of critical import to Irwin's discussion, moral autonomy, in relation to grace, is problematised. In grace the good is possible, moral action impossible (Irwin: 2002; 167). It is thus interesting to recall Augustine's declaration, "the good I do is done by you in me and by your grace: the evil is my fault" (Augustine: 1984; 210) as greater credence is given to Irwin's critique in relation to this. For "good I do" suggests a moral act, but whether this act can be considered a 'free' act is of course debateable. The "good I do" contains its own negation. The assertion of agency is problematised by the concept of grace. Hence the statement, "for me, there is no good but you, who are with me even before I am with you" is pertinent. For if a subject, divided in origin, split in subjectivity, is set in such terms, is man is ever fully responsible for the good?

If so, is it still right to suggest evil is non-existent? Or that it is simply a lack of being? And, given these questions, is it possible to read Augustine's theory of privation from an inverse perspective? Rather than seeing evil as a privation, is it possible privation pertains more readily to the good; that which is sought but never fully attributable to the subject's actions. Whether a world-view such as that proposed by Harrison, or one on which Irwin's pessimism critically rests, problems nonetheless turn on issues of moral responsibility. The conclusion would seem to be that for Augustine humanity is responsible for evil. Yet to call everybody responsible for evil is to suggest nobody really is responsible. As such, the horror of evil dissipates into another void. This is strangely compelling as an argument. Yet what it means is that the 'good' is rarely the effect of 'moral action' but has its value retrospectively discerned as a force attributed to the power of God. On this reading, the good act is wholly 'imaginary,' becoming 'real' only on reflecting upon this act. We can, in all reason, assert that autonomous moral action is impossible; but reflection on action makes moral action *seem* possible. As Charles T. Mathewes notes,

> "Augustine's demythologising of evil was of a piece with his radical metaphysics of God. God's absolute goodness so exhausted the conceptual space of transcendence for Augustine that evil had to be solely a consequence of the created order's swerve away from God" (Mathewes: 2001; 64).

In monotheism, as Mathewes suggests, evil is played down; rather, it is considered the, "created order's swerve away from God" (Mathewes: 2001; 64). But we can read any such "swerve" in two ways. For it can firstly mean evil bears no relation to God. Evil is lack. It can secondly mean the "swerve" amplifies responsibility; a force bringing evil to bear on action needs to be fought. Perhaps in deliberation, Augustine precludes himself from supporting either position. For to take the former position would mean 'we' are responsible; even if the good is never attributable to us. In the latter position, however, evil is predetermined; absolving responsibility. This debate becomes of major import in the years following Augustine's canonisation by the Church. For Thomas's interpretation of Augustine is felt to resolve this debate, making Augustine a more systematic thinker. Hence Carlos Steele believes the scholastic work of Thomas Aquinas brings Augustine's views on evil to a proper conclusion. In an article devoted to this legacy, Steele notes, "evil is not required as something necessary for the *existence* of the world: this in fact would make evil an essential factor for the creation of the universe" (Steele: 2001; 180). These are reflections on good and evil which, in their elasticity, end up positing evil as indelibly lacking in substance–evil coming from nothing as such–and are considerably orthodox renderings of Augustinian theodicy. For Steele not only emphasises privation, consolidating the orthodox reading of Augustinian evil when doing so, but also argues that Islamic philosopher Avicennae is *the* crucial support to the Augustinian position. Both, he argues, focus on concepts *poena* and *culpa*,

> "The distinction between *poena* (punishment) and *culpa* (fault, guilt) plays an important role in medieval discussions on evil and is yet another legacy of Augustine….According to Augustine all evil is either *culpa* or

poena. For evil as *culpa* God is not responsible: it comes into the world
through the free choice of rational creatures. The evil of *poena* follows
upon the evil of sin ("poena semper sequitur culpam") as a divine
punishment" (Steele: 2001; 190).

Steele believes *peona*, "follows upon the evil of sin" (Steele: 2001; 191).
Poena is a conceptual response to the fact that, "if human beings had
never abused their free will in disobedience against God, they would never
have suffered all the hardships of this temporal life" (Steele: 2001; 191).
Poena is necessary for the Good when, "hardships of this temporal life"
are punishment for the Fall (Steele: 2001; 192). In *culpa*, the good act can
never be attributed to the subject. Rather the subject can only act *in* grace.
Therefore, the moral is constituted in relation to a presence Augustine
attributes to God (or… in Marx the State, in Lacan the Other). Something,
as distinct from the self, determines good. The issue, perhaps the main
thing to be considered, is the exteriority from which grace or an other
'comes.' It is not surprising Steele sees desire as a central feature of a
debate Augustine contributes to. For while it is possible desire in
Augustine is desire for grace, we should also note that desire, as an idea,
has been central to psychoanalytic and post-Hegelian philosophers
because of Augustine. For Augustine, some argue, desire *is* more than an
idea (Augustine: 1961; 164). Desire is important if a life aim is to free
oneself from desire. But desire is also important as in addressing the carnal
impulses and their evil.

This concern can be examined in relation to a conversational account
between Augustine and a virginal bride and its specific discussion in *City
of God*, "if you have consented, divine aid has been added to divine grace,
to prevent your losing that grace, while men's reproach has come in place
of men's praise" (Augustine: 1984; 28). That the subject requires aid to
consent to sexual activity makes the idea of a relationship dubious; God
intervenes to prevent slippage from one partner to another. God is in fact
the third party. In the most private compartments, God watches over the
desiring couple (in the throes). Hence in "The question of violence from
others, and the lust of others suffered by an unwilling mind in a ravished
body" (Augustine: 1984; 27), Augustine is able to distinguish between the
temporal realm (perhaps influenced by the Neo-Platonists) of desire and
the ideal, transcendence. The world is the world of desire but what we
strive for is transcendence for freedom from desire. Augustine's analysis,
having gathered momentum in the early sections of *City of God*, ends up
with the rather dubious conclusion that "prohibition causes the desire to
commit the unlawful act" (Augustine: 1984; 514). If the suggestion made

here is that the object-cause of desire is in fact the law, should we assume the law determines our explicit desire to transgress? For, as Neil Forsyth states in *The Old Enemy: Satan and the Combat Myth* (1986),

> "The mistrust of the body, evident throughout Augustine's life, in the *Confessions* as well as the anti-Pelagian tracts, comes very close to Mani's position that man should abstain from sexual contact because that is how evil is passed along. Pelagian opponents who accused Augustine of Manicheanism and defended the goodness of human sexuality had a strong case. Augustine maintained throughout the Pelagian controversy that the purest of Christian marriages could easily be polluted by the venial sin of sexual desire" (Forsyth: 1986; 401-402).

Lang's murder mystery *M* (Lang, 1931), a film in which desire is quintessentially associated with murder, is a dangerously subversive illustration of Augustine's insights. We return to Lang later. But we are now in a position to see Augustine's consideration of desire is strongest in *City of God*, even though 'carnal desire' registers the need for God's grace. Desire comes from within and without, and for this reason it is curiously attractive in its theorisation. For Augustine, evil reappears contemptuously as desire. Forsyth's reading, on this note, is a cautionary instance of what goes wrong when taking the unity of the subject for granted, "once we have a theory of inherited guilt, original sin, then every act becomes sinful, whatever its putative object. What then can man do about this?" (Forsyth: 1986: 402). If the theory of privation deconstructs—especially when examined closely—in attempting to banish evil from the cosmic sphere Augustine ends up naturalising the desire to *transgress*. Now, we can say, for the moment at least, that evil and desire are generically linked for Augustine. Dualism shadows a somewhat protracted monotheism. Now, having discussed this protraction in detail, it is time for those much loved theorisers of dualism to make their presence felt: the Cathars.

The Cathars

The Cathars is the name given to an infamous heresy in France in the late medieval ages; a heresy for whom 'evil' was synonymous with older, less 'orthodox' positions on evil. It might seem strange to follow a discussion of Augustine with a brief turn to Catharism, but I believe the Cathars integrated Augustinian ideas, giving verse to the strange concoction of opinion in Augustine's own writings: taking the problem of evil to be the fundamental problem. That they prioritised ritual over 'duty,' asceticism over excess, prayer over matter, makes them of major interest to those for whom Augustine's legacy is the pivotal concern. Indeed, it is my belief that, as much as Augustinian evil influences the Western tradition, Catharism has had an equally momentous impact on this tradition; one such influence the suspicion of sexual desire as invariably demonic within certain strands of Christianity. As Stepher Barber aptly puts it,

> "Some historians–such as Bernard Hamilton and Yliva Hagman–therefore reject the idea of ultimate Manichean derivation, pointing out that the Paulicians, the Bogomils, and the Cathars all saw themselves as 'good Christians'" (Barber: 2000; 12).

Some would say "of course they did" because it is well-documented that the Cathar 'heresy' threatened Christian orthodoxy in the medieval period. Underground after the rise of Christianity, the Cathar movement was thought to have remained intact in pockets throughout Europe. In a recent overview, Malcolm Lambert notes, "scripture, together with unwelcome natural phenomena, was used to inculcate the belief that the visible world was evil: thunder, earthquakes, the existence of worms, toads and fleas was cited to show that the world could not have been the work of a good God" (Lambert: 1992; 119). For Cathar scholar Norman Cohn, "God created all invisible things, (whereas) the Devil created all visible ones" (Cohn: 1976; 58). In unenviable terms, the devil (as a demi-God) is the creator of physical bodies; detestable as they 'appear,' with the human body itself grotesque, 'monstrous' even. The Cathar Word, on the other hand, warns its people of how evil *can* and *will* appear. Cathars, as Lambert states,

> "Honestly thought that they were the only true Christians, that the clergy were servants of Satan's church; and that Cathar teaching presented a stream of pure underground Christianity, often persecuted, but always surviving and reaching back to the days of the apostles" (Lambert: 1992; 119).

The group "honestly thought" they were the "true" Christian religion. As Lambert stresses, they believed persecution to be a natural consequence of their membership. Moreover, Lambert further suggests that, considering the apocalypse imminent, the Cathars attempted to go "back to the days of the apostles." In other words, the Cathars yearned for apostles such as Augustine and St. Paul to return. Given this yearning was intrinsic to the heresy, a strong case can be made for situating Cathar evil in an

Augustinian framework. Passages from *City of God* appear to offer support,

> "If those who lost their earthly riches in that disaster had possessed them in the spirit thus described to one who was outwardly poor but inwardly rich; that is, if they had used the world though not using it, then they would have been able to say, with that man who was so sorely tried and yet was never overcome: 'I issued from my mother's womb in nakedness and from nakedness I shall return'" (Augustine: 1984; 17-18).

Positing themselves as "inwardly rich" (Augustine: 1984; 18) meant an anti-materialist theology in which the pure and divine nakedness Augustine mentions would be given central importance. The Slovenian philosopher Slavoj Žižek has offered a rather interesting take on this view. His retort that, "maybe these strange beliefs which seemed so shocking to the Catholic orthodoxy were precisely those that had the appearance of stemming logically from orthodox contemporary doctrine" (Žižek; 2001; 8) makes a compelling case for the Cathars and their "strange beliefs" on evil being included in an 'orthodox' tradition. Again, a textual echo is found in the noteworthy corridors of *City of God*,

> "The fire which makes gold shine makes chaff smoke; the same flail breaks up the straw, and clears the grain; and oil is not mistaken for less because both are forced out by the same press. In the same way the violence which assails good men to test them, to test and *purify* them, effects in the wicked their condemnation, ruin, and annihilation" (Augustine: 1984; 14).

To purify, to rid the Christian subject of all physical evil forces, distinct from theological debate, is a central concern; with performance and ritual a crucial component. Disdain for theological debate may well derive from grace–suggesting that no debate can instil such powers–but emphasis on purity is also a reason for the acceptance in recent years of the Cathar heresy in orthodox Christian religion and its gathering momentum. Augustine's emphasis on purity may well have been a response to humanity's responsibility for the Fall, but it is a view echoed by the Cathars. Asceticism, in a strict diet of nutrients, is also present in the debates around purity and asceticism in *City of God*, "the bodies of the righteous, after the resurrection, will not need any tree to preserve them against death from disease or from extreme old-age, nor any material nourishment to prevent any kind of distress from hunger or thirst" (Augustine: 1984; 535). The Augustinian-Cathar is the considered subject of *endura*, to the extent, "life itself was an imprisonment under Satan, and a possible psychological effect of the obsessive and perfectionist life of the perfect" (Lambert: 1992; 139).

The *consolamentum* is 'the' Cathar prayer. Perfects administer the prayer; those that hold the highest honour an initiate of the movement can attain (Weis: 2000; xxxvi). The prayer involves a ritual of two stages. During the first tributes are paid to the Holy Trinity, acknowledging the need for penance and grace. The second consists of Perfects denouncing the "works and things" of the world; the recipient, the consoled party, then joining with the community. The prayer is central; the "free, pure and incorrupt" Word described by Augustine in the *Confessions* (Augustine: 1961; 135) is regenerated around *endura* and other Cathar rituals. The *consolamentum* far transcends orthodox Christian use of prayer; the key distinction being the Word is now a weapon for the Cathar. Armed with the 'Word,' deprivation, starvation, is dealt with; the signifier an antidote to evil. In the posthumous collection *The Ethics of Psychoanalysis*, Lacan gives a curious support to this point. In a Lacanian detour through the interstices of medieval life, a curious perspective opens on the unique position offered by the Cathars. By attending to the Cathar amplification of the word, as praxis, Lacan finds a link to the emergence of 'courtly love,'

> "In many cases, it seems that a function like that of a blessing or salutation is for the courtly lover the supreme gift, the sign of the Other as such, and nothing more. This phenomenon has been the object of speculation that has even gone as far as identifying the blessing with that which is the *consolamentum:* the highest rank of initiates among the Cathars" (Lacan: 1993; 153).

A resoundingly symbolic (for the Cathar) warding off of evil is the specific use for which the prayer is put (Lacan: 1993; 153). Its capacity to delay the sexual act (for the courtly lover by Lacan), gives the prayer a certain value. Why? Well for one the sexual act is barred to the Cathar. It is also, however, barred to the 'courtly lover.' Notably then, the *consolamentum*, for historian René Weis, requires, "the dying person … in a state of grace…could no longer be touched by women" (Weis; 2000). Hence, in the fight against evil consolation is found in the prayer. In this sense the Cathar makes of the signifier a particular counterweight to the symbolic expression of evil in material and corporeal form. As Parkin remarks,

> "Evil refers to various ideas of imperfection and excess seen as destructive: but these are contestable concepts which, when personified,

allow mankind to engage them in dialogue and reflect on the boundaries of humanity" (Parkin (ed): 1985; 23).

The sign (through dialogue) helps confront what Parkin calls, "boundaries of humanity" (Parkin (ed): 1985; 23). Cathars confront evil in language. Unheralded yet not unusual, as Barber notes, (signs, discourse etc.), evil is elevated to a symbolic level; language a guard to evil. Narrative (in its link to the symbolic) is the 'thing' the Cathar summons fighting the evil body and its desires. The prayer is the weapon against evil. As Barber notes, "the *consolamentum* thus provided the cement for the whole Cathar movement, but it is a cement which could all too easily come loose" (Barber: 2000). This is an interesting take on things. For it points to the centrality of the word as a means of preventing evil from infiltrating the physical body of the Cathar, and the symbolic, of prayer as knowledge, as an antidote to the pure material presence of evil. As the word is considered the, "cement which .... comes loose" it is also matter; and it may be that Cathar notions of evil are deconstructed by the counter idea of prayer as material cement against evil. This is a basic paradox. For it means the cement–prayer–perpetuates the thing it undermines, Evil. It is not so much prayer but Evil which helps the Cathar to exist. John Milton's epic *Paradise Lost* (1667), to which we can now turn, offers a response to this problem.

Paradise Lost

Paradise Lost is perhaps the poem most commented on in the English literary tradition. Christianity is its point of narrative concern, particularly the Biblical Fall of man, hence it includes all that preoccupied the Cathars after Augustine: the war in Heaven, the Fall and the origin of evil. In this great English epic, a demonic purpose is assigned *to* evil in the same way a humanistic purpose is given to the good; aligning aesthetics to ethics. We have already seen concerns with evil and responsibility coalesce in Augustine and the Cathars, and the problem of evil in Milton certainly follows this tradition; a level of continuity kept with a tradition of prior thought.

It is not my aim to consider all aspects of the poem here. The short critique which follows might be considered in more expedient terms as an intervention, a picking apart of certain 'issues' in the poem that can be considered part of the Augustinian tradition. I consider *Paradise Lost* an important genealogical marker. The reason for this is I see the poem as a transition point between medieval and modern, the humanist and anti-humanist, in its precise consideration of the will and language. It is also an interesting battleground in the debate around orthodoxy, which Catholic novelists and academics such as C.S. Lewis and C.K. Chesteron have contributed so immensely to; and which emerges on the back of Augustine and the problem of evil. Hence, the poem serves as both a marker for the emergence of the modern, and a text theologians return to by way of escaping the humanism which would come to define the modern.

The Language of 'Sin'

On the role of allegory in *Paradise Lost,* C.S. Lewis claims,

> "We need not ask 'What is an Apple?' It is an apple. It is not an allegory… We can also dismiss that question which has so much agitated some great critics. 'What is the Fall?' The Fall is simply Disobedience–doing what you have been told not to do: and it results from pride–from being too big for your boots, forgetting your place, thinking that you are God" (Lewis: 1967; 70-71).

The concepts of allegory and 'evil'–discussed by Lewis–return in the curious assertion, "evil as such, which is (allegory) cherished as enduring profundity, exists only in allegory, and means something different from what is" (Benjamin: 1977; 233). Indeed, it is possible Benjamin's assertion can be seen to counter Lewis's reductive response, as a precise and epistemological rendition of Augustinian notions of perversion. As such, evil, "means precisely the non-existence of what language presents" (Benjamin: 1977; 233). Evil, as such, is the excess *in* language. I would say that this 'excess,' which pertains to the epistemological notion of evil as it gathers momentum in the verse, is increasingly evident as the verse progresses. In that God's description is defined in relation to 'Darkness,' while 'Satan' is considered in relation to 'Light,' words perversely interchange. Hence, the Language of Heaven becomes the Language of Hell,

> "The shining heav'nly fair, a Goddess arm'd
> Out of the head I sprung: amazement seis'd
> All th' host of Heav'n; back they recoiled afraid
> At first, and call'd me Sin, and for a Sign
> Portentous held me" (Milton: 1994; II: 56-61).

"Signs," as R.A. Shoaf notes, "emerge from sin (which) is the precondition… of the sign" (Shoaf: 1993; 23-59). Forsyth believes, "this naming of Sin, to make the pun with "sign," is arbitrary, shifting language from a natural to a merely artificial or customary basis" (Forsyth: 2003; 207). What Forsyth means is the expedient mutation of words and things is found in sin. Let us say the bind between words and things desolves in sin. In the enunciation of the sign, signification is increasingly destabilised,

> "To intellectual; give life and sense
> Fancy and understanding whence the Soul
> Reason received and Reason is her being
> Discursive, or intuitive: discourse
> Is softest yours, the latter most is ours
> Differing but in degree, of kind the same"
> (Milton: 1994; V: 485-490).

Milton is attuned to the nuances of language. Unlike the Cathars, for whom language is a symbol of higher power, the deceptive features of language are addressed. "Sense"–in this case concerning discourse–as "Differing but in degree, of kind the same" (Milton; 1994; 490) is perhaps crucial. Of course, to differ while 'the same' is a paradox remaining. Nonetheless, the paradox makes language powerful enough to overturn the very essence of what values mean or can mean. Evil is an apparent cause of this. As Forsyth notes, "from a theoretical word '*ubiloz*, cognate with "up" or "over" ... the etymology of "evil" connects up with the concepts of "too much," "exceeding due measure," "over limits," what used to be thought as "hubris"" (Forsyth: 2003; 208). Evil has excessive power; a 'hubris' of definition. After the Fall a demonic language emerges. Satan's declaration, "Evil, be thou my good" (Milton: 1994; IV; 108) is an example of this. For if the Cathar debate is reopened, it is because, by contrast, Miltonic Evil is the considered excess *of* language; that which disrupts any such stable meaning. As a consequence, heaven, as a concept, can then assume devilish association. Finally, excess is brought to bear on language; *Paradise* as a poetic venture is a serious commentary on the instability of language as an absolute. Language is not what warns us against evil but that which is infected by it.

Milton and Augustine

Other issues of concern are the way the poem deals with Augustine's legacy, its genius use of 'character,' and indeed its emphasis on how opposing values interconnect. In *A Preface to Paradise Lost,* C.S. Lewis has taken issue with these concerns, making the point that Milton's version of the Fall story is pretty much that of St. Augustine, or the church in general (Lewis: 1967). With regard to the battleground I mentioned at the beginning, the poem examplifies, at least from this perspective, the literary text as religious support. The debate can be said to involve the complexities of language and meaning; something I believe the poem confronts in a more radical way than Lewis admits. In the aftermath of Augustine, attempts at understooding good without evil emerges as a frustratingly difficult exercise. Like Augustine, Lewis wonders if good opposes evil,

> "From this doctrine of good and evil it follows (a) That good can exist without evil, as in Milton's Heaven and Paradise, but not evil without good (De Civ. Dei, xix, II). (b) That good and bad angels have the same Nature, happy when it adheres to itself (ibid xii, I). These two corollaries explain all those passages in Milton, often misunderstood, where the excellence of Satan's Nature is insisted on, in contrast to, and aggravation of, the perversion of the *will*" (Lewis: 1967; 67).

One of the interesting things of note here is Satan acts alone, autonomously; his autonomy intricately linked to evil. In one sense he is locked into his 'Nature,' yet has choice. In another he is the victim of his disposition, needed to exist alone if good is to exist. As we'll see, this position and counterposition serve as anchor points in later depictions of evil. For it means evil must be present in the world, if good is to be present. Hence, the most insidious of evildoers can be considered necessary if good is to exist in all its plentitude. In other areas of the poem, a more 'orthodox' Milton is present, but a Milton whose interest in Augustine lies in controversial areas dwelling on autonomy and moral freedom,

> "He and his faithless progeny. Whose fault? Whose but his own? ....
> Sufficient to have stood, but free to fall" (Milton: 1994; III; 96-98).

Augustine appears in Milton's next assertion, "Man shall not quite be lost, but saved who will; Yet not of will in him, but grace in me" (Milton: 1994; 174-175) in the sense that Augustine's cry, "the good I do is done by you in me" (Augustine: 1961; 210) is clearly evoked. Moreover, Lewis's belief that Milton and Augustine have a similar view on evil is given credence; a credence also given in other defining areas of the poem,

> "Th' image of God in Man, created once
> So goodly and erect, though faulty since
> To such unsightly suffering be debased"
> (Milton: 1994; XI; 508-509).

For Milton, good and evil are bound together. Language is the glue. If excursions into the Augustinian legacy, exploring the link between good and evil, then for Milton, we cannot escape the fact that to understand good we must understand evil. *Areopagita* (1644) goes a way to furthering this analysis,

> "It was from out of the rind of one apple tasted, that the knowledge of good and evill, as two cleaving together, leaped forth into the world. And perhaps this is that doom that Adam fell into of knowing good and evill, that is to say of knowing good by evill….Since therefore the knowledge and survey of vice is in this world so necessary to the constituting of human vertue" (Milton: 1988; 287).

Thus the survey of evil–for Milton–is a necessary feature of the good. Yet in areas of the poem, the difficulty in using language to make absolute claim about either is felt. Even if, it seems, knowledge of vice requires knowledge of the good,

> "Amidst the glorious brightness where thou sitt'st….
> Dark with excessive bright skirts appear" (Milton: 1994; III; 376-380).

The contrast is telling. 'Excess' comes into play. It is the excess of language. When darkness enables a system, call it knowledge, to function, an interesting take on evil can develop. As Joseph Weittrich notes, the 'culture-demon' can turn, over the course of the epic, to 'culture-hero' (whom the Romantics identified in Satan) (Wiettrich in Rumrich and Dobranski (ed): 1998; 245), or vice versa. This turning of one into another is important. For it exemplifies the idea that good and evil, seen from a distance, are oppositional, but up close form a strange unity. It also means, "the wiser course may be not to choose" which 'character'–God or Satan– is of greater value to this understanding. Rather, the important point is that the epistemology involved in seeing this is given prominence. Milton, like Augustine, encounters problems when trying to expel evil. Instead, he shows us the link between good and evil and its epistemological energy. By advocating the 'empowered' choice *not to* choose, good/evil can be seen as a conceptual 'two' that in their merging ultimately, "cleave together;" as such one is considered a crucially necessary facet of the other (Milton: 1988; 287). It is, as an overlap, a compelling position. For, we see a Satan,

> "Still drawn to love, but his will is what drives him to revenge. For a brief moment, his evil separates off, as Fowler commented *ad loc*; it is no longer his essential nature. …. Hatred, then, is what his will tells him to

practice, but his other, better, more unreflective self would allow him to love, even to hope he might somehow be admitted to this Paradise, not forced to spy on it like a lonely *voyeur*" (Forsyth: 2003; 262).

That he *loves* while *doing evil* (Forsyth: 2003; 261) makes 'understanding' Satan a moral challenge in itself; a challenge requiring the critic to question the means for condemning. In confronting evil we need to use something infected and corrupted by it. A paradox comes to the fore. But it is an interesting paradox allowed for here: a level of redemption is offered with it. For Milton our greatest moral challenge is in realising what we hold as evil has a trace of the good in an inverted and misunderstood form. It is 'language' which, while holding the key to this, is also the object to it.

Milton's legacy, I would argue, is almost as profound as Augustine's. What makes it so interesting, and this interest will surface throughout the book, is the emphasis on knowing. Evil may well cling to knowledge, but it is also that which pertains to knowledge, and language is how we express knowledge, which also escapes it. Evil has no measure, it upsets reason, but it also allows reason to function. And reason, as Milton could see, was coming to dominate the metaphysical landscape.

Kant and the Moral Law

Immanuel Kant's status as one of the great moral philosophers of the modern age can be considered to have its basis in understanding the moral as well as the evil act. It is not surprising that Kant would be so concerned with that greatest of moral problems: freedom. While Kant expands on certain Miltonic concerns in his great studies of moral freedom, only in maturity is evil confronted head-on. For Kant believed,

> "An action from duty has its moral worth not in the purpose to be attained by it but in the maxim in accordance with which it is decided upon, and therefore does not depend upon the realisation of the object of action but merely upon the principle of willing, in accordance with which the action is done" (Kant: 1996; 399-400).

Kant gives priority to the will over the action. Humanity as an "existent end" is a formal "limiting condition of our actions, and thereby requires us both to refrain from certain deeds and to act harmoniously with it" (Garcia: 2002; 196). In such a 'condition' the categorical imperative–the essential and substantial ideal of human ends–is of issue. The categorical imperative is defined as the 'two' obligatory ends brought about in moral life, according to Garcia, "our own moral perfection and the morally permitted happiness of others" (Garcia: 2002; 197). Perfection relies on how the will impinges on action. Our moral happiness is therefore a conduit of this duality. If moral action is considered as a conduit of the autonomous subject, whether it results from self-oriented imperatives is key; for either self-initiated imperatives are demanded in freedom or a higher power is the origin of the moral law. Put simply, a Kantian inquiry looks at imperatives, as Alenka Zupančič notes in *The Odd One In* (2008) as the criteria of a moral act (Zupančič: 2008; 7). One way of locating these criteria involves considering what happens in the moral act as posited in Kantian ethics. Who is prioritised, when, for Kant, an act is moral? For if pathological desire cannot be identified in moral action per se–that is, the 'me' acting freely–a full abstention from desire is needed. It is for the same reason a moral act is said to operate as the categorical imperative in Kant, the key concern being whether the subject knows they are sizing up to this imperative; that is, whether they know if they are acting in a non-pathological manner. This question (or even problem) is central to *Touch of Evil* (1958), but before our turn to Welles, immoral act(s)/action needs clarification.

Immoral Action

Defining immoral action can flesh out what is significantly *evil* in Kantian ethics. In self-gratification, a central attribute is desire. Simply, desire is central to life. Yet a problematic role is taken by desire when the 'material' trumps the 'formal,'

> "Life is the faculty of a being by which it acts according to the laws of the faculty of desire. The faculty of desire is the faculty such a being has of causing, through its representations, the reality of the objects of these representations" (Kant: 1993; 9-10).

While the subject rises from a fallen state in Augustine, it is, moreover, a desire-oriented state from which the Kantian subject emerges. Duty and the moral law hinge on a categorical imperative, which, for Kant is the fundamental axis on which moral action rests. So, any alternative imperative, for which desire is integral, when abusing another, is immoral. Using others for self-gain is a considerably immoral act. For example, in the Dardenne Brothers' *Le fils* (The Son (2004)), a story of moral duty is set around the narrative of a child (Morgan Morrine) killed in a robbery, the film then portraying the father (Olivier Gourmet) of the child coming to an understanding of the murderer he encounters as a teenager. In the context of the present inquiry, in Kant's observation an object is found which cannot be willed universally through the "receptivity of the subject" (Kant: 1993; 22) as a particular form of 'self-love,' as illustrated by the child–shown in the final scene–as he is wrestled to the ground by the adult teacher. Without speaking, the immoral act of forcing the child to accept moral advances turns into an explicit act of universal will. Without an object, one which is based on the conjecture of acting according to purely formal dictates, the moral is simply and properly shown. The end is an illustration.

The Act of Evil

Kant's most perplexing examination of evil is in *Religion Within the Limits of Reason Alone* (1960), one of his last texts. Considerably different to his earlier writings, the question of evil–an eminently religious problem–is confronted as an eminently philosophical one. The concept of *radical evil* emerges as a recant in late Kantian ethics, part of a larger metaphysical reconsideration of problems such as perversion, free will, evil. In the text acts more radical than those, Garcia observes, are properly explored,

> "Our object is some specific state of affairs, where the humanity of another person figures only indirectly into our actions as a useful incidental means towards the realization of this independent aim" (Garcia: 2002; 201).

Garcia believes that exploiting others is the mainstay of immoral if not necessarily evil acts. He goes on to state that a conman fails to dehumanise the person he cons; he simply uses the victim in question to enact a desired state of affairs. Evil differs. In evil, the other person is dehumanised. The evildoer accepts the other's humanity while attempting to attack it (as is the case in forms of racist assault). The distinction is crucial. For immoral action concerns others being used for a desired end, while evil is an assault on another for no end. From this, and more complex in its evaluation, is a *radical evil* which treats 'humanity' as an 'end in itself.' And because humanity cannot be considered as an object, in that it encompasses humans in their entirety, its peculiar status is maintained. In *Religion Within the Limits of Reason Alone* the audacious claim, "the *perversity* of the human heart... it reverses the ethical order......man is hence designated as evil" (Kant: 1960; 25), takes this quasi-object as its point of emphasis.

Having focused on screening objects from acts (with virtuous preconditions, as distinct from the virtues, central to moral action), Kant went on to state that, because it was imperative that objects involve gain, they cannot be moral. Now, for Kantian scholars the last thing Kant wants is an ethics hinging on acts in which we do, "evil simply for the sake of doing evil" (Copjec: 1996; x). But this is precisely what a certain strain of Kantian scholarship has identified in this debate. Not only is a moral act said to preclude any defined *object*–autonomous–but when so, structured like an evil act. The infamous 'desk murderer' and profile Nazi war criminal Adolf Eichmann can be referenced here. Captured in Argentina years after the war Eichmann was then brought to trial in Israel. His trial hinged on genocide. Yet Eichmann excused his criminal activities on explicitly moral grounds. And this involved specific reference to 'duty.' Arguing that he had been obeying the Law as a good Kantian, his critics quickly reacted by stressing his 'duty' as a screen for state evil. For while is it demanding for Kant, as distinct from appearing so, the law *appears* demanding for Eichmann. Unable to distinguish his own will from others, Eichmann's perverse lack of awareness was evident. Without the moral compass to scrutinise, he simply followed orders as a 'dutiful citizen,' emphasising the perversion of 'duty' in evil. Andrew Hewitt's belief that in such instances, "radical evil is an evil in which the means of overcoming evil are themselves contaminated by the evil that is to be overcome" (Hewitt in Copjec (ed): 1999; 81) serves to illustrate the nature of such evil: Eichmann could argue he was a Kantian subject doing his duty. As Henry E. Allison notes,

> "It is precisely the testing of maxims that provides the major occasion for self-deception, which here takes the form of disguising from ourselves the true nature of the principle upon which we act. In short, immoral maxims appear to pass the universability test only because they ignore or obscure morally salient features of a situation" (Allison in Lara (ed): 1999; 98).

For Allison, the fundamentally deceptive nature of the will means we can never be sure if we have removed objects of our desire from what causally structures our will. For objects can appear to exist. Claiming to have stringently obeyed the law, screening pathological motives in doing so, Eichmann said he was using Kantian terms correctly; distancing himself dispassionately from his acts while replacing his own will for that of another: his leader. The thing most frightening in Eichmann, however, was he believed that he had acted dutifully in the circumstances he was put in. As a result his Evil would appear structurally identical, from a distance at least, to that which is generally considered Good: following orders and obeying superiors to the State. In Orson Welles's unpublished screenplay–based on Conrad's *Heart of Darkness*–a text which is concerned with the way in which evil acts are structured similarly to good, Marlow meets Kurtz, the renegade colonialist he has hunted down, only to make the statement,

> "I'm a great man, Marlow–really great….The meek–you and the rest of the millions–the poor in spirit, I hate you–but I know you for my betters–without knowing why you are except that yours is the Kingdom of Heaven, except you shall inherit the earth. Don't mistake me, I haven't gone moral on my deathbed. I'm above morality. No I've climbed higher than other men and seen farther. I'm the first absolute dictator. The first complete success. I've known what many others tried to get …. I won the game, but the winner loses too. He's alone and goes mad" (Welles in Thomson: 1996; 289).

The fact that he considers himself in an *almost* moral capacity can be more clearly felt in the fact that he has, "climbed higher than other men" (Welles in Thomson: 1996; 289). For Kurtz believes he conquers 'ordinary' morality, but loses in being alone. If there is a moral principle involved in striving to be beyond everyday morality–the basis of legality–while others are (at the same time) terrorised, then Kurtz is a properly Kantian figure: unbeholden to any external guarantor. He looks for a moral felt internally and dependent on the 'strong' for its immediate expression. The law concerns Freud and his great interpreter, Jacques Lacan. Lacan confronts the moral/pathological subject around the central axis of the Law. And so it is to Lacan that we now turn. But, before doing so, let us take a brief interlude.

Interlude on Good and Evil

> "To my mind Myra is evil in its purest form. It might not seem that way to the people who are already beginning to defend her as a woman who simply did what her lover told her…they didn't know her as I did," David Smith, Chief Prosecution Witness in the Moors Murder Case.

A breather helps elucidate problems discussed thus far. A series of films surrounding British serial killers have been produced in the past decade, many of which are significant attempts to confront the problem of evil, and many of which echo the struggles Augustine undertook. Tom Hooper's *Longford* (Hooper, 2006) is a fascinating account of the legendary Lord Longford's (Jim Broadbent) lifelong campaign to free the notorious serial killer Myra Hindley (Samantha Morton). Longford, both a socialist and Catholic, was a renowned public figure, instrumental in the formation of the British welfare state and the reform of the penal system. Hindley, on the other hand, is one of the most disdained criminals in penal history; one who, in collaboration with Ian Brady, tortured and murdered children. The now infamous murder case, in which she and Brady were tried and sentenced to life imprisonment, is known as the Moors Murders. This is because the victims were buried on the Moors on the outskirts of Manchester. Longford's relationship with Hindley, looked at through the lens of an Augustine grappling with the problem of evil (a grapple the first chapter of the book attends to) is a serious consideration of the viability of evil considered as a privation of good; lacking status as a substance in itself. Longford believes in the redemption of the human subject, believing that all criminals can be rehabilitated, or as he points out in an interview near the end, "that anyone, no matter how evil, can be redeemed" (*Longford*; 2006). Indeed, the film can be read as an examination of evil acts, in this case the active dehumanisation of others, most cruelly felt in relation to killing children, against the gain of an immoral act: the criminal. In this sense, 'evil' has a much more disturbing end than criminality. Here the Kantian distinction is crucially felt when the question 'why' murder others, other than to dehumanise as the only significant 'end,' is also asked.

Longford believed Hindley had paid for her crimes and deserved to be released. Yet in the course of a lengthy correspondence Longford cuts an increasingly forlorn figure, toyed with by a deceptively wicked Hindley. Longford's 'do goodery' in the face of evil which makes him appear increasingly naive, is brilliantly illustrated in Hindley's betrayal. About to have her case reviewed, Hindley decides to reveal the grave of another victim, in the process demonstrating her allegiance to estranged partner Brady. Reeling from this, Longford decides to seek out the infamous tape recording of the killers (which was sent to him years earlier); recordings in which Hindley and Brady are heard torturing before cruelly murdering their victim (a tape he previously avoided). Longford stands listening to the abuse. He then begins to squirm in anguish, as he is unable to process the gravity of what he hears: the barbaric dehumanisation of the child. With gestures suggesting he questions his own faith when confronted with a more pronounced, more invariably wicked evil than he had previously imagined, just as Augustine looked upon his breakthrough in moral theology with scepticism in later years, Longford appears sceptical, confronted with an evil so destructive that no amount of rehabilitation can change it for the better. Hence, in Augustine's *Confessions*, when he concludes,

> "That if things are deprived of all good, they cease altogether to be; and this means that as long as they are they are good. Therefore, whatever is, is good; and evil, the origin of which I was trying to find, is not a substance, because, if it were a substance it would not be good. For either it would be an incorruptible substance of the supreme order of goodness, or it would be a corruptible substance which would not be corruptible unless it was good" (Augustine: 1961; 148).

He offers an account of Longford's belief. Committing to Christian theology, Longford wants to believe that Augustine's theory accounts for human corruption–when a lower good replaces a higher one–yet he struggles against the tortuous realisation that perhaps the opposite is true: Hindley revels in evil. Longford's faith is, however, rewarded in one of the final scenes of the film. Hindley, knowing she will never be released, writes to the retired Lord requesting him to visit. Sitting on a park bench, smoking a cigarette, old and decrepit, she apologises wholeheartedly for her action. She then talks about the Moors. She makes the audacious claim that, sitting in the moonlight upon the Moors, basking in the glow of evil, evil could be "a spiritual experience too" (*Longford*; 2006). For Longford however, this confirmation, far from pushing him further into the realm of despair, reaffirms his belief, like orthdox Augustine, that there is substance and nothing outside it. What Hindley perceived as a spiritual evil was her distorted incapacity to know the true good. The film ends at this point: the reconciliation the sign that all can be redeemed.

The Coen Brothers' Oscar winning adaptation of Cormac McCarthy's novel *No Country for Old Men* (The Coen Bros., 2007), is an equally compelling exploration of evil. Forms of pathology are explored around the two main characters, Anton Chigurh (Javier Bardem) and Llewelyn Moss (Josh Brolin). Chigurh, a hit man, hunts his victims without remorse, maiming anyone who crosses his path. When small time hunter Llewelyn Moss stumbles across a suitcase of drug cartel money in the desert, which Anton is the psychopathological custodian of, Moss decides to cut his losses and run. Chigurh then hunts him down. While the moral disclaimer is Moss doesn't go to the police and reveal what he finds, doesn't come clean, the blue-collar Moss, living in a trailer park with little chance of social mobility, precisely in the immoral nature of his acts, elicits sympathy. Once again, the immoral, presented here as financial gain at the expense of others–in this case the fact the stolen money is drug money–is set against the more precarious presence of dehumanising evil. Moss is a crook by chance rather than design, and sneaking off with the money procures a point of identification for an audience suffering similar money problems. In similar circumstances it is likely we would do the same. Nonetheless, in the course of a suspenseful sequence of events, Chigurh locates Moss with a monstrosity equal to any other vice. Whether he kills in revenge or is ontologically programmed to kill is the morally perplexing conundrum on which the film rests. On first impression, he appears wholly wicked, making it implausible to assess his behaviour morally. On second, he appears human, compelled by revenge. If the betterment of his family is what Moss seems to want, he is morally deficient–pathological–but Chigurh appears far more intent on harm. He is, within the context of the Kantian tradition, a killer who simply kills for no apparent end; indeed, the film generically toys with the audience expectation of what this end is (Chigurh dehumanises his victims with the use of a cattle-gun, a feature of the film, along with the spellbinding performance of Bardem, that is difficult not to appreciate).

Killing Moss, Chigurh brings the main narrative to an end. He remains on the run (free) and is never brought to justice. Instead, the film ends, as Ed Tom Bell (Tommy Lee Jones), the police detective involved in the manhunt, reflects on the event. On a murderer he had sent to the electric chair for killing a fourteen-year-old girl he states, "the paper's said it was a crime of passion" only for Bell to inform us, "that there wasn't any passion to it at all...he'd been planning to kill somebody for as long as he could remember" (*NCFOM*; 2007). Bell is adamant that in such crimes the metaphysical embodiment of an evil committed without passion and without an object is found. Evil such as this, Copjec says, "burdens us with full responsibility for our actions" because we can't "exonerate ourselves by claiming to be victims of our passions and thus external circumstances" (Copjec: 1996; xi). In addition, Marcus G. Singer attests, "knowing it to be evil, but not caring is the only way of confronting such malignant crime" (Singer: 2004; 205). In the final instance, Bell's account serves as a customary illumination of the ethical problem on which the 'perversity of the heart'–registered in Kantian terms–hinges.

Another award-winning film, which presents a similar set of moral problems, in a somewhat inverted manner, is Florian Henkel von Donnersmarck's *Das Leben den Anderen* (The Lives of Others (2007)). The story is set in the former DDR during the last days of the socialist dictatorship, and concerns the surveillance of writer George Dreyman (Sebastian Koch) by a member of the Stasi, Gerd Wiesler (Ulrich Muhe).

Dreyman, allegedly loyal to socialism per se, is under threat for expressing considerably unorthodox views. The narrative develops as Wiesler becomes more aware of Dreyman and is forced to make a decision that goes against his duty to the state; a Kantian act of sorts. He can charge Dreyman for treason, or he can acknowledge his integrity and let him go. In this latter sense, the fact that he lets him go serves as a kind of cathartic antidote to historical traumas such as the Eichmann trial. The reason is it illustrates the manner in which members of a totalitarian state can become morally aware, independent of what that state dictates. In other words, the film expresses, in the faith of Wiesler, a moral triumph. The proverbial twist comes at the end when Dreyman is made aware of Wiesler's actions. Dreyman discovers what Wiesler has done–saving him from possible death–when gaining access to his files. On tracking him Dreyman discovers Wiesler to be working as a postman. The film concludes with the assertion that a moral act doesn't require an other–Wiesler never looks for recognition–in order to be legitimate. Moral acts are free of charge. As Kant says, we don't act in order to impress the other: we act because it is the right thing to do. Wiesler acts freely, free of any motivating factor, passion or pathology (although Slavoj Žižek identifies a "homosexual undercurrent in the film" (Žižek: 2008; 63)); other than doing what is right.

If the principle aim of this interlude was to show what appears divergent in Wiesler and Chigurh (as not so) then both act in a manner free of the desire *for* an object. As the film comes to a conclusion, Anton rides into the sunset to penetrate more horror, purely because what he does is evil. Similarly, Wiesler continues unaffected by allegiance to a State, because his actions are, by proxy, radically moral. This discussion can now be extended, by further analysis of radical (good and) evil in the writings of Jacques Lacan; in what amounts to a further deliberation on the *problem* of evil.

Lacan and Evil

French psychoanalyst Jacques Lacan is one of the most researched theorists in critical and film theory, his work on spectatorship and identification the bedrock of contemporary analysis. Yet Lacan's writings on evil, however, are relatively scant; apparent in two texts: the essay *Kant avec Sade* (1989) and seminar *The Ethics of Psychoanalysis* (1993). The first of these confronts Kant's legacy through the lens of the notorious Marquis de Sade, arguing that the categorical imperative so imperious in Kantian ethics is brought to a logical conclusion in the notorious writings of de Sade. This argument resurfaces in *The Ethics of Psychoanalysis*. In this text, published on the back of seminar notes, Lacan explores the problem of evil directly. Lacan is interesting in that his more than probing analysis is directed at Kant, even if its conclusions appear more directly related to Milton (emphasis on the 'Other,' the close unity between Good and Evil etc.). Yet where Lacan differs, and this is crucial, is that he's not really interested in knowledge. Rather Lacan's interest lies in sensuous experience which cannot be conceptualised under the epistemological remits of thought.

Lacan draws attention to desire and the role it plays in the dialectic constitution of the subject, offering a forthright description of another key concept: *jouissance*. While this concept is notoriously difficult to define, the impact the concept itself has had on the Kantian tradition is immense. Lacan's insights, obscure at times, are radical in scope. For let us now familiarise ourselves with a Lacanian form of analysis,

> "The right to *jouissance*, were it recognised, would relegate the domination of the pleasure principle to a forevermore outdated era. In enunciating it, Sade causes the ancient axis of ethics to slip, by an imperceptible fracture, for everyone this axis is nothing other than the egoism of happiness" (Lacan: 1989; 71).

The "egoism of happiness" is set in a direct contrast to the *jouissance* of the Other. In Lacan, the concept of 'the Other' (whose origins lie in Hegelian idealism), is used to designate the totality of social discourse: counting for everything the subject relates to as a subject. Neither 'satisfying' nor 'enjoyable' *jouissance* is more suitably translated as the pleasure beyond pleasure (Rabaté (ed): 2003; 103). For Braunstein, *jouissance* is more than, "a combination of "enjoyment" and "lust"" (Braunstein in Rabaté (ed): 2003; 103). *Jouissance* is a state of being from which autonomy is felt by the subject;–in expression–reconfiguring the subject's relation to the symbolic Law; the Other on which the Good depends. In Lacanian critique, because desire of the subject is desire of the Other, it means that desire is symbolic in its externalisation. This, as we can see, is of comparable testament to a 'God' similarly deployed in Augustine. Lacan nonetheless points to de Sade's writings as the pertinent historical moment in his analysis, when the dark interior of Kantian morality finds a mirror image,

> "Sade is the inaugural step of a subversion, of which, however amusing it might seem with respect to the coldness of the man, Kant is the turning point, as never noted, to our knowledge, as such" (Lacan: 1989; 56).

For Lacan, the pertinent point is that the steps needed to act categorically (in de Sade), can appear 'identical' to the highest evil, Kant, in his early writings at least, sets out to expel (Lacan: 1989; 57). For Kant the categorical imperative requires an autonomous and therefore 'free' will. But Lacan adds considerably to this: looked at this way the moral act is akin to *jouissance*. In the sense that autonomous action is critical, we are only ever autonomous in evildoing. The Augustinian notion of autonomy, central to his thought, serves as a salubrious bridge to Lacan and a resurrection of earlier debates on evil. The text *On Free Choice of the Will* is a significant illustration of this. At a crucial point in the text, Evodius questions Augustine and is offered the rather audacious reply,

> "Since God foreknows our will, the very will that he foreknows will be what comes about…It follows then that his foreknowledge does not take away my power since he whose foreknowledge never errs foreknows that I will have it" (Augustine: 1993; 76).

God, Augustine believes, "foreknows our will" (Augustine: 1993; 76). God–like the Other–"foreknows." God dispenses grace but the Other materialises with the subject entering the symbolic. The Other grounds the desires of the subject as desire of the Other. All of this takes on greater importance when Lacan deliberates, in his ethical writings, on the nature of autonomous acts. His work is of most importance in addressing the relationship between the moral law and what he calls the 'highest Evil.' In this precise sense, Lacan's writings confront the big questions of moral discourse from the medieval period, using these to explore the family, sexuality etc. 'God,' as Malcolm Bowie states, means,

> "Two things at once ... it is 'the One' that male sexuality ordains, and that psychoanalysis in temporary partnership with Christian theology, is able to unmask in an indefinite variety of human contexts. Yet it is also the Other, whatever inextirpable impediment it is that comes between the partners in the well-known arrangement that one is not strictly entitled to call a 'sexual relationship'" (Bowie: 1991; 154).

We can follow Bowie's assessment. We can see the autonomous agent, free from the Other *quo* God, in *jouissance*. This means that Sadean/Kantian 'acts,' in Lacanian ethics, are excessively 'pleasurable' forms of 'enjoyment' free of a defining object. A thought out of kilter with much of modern morality is developed here. In the evil act, the desire of the Other is suspended. Of course, this is distinctively different to how moral philosophers like Onera O'Neill, who believe that, "*finite* rational beings can reject autonomy sporadically" but when this is so "evil and error (is) to be expected" address the topic (O'Neill: 1990; 64). For O'Neil, autonomy and morality are linked–an issue Lacan sees as problematic. In contrast, autonomous acts (independent of the Other), in Augustine *and* Lacan, are evil. "Well in evil," a phrase Lacan uses, has curious affinities with autonomy as outlined in Augustine. Lacan's plea, "we cannot avoid the formula that *jouissance* is evil" supports this affinity (Lacan: 1993; 184). As Richard Kearney states,

"Citing Kant's equation of 'diabolical evil' with the monstrous sublime in the Third Critique Žižek claims that 'the impossible content of the moral law as pure form is "diabolical evil."'" In other words, in the highest instance of noumenal experience–contact with the Law–the human subject finds itself obliterated in a sort of Kafkaesque confusion of sublime proportions. For what it encounters here is nothing other than the 'unconscious' of the Good: that is, the monstrous" (Kearney: 2003; 96).

Perhaps, like Milton, evil of the sort outlined here is at the heart of Lacan's writings (Kearney: 2003; 96). Given sustenance in *The Ethics of Psychoanalysis* (Lacan: 1993; 184) *jouissance* is crucially linked to evil. Slavoj Žižek, the most cited Lacanian philosopher today, has written extensively on the malignant operation of *jouissance* around the everyday workings of the law. In his commentary on the Nazi torture conducted in the camps, he argues that–given *jouissance* is knitted into the legal system–it becomes,

"More satisfying to torture prisoners as part of some orderly procedure– say, the meaningless 'morning exercises' which served only to torment them–didn't it give another 'kick' to the guards' satisfaction when they were inflicting pain on their victims not by directly beating them up but in the guise of an activity officially destined to maintain their health?" (Žižek: 1997; 56).

Safeguarding the pain it horrifically represses, the law, has an altogether more pathological "kick;" that is, than forms of explicit evil which strive to reject legal frameworks completely. Implicit is the "dirty secret," with its 'duty' to hide behind the law (Žižek: 1997; 56). The Eichmann case, mentioned earlier, is a suitable means of analysis for this. Eichmann's belief that his 'dutiful' actions were simply a perverse effect of the law, sprung from a harrowing detachment, an autonomy, from what he was actually doing; an indifference to the contents of his actions. Chigurh in *No Country for Old Men*[1] elicits a similar sense of indifference; even if he

---

[1] An interesting on-line debate has developed in recent years theorising Anton as an Angel sent by God to purge Mankind of its sins. Anton's terminator like status

lacks legal sanction. To conclude, Lacan centres on the law and freedom. Autonomy is both good and evil. From this we assert that Evil is structured like the highest Good. At a structural level, both are autonomous acts Lacan refers to, in a crucial distinction, as *jouissance*. Moreover, Lacan sees the *will-to-jouissance*, will for autonomy, as the Law's unconscious. The subject of extreme Evil bears all the hallmarks of the subject of Good.

In Finale: Kant avec Bataille

In an essay on French writer Michelet in *Literature and Evil* a bizarre position regarding evil is put forward by the *enfant terrible* Georges Bataille. Rendering evil immeasurable in its scope Bataille states, "we can consider any road valid if it helps us to come closer to the object of our disgust" (Bataille: 1973; 71). Now, the object of disgust is rather difficult to define ethically, although it does have a curious attraction in its indefineability, as developed by Bataille in *Literature and Evil* (1973),

> "We cannot consider that actions performed for a material benefit express Evil. This benefit is, no doubt, selfish, but loses its importance if we expect something from it other than Evil itself–if, for example, we expect some advantage from it" (Bataille: 1973; 18).

Bataille closes our enquiry by suggesting Evil has no object, has no positive material gain for the evildoer. Precisely because it, "appears possible to represent moral judgments," Alice Crary notes *quo* Kant, as "both objective and instrinsically practical without needing to appeal to any objective and instrinsically practical properties" (Crary: 2007; 14), a step can align the highest Good as categorical imperative with that of the highest Evil. Bataille, taking this view, is an extreme mirror position. When theorising Evil as an act without an object as its principle (Bataille: 1973; 18), and unbound by practical properties, Evil is elucidated by Bataille in perversely Kantian terms,

> "Evil, therefore, if we examine it closely, is not only the dream of the wicked, it is to some extent the dream of the Good: Death is the punishment, sought and accepted for this mad dream, but nothing can help the dream having been dreamt" (Bataille: 1973; 21).

Bataille's Evil is inspired by a lifetime flirtation with Surrealism. There is a similarity to good and evil: one contests yet defines the other. We find in

---

accords with his lack of empathy towards his crimes. He is simply carrying out divine plans.

Evil a peculiar form of moral imperative; "the dream of the Good;" echoing the position on evil taken by Lacan, Žižek and Kant. In other words, excess pervading goal-oriented impulses, objects, has–rather paradoxically–an instrinsic purpose. For Bataille, such imperative excess is approached in the following way,

> "Humanity pursues two goals–one, the negative, is to preserve life (to avoid death), and the other, the positive, is to increase the intensity of life. These two goals are not contradictory, but their intensity has never increased without danger. The intensity desired by the greatest number (or the social body) is subordinated to the care of preserving life and its works… The notion of intensity cannot be reduced to that of pleasure because, as we have seen, the quest for intensity leads us into the realm of unease and then to the limits of consciousness" (Bataille: 1973; 73-4).

The limit comes to play a prominent role, whether in sexuality or pleasure, in modern views of evil. Evil is excessive, beyond measure, a limit point. And yet even outside the Christian tradition, it remains ultimately Christian in its usage. Bataille's work is concerned with evil in an aesthetic and ethical context but it must be kept in mind that what pertains to literature doesn't necessarily pertain to ethical life. There is little doubt Bataille's are views on the notorious end of the scale since the ethical turn in continental philosophy, most clearly challenged in the work of Emmanuel Levinas and Hans Jonas, but this discussion is beyond the scope of this book. Two films that challenge popular notions of Good and Evil will now be examined in greater detail: Fritz Lang's *M* (1931) and Orson Welles's *Touch of Evil* (1937). As directors who bring to light a morality that–although inherited from the Judeo-Christian tradition– challenges the fundamental precepts of the tradition itself, Lang and Welles provide a starting point for the problem of evil in film.

CHAPTER TWO

THE 'DISCOURSE ON EVIL' IN FRITZ LANG'S *M* (1931) AND ORSON WELLES'S *TOUCH OF EVIL* (1958)

Introduction

"Thus I struggled with myself and was torn apart by myself,"
—Augustine, *Confessions.*

Two notably similar movements tend to arise in the study of cinema and evil: noir and expressionism. Although lacking the criterion to qualify as genre, noir can be felt in every genre of film today. I would even say noir is the quintessentially American form; with its roots nonetheless in Europe. Fritz Lang's *M* and Orson Welles's *Touch of Evil* are indeed brethren of noir from the perspective of expressionism and its subsequent impact on American film. Both are critically examined in this chapter. The chapter begins by exploring the problem of evil in Lang's post-expressionist *M* before briefly contextualising the discussion in relation to Welles's *The Lady of Shanghai* (1947). After a subsequent turn to noir is considered in Welles's oeuvre, a platform to attend to the later *Touch of Evil* (1958) will emerge. 'Dangerous' in that it dramatises moral difficulties in an exemplary form, it is argued that *M* relays emotional difficulties back onto the audience. Indeed, in order to experience the film in its properly moral context, the audience is required *to judge* the emotion felt in judging evil.

Fritz Lang's *M* is undoubtedly one of the great masterpieces of twentieth century cinema. Made during the rise to power of the Nazi movement in 1931, *M* is also a distinctly modern film. In style alone the space of the modern city is brought to bear on factitious concerns about evil. Originally titled *Murderers among Us,* notwithstanding, one of the film's many qualities lies in illustrating the anonymity of the metropolis, when crime begins to threaten everyone. Yet *M* is a film 'about' Peter

Lorre as much as Fritz Lang. Lorre's is one of the great 'criminal' performances in film history; adding another layer of artistic value. *M* responds–in both script (written by Lang with his then collaborator wife Theo von Harbour) and style–to crime. During the Weimar period, a murder industry increasingly demonising agents at the expense of acts had arisen (as well as the real-life hunt for the serial killer Peter Kürten) which impacted on Lang and von Harbou's script in no uncertain terms. The film therefore confronts criminal evil. It is of little surprise that the anger which begins to arise in the court scene is mirrored in those watching, "as viewers in *M* we participate in hatred of the psychopath and (ambivalently) want him dead. But explaining the feeling or the act it motivates does not justify it" (Hoffheimer: 1990; 507).

There is an ethico-sociological strain to the film, particularly when the hunt and trial of a child murderer, Hans Beckert (Peter Lorre), in the metropolis, is the implicit concern. Beckert is an archetypal 'visionary' serial killer, using the criminological criteria devised by Holmes and de Burger in their quintessential study of the condition (Holmes and be Burger; 1988). His stigma is the vision impelling him to kill. But he is also 'disorganised;' lacking the self-serving mark of a classic organised killer. In fact, Beckert's is an ultimately 'child like' demeanour; with the contradiction in *his* role as murderer and child brilliantly espoused by Lorre. Beckert, the hunted criminal, however, has an elusive presence until the end (when captured). Having eluded the Berlin police and detective forces, he is tried (in a court overseen) by criminal gangs, from which he pleads innocence on the basis his actions are not his own. Beckert defends himself by suggesting 'death' motivates him to murder. By the end of *M* Beckert has claimed 'death' experienced at the point of murder is what compels him to act. Childlike and naïve, Beckert's defence contributes to a discourse on evil focused on the "moral status" of a killer (McMahon: 2002; 265). This considers Beckert as rational agent, 'free' in conventional moral discourse, as well as Beckert as the pawn of some cosmic struggle; a battle between the humanism which came to dominate the courts at this time and something else, call it anti-humanism for want of a better word. Before examining the discourse on evil and the court involved, a certain degree of context can be given to Lang and the issues his films deal with. Having made his name as a filmmaker in Weimar Germany during the age of expressionism Lang nonetheless directed a number of post-expressionist 'talkies' before fleeing to the U.S. in the 1930s. Following his move to Hollywood he broke with his 'allegorical' style. Reynold Humphries points to a 'dumbing down' required for more populist audiences (Humphries: 2003; 22). In addition, Colin MacCabe, who equates the quality of these with Lang's earlier work, saw the French *Cahiers* critics' interest in Lang's American films as recognition of the continuity between early and late. For MacCabe, the New Wave–Godard, Truffault etc.–saw the American films as equal in value to the German ones (MacCabe: 2003). In low-culture, dangerous realism was found.

Similiar oscillation–between low and high culture, Shakespearean drama and crime–in Welles's career is noted by David Thomson (Thomson: 1996; 289). Such oscillation is of interest precisely because what is considered 'low' often presents itself in low-grade, often aesthetically questionable modes of visualisation. *Touch of Evil* is arguably the greatest B-movie ever made; its lack of beautification ironic as it now stands as an art-house classic. It is not surprising then that *Touch of Evil* ends with the anti-heroic representative of the law floating downstream, to all extents dead, or that *M* ends with a 'discourse on evil' deliberating on child murder. For both films offer a considered and varied response to the famous Nietzschean retort,

> "Shall we not have to light lanterns in the morning? Do we not hear the noise of the grave-diggers who are burying God? Do we not smell the divine putrefaction?–for even Gods putrify! God is dead! God remains dead! And we have killed him!" (Nietzsche: 2001; 126).

The implication being that in the pivotal space constructed in each film God is not so much dead as murdered; in this sense an evil reigns over the city. It is within this context that the 'official' law as represented by the police in *M* are those who fail to reprimand the murderer Beckert: he is tried by a mob of ex-cons. For *M* ends in the dungeons of the modern city. As Tom Gunning observes,

> "The death's head that Benjamin finds lurking behind allegory's emblems, Lang reveals …. the arrangement of the modern city. As Benjamin intuited a relation between baroque allegory and modernist practices, Lang's career demonstrates the progression from one to the other. Ultimately the modern space of *M*, as the opening sequence shows, is read allegorically as well, as the space that measures separation and death" (Gunning: 2000; 173).

The measurer of death, Schranker (Gustaf Gründgens), the criminal leader of the trial, is, ironically, wanted on three counts of murder. If the finale is inspired by the great 'sham' trial of German culture, Franz Kafka's *The Trial* (1985), there is little doubt Lang nods to the Kafkaesque. Kafka's novel ends with a deliberation on innocence and guilt, as K is told, "it is not necessary to accept everything as true, one must only accept it as necessary" (Kafka: 1985; 243). A similar deliberation on Beckert would suggest his desire to kill is also a necessity; one he also has to accept.

Yet Beckert's death is also considered necessary. In the sham court, where Beckert is allowed to defend himself, he is given a lawyer in order to do so–Lang's tongue in cheek–and the court materialises as a mock-up, when Franz (Freiderich Gnaß) the burglar is coaxed into confessing. When Franz is asked to confess by the police, the courtroom scene magically unfolds. Franz speaks of a court made up of three figures: Schranker as prosecutor, Beckert as defendant, and Beckert's defence lawyer (Rudolph Blümner), as a baying mob appears with a slow pan around the room. The trial progresses as the defence becomes more emotional, as Beckert screams into the camera. We sway between compassion for the murderer and hatred of his actions. But if there is a difficulty in castigating a criminal so obviously deranged in his eloquence, further difficulty is found when a beggar, afflicted by poor sight, is presented as a witness to the prosecution. When the beggar appears in court, Schranker says,

> "You talk of rights…You will get your rights. We are all law experts here, from 6 weeks in Tegel to 15 years in Brandenburg. You will get your rights, you will even get a lawyer. Everything will be done according to the rule of law" (*M*; 1931).

Far from subtle is the way the law and crime (recalling how Lang based the film on a hunt for a murderer on the streets of Berlin) are structurally linked; in the Kafakesque court everyone is a criminal. As the murky underworld of the city takes centre stage, criminals assume power of judgment; the archetypes of German fascism allegorised in mocking appraise. Indeed, the trial is "one of the finest moments of sound cinema" (Gunning: 2000; 194), in that ruthless fascist punishment is pitted against its humane other. If to kill "a person who lacks responsibility" (Hoffheimer: 1990; 505) is its focal point, it is the, "evil thing inside me, the fire, the voices, the torment" (*M*; 1931) Beckert speaks of which makes it difficult to judge. The primordial murder requires our moral evaluation, but the confession may well be the unravelling design of a highly orchestrated murderer: the well-known deviousness of a child killer. The twofold nature of the evil depicted here makes Beckert, firstly, a victim with "rationality, irony and a liberal tradition behind him" (Gunning: 2000; 196).

It (secondly) also makes Beckert an intrinsically evil agent. As a woman screams, "you never had children, huh? So you haven't lost any" (*M*; 1931) her desire to see Beckert killed is sprung from the depths of victimhood. For Beckert has killed children and it is felt he could do so again. Not only is the judge, who deliberates on the nature of the will, a criminal himself, wanted on three counts of murder, but a dangerously subversive figure who expresses all the moral authority of his real life other. If his deliberation on criminal corruption per se, base evil, sets the tone of the debate, the confession of doing evil unfolds with explicit talk about how Beckert strives to do good, while urges to kill consume him. Hence, at the end of the film, when a hand "in the name of the Law" (*M*: 1931) intervenes to save him from this mob, the body remains hidden in an off-screen position. Indeed, the "restoration of order remains elliptical, dramatic in its effects, incommunicative in its meaning" (Gunning: 2000; 197).

What intervenes to save Beckert is never revealed, but its presence serves only to hint at the Law and indeed impossibility of knowing it; of conceiving the Law as a full body. It may well be a gesture symbolising the power Augustine delineates as *grace*. Yet a less optimistic reading is it points to Beckert's will as the repository of a confliction of 'darkness' and 'light;' a murderer taken by the forces of evil.

In a film in which 'conflict' occupies so prominent a place, the expressiveness of Lorre's 'character' needs to be acknowledged. For it is in 'expression' where the humanistic element of psychological profiling–call it 'the will'–can be discerned. Yet, by downplaying the 'expressive' in this final scene, and thereby enhancing the status of the post-expressive in counterpoint, the 'expressive' is given a secondary status to the idea of destiny; that certain people are destined to kill. Although it is easy to allow a character study to take the place of a discourse, Lang is brave enough not to fall into the trap. For this isn't Beckert's story; it's a discourse on whether people are destined to act as they do. It is therefore a story, a narrative above all, in which Beckert is not just a killer, but the potential killer in all of us.

M and Evil

The features of a real criminal court are suitably present in the trial, so the issues raised have real moral purpose. The profiling of child murderers is a defineable feature of modern psychiatry, and Beckert's insanity plea is integral to our subsequent consideration of the concluding discourse. For at a crucial stage he makes his plea: the insanity clause. To this, Schranker vehemently responds,

> "That would suit you wouldn't it? Then you'll invoke Paragraph 51 and spend the rest of your life in an institution at state expense. And then you'll escape, or else get a pardon, then you are free as air, with a law-protected pass, because of mental illness" (*M*; 1931).

By activating the insanity clause (Paragraph 51), Beckert attempts to reduce the level of personal responsibility he holds for the crime in no uncertain terms. If successful in the eyes of the court, even one such as this, he can be absolved of all culpability. It is noteworthy then that Schranker's response is two-pronged; firstly condemning Beckert's evil, while secondly assuming he is responsible. When legalistically posited as a metaphysical attribute, the very idea of 'evil' as the design of one person is a contentious one: it remains an explicitly questionable groundwork on which to base moral argument. Indeed, the 'discourse on evil' brings this to light. *Discipline and Punish: The Birth of the Prison* (1977), Michel Foucault's genealogical account of the modern judicial system (regarding the nature of punishment), is just one of a few texts to properly explore the emergence of psychiatry regarding the kind of crime illustrated in *M*. There is a certain value to what Foucault says about this regarding our discussion,

> "The affirmation of the rights of the prison posits as a principle: that criminal judgement is an arbitrary unity; that it must be broken down; that the writers of the penal codes were correct in distinguishing the legislative level (which classifies the acts and attributes the penalties to them) and the judicial level (which passes the sentences); that the task today is to analyse in turn this later judicial level; that one should distinguish in it what is properly judicial (assess not so much acts as agents, measure 'the intentionalities that give human acts so many different moralities')" (Foucault: 1977; 247).

Bi-furcating into the kind of 'different morality' which would quantify the responsibility Beckert holds, the court appears distinctly Foucauldian. Initiated as a more puerile reaction to the increasing tension in the city; (and, indeed) its subsequent call for justice, it is the prevailing fear the murderer would be 'free as air' if tried in a normal judicial setting which serves as cause. Schranker identifies in Beckert a force greater than criminal immorality, believing Beckert evil and responsible for the evil he commits. Beckert's response is telling. He says that he is free, yet compelled to kill. The contradiction in a term like 'evil' is now brought to the table. Laying emphasis on forces extraneous to the will, considered as a cause of action, and thereby impelling him to kill, Beckert assumes he is not alone when killing children. The court obviously reject this claim. And in doing so they insist on death, irrespective of the agent involved, as *the* necessary and required punishment. This means Beckert cannot be reprimanded: he must be killed.

It is crucial, within the trajectory of what Lang achieves in this remarkable film, that Schranker and his colleagues consider 'death' an appropriate punishment for an evil that is shown to transcend the structure of power which he and the law constitute. I have titled the final sequence the 'discourse on evil,' due to the fact that the first half of the discourse concerns the Law (temporal and eternal), while the second confessions in relation to the jurisdiction of the law; evil and will. The moral, or its basic principle, intersects with 'modern' problems such as insanity: so that Beckert's response to *not* willing the murder of the children corresponds to a belief that forces of an extraneous nature–of which he is the host–have infected his will. Of course, this implies something in him more than him makes him act,

> "But I....I can't help myself! I have no control over this, this evil thing inside me, the fire, the voices, the torment....It's there all the time, driving me out to wander the streets, following me silently, but I can feel it there. It's me pursuing myself" (*M*; 1931).

A compelling sequence set against the backdrop of Franz's testimony materialises, so that, like the 'gimp's' testimony in Bryan Singer's neo-noir masterpiece *The Usual Suspects* (1995), it may well be a hoax, a fantastic invention on the part of a dubious crook. The final scene has a dreamlike quality. It seems out of synch, abstracted from the detective hunt across Berlin which it comes after. This level of abstraction is echoed in Beckert, having been accosted, stating that his actions are *beyond,* "it's me pursuing myself" regarding the will. That demons pursuing him cease only when "I do it" (*M*; 1931) means Beckert, as Roger Dadoun argues, "dies phantasmatically within or without the real death of the victim" (Dadoun in Gunning: 2000). The 'death' he speaks of, as Dadoun observes, requires killing others as a perverted way of saving the self. If this is a paradoxical bind, one in which Beckert is held, the question it poses is whether he can be exonerated on these grounds? Is he innocent in the greater scheme of things, if the *thing*–the darknesss of a primeval 'evil' posited by the Manichees–is thought to be working itself out in him? Of course, both interpetations have merit. To say, "someone who admits to being a murderer should be snuffed out like a candle" (*M*; 1931), like the court, is a simplistic evaluation. Pleading to the mob, the lawyer maintains that Beckert's will–intention–is the main issue of concern,

> "It is this very obsession which makes my client not responsible. And nobody can be punished for something he can't help…I mean this man is sick. A sick man should be handed over, not to the executioner, but to the doctor" (*M*; 1931).

Which questions responsibility. In this context, the lawyer's plea a "sick man should be handed over" (*M*; 1931) can help alleviate Beckert's guilt. This debate brings to light, well ahead of its time, the problem controversial crime elicits in criminal behaviour. Recent texts, *Zero Degrees of Empathy: A New Theory of Human Cruelty and Kindness* (2012) by British neuroscientist Simon Baron-Cohen and Jon Ronson's *The Psychopath Test: A Journey Through the Madness Industry* (2011) have been instrumental in exploring empathy, or the lack of in subjects prone to acts of insidious evil. For Baron-Cohen, "one objection to the notion that cruelty is the result of low (affective) empathy," meaning the agent cannot identify with the emotions of the victim, "is that it removes responsibility or free will" (Baron-Cohen: 2012; 116). In light of this, there is little doubt Beckert is emotional, and takes a certain responsibility for his actions. Yet he suggests something insidious and demonic is impacting upon the will. The physical emphasis on his emotions as empathic in origin makes it difficult to judge Beckert. Yet, as Jon Ronson notes, the problem psychopathic behaviour brings to the table is the very means for intervening in it, psychotherapeutic therapy, can serve to increase the very problem it seeks to resolve. Following his investigation of *The Oak Ridge Programme*, a Canadian research centre for the study of psychiatric intervention, Ronson was faced with the rather paradoxical conundrum that psychopaths, as understood through the lens of modern science, were *incurable*. The means science has devised to cure psychological disorders finds itself inverted with psychopathology. Or as Ronson puts it, "teach them empathy and they'll cunningly use it as an empathy-faking training exercise for their own malicious ends" (Ronson: 2011; 94).

Beckert appears emotional; Lorre's dramatic gesture problematising the issue of a psychopath faking emotion. But, rather than assume Lang is conducting a psychological experiment–call it a play on the celebrity personality of serial killers (which emerged at this time)–is it not more important–as mentioned earlier–to de-emphasise 'expression?' (Particularly as the film is a landmark in post-expressionism). Because the discourse suggests something greater: destiny.

Destiny brings us back to the will. If Beckert's cry "how I must.... Must...Don't want to" (*M*; 1931) implies that evil is something corrupting the will from outside, on which the defence lawyer can claim that Beckert has limited responsibility for the actions he performs, the debate about him being insane is made. If there is a significant question arising from this then it concerns whether or not Beckert is aware of what he does. Moreover, the idea that Beckert is faking emotion is paralleled by a suspicion of the body elicited in the gestures he makes to the crowd; marked by Beckert's squirming expressions. Around the body–and indeed evil, as discussed in Chapter One, manifest problems unfold. Recapping, Cathar views of the physical as constitutive of a demonic evil were reiterated in Augustine,

> "We set out to discover what evildoing is. This whole discussion was aimed at answering that question. So we are now in a position to ask whether evildoing is anything other than neglecting eternal things, which the mind perceives and enjoys by means of itself and which it cannot lose if it loves them; and instead pursuing temporal things–which are pursued by means of the body, the least valuable part of a human being, and which can never be certain–as if they were great and marvellous things. It seems to me that all evil deeds–that is all sins–fall into this one category" (Augustine: 1993; 27).

That bodies are, "the least valuable part of the human being" (Augustine: 1993; 27) puts them in a certain opposition to the eternal unchanging notion of the soul. In the sense of it being opposed to the eternal soul, the idea of Beckert as a victim wrestling with some kind of bodily *thing*, coercing and corrupting his will from outside, can be addressed. In this light, the *thing* of the body is considered a manifest evil force. Gerard Loughlin has pointed out that, "the sexual organs have become an alien within the body: the very sign of the disobedience which constitutes our fallen world" in Augustine's writings (Loughlin: 2004; 114) and this bears implicitly on the kind of intent Beckert refers to which, irrespective of the will, manifests in the physical gestures made to the crowd. Beckert believes, as he says himself, his murders are 'caused' by something in but not part of him. The body is considered alien, forcing him to act the way he does. It is not surprising his physical squirming is accompanied by the plea,

"Who are you? Criminal? Are you proud of yourselves? Proud of breaking safes or cheating at cards? Things you could just as well keep your fingers off. You wouldn't need to do all that if you'd learn a proper trade, or if you'd work. But I…I can't help myself" (*M*; 1931).

It is not so much the plea (but the physical expression of it) which distinguishes the calculated crime from one with origins extraneous to the will. It is the body ("I can't help myself") Beckert believes has a life of its own. For the lawyer, Beckert has lost control of his will, while for the dweller on evil, Beckert is caught in the grips of desire beyond his physical control. Hence, Beckert's pathos, *wanting* to do good yet *impelled* to do evil, constitutes the film's danger; making us wonder if the body which saves him is also what entices him in the first place (while preserving prohibition)? In other words, Beckert is saved by the hand enticing him to kill. Hence the proposal that Beckert is responsible because he is a particular behavourial type, with a minimal capacity for empathy, is set in opposition to a not wholly different idea of evil as being, persecuted by a physical desire he has no control over. Here is the irony. A behavourial type, call it a psychopath, is akin to the bedrock we call evil. Beckert might confess, but being is beyond confession. Beckert's status as a killer of children no less, contrasts his own childishness; his wide-open eyes glaring at the mob that stand in our place. His destiny is to be the child he kills. And to remain so, he must kill again and again.

Confessions

> "Does anybody feel,
> The same way I do?
> And is Evil just something we are,
> Or something we do?"
> —Morrissey, *Sister I'm a Poet.*

It is the complexity of a legacy which has been attributed to Augustine in all *his* complexity as a person, which can be identified in Beckert's simple cry, "I can't help myself." After Beckert's plea, the jury respond with a final punishment of death. Essentially, the judge's quandary–*ex post facto*–lies in believing that evildoers are responsible for the acts they perform, Beckert the focal point of this, while considering Beckert an evil person. This is a major contradiction. Evil is considered to be an attribute of human behaviour while the subject is responsible when displaying this evil. Beckert is punished yet the fact he should be punished for being something he has little control over, whether insane or not, a psychopath or personality type, is deeply ironic. For how can someone be killed as punishment for something hard-wired into his or her being? Notwithstanding, the film ends with a suitably dangerous link to Orson Welles's *The Lady From Shanghai* (Welles, 1947). Let us now explore this link further.

Welles and the Law

"It is not so much the grandeur of evil–although the grandeur is there–as the innocence of the sin, fault or crime. Minafer, Michael O'Hara, MacBeth, Othello and Arkadin are all in one way or another condemned by our legal system, our intelligence and our hearts, but we also feel that they elude our judgment," André Bazin, *Orson Welles: A Critical Review.*

Peculiar lighting, widescreen close-ups of distorted faces and of course, the *femme fatale* are all noir conventions which in *The Lady of Shanghai* make for a classic backdrop to Welles's later and more expansive study of evil in *Touch of Evil*. Certainly, "the role of a passive hero who allows himself to be dragged across the line into the gray area between legal and criminal behaviour" (Borde and Chaumeton in Silver and Ursini (ed): 1995; 22) is characteristically noir. But beneath its surface, the film explores the charismatic allure of evil. Fighting corruption, the antagonist is interrupted by agencies beyond his control, in some way similar to the Cathar battling evil. The plot centres on a power struggle between two criminal lawyers, seeking sole ownership of a law firm both had founded, the film's narrative tension based around an antagonistic struggle. The individual caught in this, the Irish sailor Michael O'Hara (Orson Welles), wants to be pivotal to the drama, but a woman he becomes pathologically attached to leads to his downfall.

The *femme fatale* in question, Rosalyn Bannister (Rita Heyworth), wants sole ownership of the law firm. Eventually Rosalyn outwits the male protagonists–inclusive of which is O'Hara–as she implicates her husband in the crime. Welles's *femme fatale* is oblivious to the good of others, accentuating Borde's and Chaumeton's observations in their defining study. In this classic text the critics argue,

"In a true *film noir*, the bizarre is inseparable from what might be called the *uncertainty of motivations*. For instance, what are Bannister and his partner hoping to accomplish with their shadowy intrigues in *The Lady from Shanghai*? All the weirdness of the movie is focused on this: in these mysterious and metamorphosing creatures who tip their hands only in death. … the enigmatic killer, will he be an executioner or a victim? Honor among thieves, an extortion network, unexplained motives, all this verges on madness" (Borde and Chaumeton in Silver and Ursini (ed): 1996; 24).

In its visuality alone *The Lady of Shanghai*–with facial expression distorted in widescreen close-ups–fashions an "uncertainty of motivations" (Borde and Chaumeton in Silver and Ursini (ed): 1995; 24), what can be considered as a weirdness of demonic proportions around the will. Bizarre moments and innuendos, seemingly with no relation to the narrative, are echoes of a dangerous cosmic plot. When Rosalyn says, "everything's bad Michael, everything. You can't escape it, you gotta get along with it, deal with it, make terms with it" (*The Lady from Shanghai*; 1947), how the noir world is viewed is given expression. Later, Michael's declaration, "you could feel the lust and murder like a wind stingin' in your eyes, death reekin' up out of the sea" (*The Lady from Shanghai*; 1947), makes of the natural world a vehicle of evil. When Grisby (Glen Anders) fakes his own murder to claim insurance the act in itself accentuates his role as 'criminal lawyer;' in the process committing the very set of action what he defends. As Grisby notes,

> "There's no such thing as homicide unless they find a corpse. It just isn't murder if they don't find a body. According to the law, I'm dead if you say you murdered me. But you're not a murderer unless I'm dead" (*The Lady from Shanghai*; 1947).

The paradox is that O'Hara will be tried only if Grisby's body is recovered. O'Hara confessing to murder means he cannot be tried and convicted unless a body is found. The body in question can never be found as the subject in question isn't dead. Around Hans Beckert is a confession of sorts, but confession is superfluous in *The Lady of Shanghai*. The courtroom scene is similar in stature to *M*. In Welles, however, instead of criminals who appear as lawyers, lawyers parade as criminals. Repentance and confession have scant regard in the morally corrupt world of noir.

In this context, the plot fails to progress towards the prosecution of a designated evil person; rather the system unfolds in an extraordinary, dangerous capacity as the design of a dark God. Any view that the noir world is good and corruption is its by-product is undermined. It is particularly undermined in the shooting at the end, when a neon sign with the heading 'Walhalla' is situated in the corner of the frame. The characters are gravitating towards the depths of hell, living out their existence in a reincarnation of Dantean proportions. In the final scene O'Hara reiterates Rosalyn's earlier remark that, "one who follows his nature, keeps his original nature in the end" (*The Lady of Shanghai*; 1947).

By suggesting those motivated by corruption end up 'fully' corrupt in the end, Welles undermines the somewhat naively posited belief that humanity is born of the good, and irrespective of sin can still be redeemed: O'Hara therefore invokes a Manicheanism in which those motivated by evil are impelled by an essential part of their nature: the Manichean divide not just *in* noir but noir itself. Evil encroached upon in these terms is politicised around the *realpolitic* of immigration in *Touch of Evil*, Welles's later and most sustained engagement with politics, to which we can now turn.

Welles and the Noir Landscape

Marc Vernet stresses that,

> "Expressionism is officially evoked in the name of the strong opposition between black and white (the coal-like aspects of the images)–an opposition which is valid not only in terms of light contrasts but also in terms of the relation between the expanse of dark areas and the scarcity of strongly lit areas–in the name of the disproportionate shadows accompanying the character" (Vernet in Copjec (ed): 1994; 18).

Theorists claim expressionism precedes noir. In fact, much historical research into noir has been concerned with the links between a uniquely German film form, whose influence on the history of cinema is immense, and that of an American phenomenon, steeped in the popular consciousness and frowned upon by the same scholars who had championed the expressionist film form. Hence the division of the noir hero has European origins. For Vernet, disproportional shadows, low-angle shots and fill lighting, shape the expressionist and noir agent. Hence, the protagonist of 'light' (struggling against evil) is aptly replaced by the morally complicated hero of noir,

> "In each case, it is a question of the failure of institutions to defend the Good, the unequal struggle of an innocent individual against evil combinations, and the general response that seems to reside in the love of a being of the opposite sex" (Copjec: 1994; 17).

Given Copjec's analysis, it is now possible to hypothesise: *Touch of Evil* explores, "the failure of institutions to defend the Good," bringing the "evil combinations" particular to film noir to the fore. Hank Quinlan is cast as a slippery detective working the margins of the Law, with Welles taking root in a now burgeoning filmic trope. Captain Hank Quinlan (Orson Welles) is a police detective; a defender of public (rather than strictly private) virtue; a chief of homicide rather than a private 'eye.' The noir setting changes as, "the modern city with its networks of communication and intersections" (Gunning: 2000; 164) shifts to fictional border town Los Roblos between the U.S. and Mexico. *Touch of Evil* alters the topology of traditional noir. The borders set out by the State of Emergency meant the film's backdrop was a law used to stem workers migrating between Mexico and the U.S. Importantly, Welles's activism during the 50s was brought to bear. It is likely this led him to include political issues in the original screenplay with greater purpose (Thomson: 1996; 335). The opening sequence moves between Mexico and the U.S. as a car explodes in the town. The now infamous tracking shot of the border is marked by a sudden explosion; triggering a sense of urgency.

Killing the town's wealthy real estate agent, Rudy Lennaker and a prostitute he has been having relations with, the bomb attracts the attention of the town's inhabitants. Links between Lennaker's death, his estranged daughter and her Mexican boyfriend Miguel Sanchez (Victor Milan), who had an acrimonious relationship with the deceased father are made, leading to suspicion that Sanchez is involved in the murder. When travelling through Los Roblos, the newlywed narcotics agent Miguel Vargas (Charlton Heston) stumbles upon the crime. Vargas works for the U.S.-Mexican border committee and has just married an American citizen, Susan Vargas (Janet Leigh). When he witnesses the car explosion that kills Lennaker he takes an immediate interest in the case, cancelling his honeymoon. On meeting Quinlan he suspects him of racism against Mexicans. Quinlan's and Vargas's relationship is antagonistically set in a widescreen shot of Quinlan bearing down on Vargas unsettling in its monstrousness. Quinlan will–due to an impending narcotics case–interfere with Vargas, typical of the low-grade corruption both police and criminals partake in.

Quinlan and the Grandis are part of an underworld border culture. The mob exchanges information for clemency towards them. In *Touch of Evil* the affiliation between minorities and the world of detection echoes contemporaneous noirs such as *Kiss Me Deadly* (1955). It is Sanchez, member of such a minority, who is framed by Quinlan. By planting dynamite, using information from the 'Mexican side of town,' Sanchez is innocuously framed. Set outside his jurisdiction, Quinlan shows a disregard for boundaries; further evidence of a disregard for law. Framing Sanchez (on the other side) is emblematic of a hazardous approach to law-abidance: Vargas had searched the apartment earlier. As it becomes apparent that Vargas is seeking to uncover Quinlan's guilt, key developments emerge. First of all, the Grandi mob, at Quinlan's behest, frames Susan Vargas for doping–inciting Vargas's fury. Discrediting Vargas has two objectives. It stalls Grandi's impending trial for extortion, of which Vargas is the leading prosecutor. It also lets Quinlan 'off the hook.' Vargas acquires proof of Quinlan's corruption, at which point a significant twist emerges: Sanchez then confesses to the crime. Quinlan's famous 'intuition'–as referred to throughout the film–is affirmed once again.

'Catching murderers,' obeying or disobeying the Law (in this case the categorical imperative), is the morality on which Welles's complex vision is grounded: the Kantian dilemma in the border noir world. To act against evil is complicated by a morality in which allegiances are marred, and black often fades into grey. In this moral universe, "Vargas is in the position of desire, its admission and its prohibition. Not surprisingly he has two names: the name of desire is Mexican... that of the Law, American" (Heath; 1975). For Heath, the allegiance Vargas pledges to the State of Emergency *and* Mexico (Heath; 1975) means he identifies with Mexicans who desire legitimate U.S. citizenship, something he holds, while at the same time forces prohibiting that same desire. In the finale, a certain suspicion prevails that Quinlan's siding with such outsiders displays a pronounced allegiance to the moral Law. Why?

A clear sense of what happens is needed to answer this. On one level, "the discourse of American cultural colonialism and Mexican dependency, the fear/ desire of miscegenation" (Bhabha in Baker, Diawara and Lindeborg: 1996; 91) makes the moral subject far from stable. On another, "the site of dislocation between the state and its citizens" constructed in the film, according to Donald B. Pease, is the foundation on which Vargas's "extra-legal" status is set, a Mexican citizen answering neither to Mexico, nor to the U.S. (Pease: 2001; 79). In the years leading up to the production of *Touch of Evil*, a State of Emergency had been introduced in the U.S. to instigate a deportation policy for illegal and 'non-assimilable aliens.' Mexicans considered politically subversive, as well as those who were involved in illegal crossing from Mexico to the U.S. could be detained. Guilty until proven otherwise. In the final scene, testament to this, stereotype images of 'wetbacks' cut to a shot of Quinlan's body floating downstream, in a manner which crucially inverts the process by which entry to the U.S. was acquired by such emigrants.

Electing, as David Thomson notes, "to shift the action to the U.S.-Mexico border; ....as if to dramatize juxtaposition and its explosive risk" (Thomson: 1996; 337), the State of Emergency is a backdrop to state violence. Because it validates Vargas's transgression of constitutional law, the U.S. State of Emergency is *the* ethical issue in the film. If Quinlan's is a moral 'touch of evil,' it is set against the more suspect notion of an extra-moral evil expressed by Vargas,

> "Vargas thereafter enjoys the violation of the law to which he has subordinated others (and) it is difficult to imagine the position he occupies as just a *touch of evil*. The relationship he now enjoys with Susan instead enacts what Kant would call radical evil" (Pease: 2001; 99).

The U.S. State of Emergency may well have justified the transgression of rights. For it enables Vargas his allegiance to a non-state. The emergency was blamed on illegal workers. If it allowed agents like Vargas, in modern legalese, to enjoy the liberties of a 'third state,' neither the U.S. nor the Mexican, this is significant ethically. For Pease, Vargas's role,

> "Renders the emergency powers he exercises less visible through the accusation that Hank Quinlan is alone guilty of using excessive force– which facilitates Vargas's usage of these powers" (Pease: 2001; 96).

For Pease, Vargas's 'official' mandate is an evil masked by the immorality accredited to Quinlan. There is a kind of subtlety to the contrasting of Quinlan and Vargas. For if one acts immorally, the other is on a much bigger scale. One is a detective, large in size, whose immorality is defined by a deep-lying intuition for how good, at least the good in the noir world, needs to be maintained. The good is keeping things in line, and preventing the horrors of murder and evil. In this world, like Milton showed, it is necessary to understand good if one is to know evil. The other is an official, beholden to neither state, an agent for a quasi-state programme, which can override the basic principles or 'rights' and call them law. With this type of evil, human rights cease to exist, and power exerts itself without restriction. The State of Emergency depicted is almost prophetic in this sense, foreseeing the State of Emergency that would suspend individual liberties, lead to mass arrest without trial, during the recent War on Terror. Welles's film isn't simply a fictional representation of a particular time, but our present world. It is therefore noteworthy that the gypsy fortune-teller (played by Marlene Dietrich) demonstrates an astutness unbecoming the others, when claiming Quinlan was, "a good detective but a lousy cop" (*Touch of Evil*; 1958). At this point Vargas's (perhaps explaining Quinlan's moral triumph at the film's end) *apparent* patriotism is set against a crucially different reality: Quinlan's (disrespectful of minorities yet less careerist in his use of them) actions. Simply put, Quinlan's immorality has a moral purpose,

> "Quinlan is physically monstrous but is he morally monstrous as well? The answer is yes and no. Yes because he is guilty of committing a crime to defend himself; no because from a higher moral standpoint, he is, at least in certain respects, above the honest, just, intelligent Vargas, who will always lack that sense of life which I call Shakespearean" (Bazin: 1978; 101)

By the end of the film, the idea of a hidden reality is subservient to the idea that all appearances are in themselves deceptive. If a suspicion of the state pervades noir, it finds a particularly astute platform in the figure of Vargas. Vargas 'appears' beholden to a kind of 'do goodery,' taking time out of a honeymoon to tackle crime. The casting of Charlton Heston, a poster boy for the Hollywood good guy, confirms this 'identification;' if only on a subliminal level. Heston is the hero next door. That he is actually Mexican in the film has an almost comical ring, set in brownface, given that he possesses none of the ethnic features of a typical Mexican (nor talks like one). 'Opposing' ethnicities, of course, remains crucially subservient to the idea that ethnic cultures are subservient to a law that transcends either states, and that Heston in his bizarre hybridity perfectly encapsulates in the film. Quinlan, however, displays a clear knowledge of evil; his famous intuition morally vindicated if not legally so. Vargas, on the other hand, exemplifies 'order,' one in which the structures of law are mimicked by something opposing them. His hybridity, and the fact it's so noticeably 'fake,' is a nod to this. With his hybridity a quotidian of the false, he is shown to be less concerned with the partnership between border agents, than the divisions associated with what they stand for. For Pease,

> "Heston's brown mask is used to consolidate Vargas's power to instruct Hank Quinlan of the higher standards to which officers of the law are beholden. Welles, pace Bhabha, had not undermined the border law's authority. Welles had instead disclosed the ways in which emigration laws had appropriated the hybridity that had been deployed as a counterhegemonic strategy throughout the borderlands and placed it into the service of governmental rule" (Pease: 2001; 85).

For Pease, Vargas reminds Quinlan of standards the origin of which he is suitably unaware. That those such as Quinlan are more engaged with the otherness they confront, means good and evil, closely connected, form a strange unity. Because he is more alert to the othered Mexican he encounters, Quinlan is both hero and anti-hero. "There is unity between sign and object, between reason and sense, between pain and pleasure, between good and evil," (Kleberg in Copjec: 1994; 240) says Lars Kleberg of expressionism. A similiar unity pertains to *Touch of Evil*. Vargas's retort, "it's a dirty job enforcing the law, but it's something we're supposed to do" (*Touch of Evil*: 1958) illustrates the dubious unity in Wellesean film noir, the subject the subject of a 'dirty' law. In the final instance the detective, and not the state official, has defineable and recognisable moral status: upholding the Law while failing the imperatives of the law. For this reason Quinlan is a good detective and a lousy cop.

Perhaps, at this point we should pause to reflect on the bearing of this insight on the history of American film, or indeed moving imagery in general in the context of noir. So many American films focus on the bent cop, immorally breaking the law to instigate a more satisifactory moral outcome. Two recent examples bear thinking about. The first is Werner Herzog's exemplary *Bad Lieutenant: Port of Call New Orleans* (Herzog, 2009), starring Nicolas Cage as the particularly vile cop Terence McDonagh, which takes the noir sensibility as a major reference point. McDonagh's actions are irrevocably nasty; whether in drug use, prostitution, or rape, yet he manages to rise momentarily above the nastiness he involves himself in. There is something we could call 'moral' about McDonagh's consistent disrespect for beaurocracy, however 'evil' this can appear, and the triumph involved in McDonagh's act of duty near the end.

The Wire is a police drama almost Dickensian in its lengthy exploration of the city of Baltimore. The police, and in particular Jimmy McNulty (Dominic West), a cop of Irish decent (like Quinlan and McDonagh), continually brush up against the limits of legality, and indeed bureaucracy, when trying to uphold the law. This climaxes in the fifth series when McNulty invents a serial killer as part of a scheme to reignite financial investment in policing. Like Quinlan, McNulty is admired if not loved by his colleagues. As a cop whose private immoralism masks a deeply ingrained moralism, he is a curious noir take on the political impact of private versus public so specific to U.S. public life. Cops who have a private handle on the moral are more often more identifiably 'good' than those who follow the letter of the public framework of legality. One could see this as being part of a greater ideological framework, where private initiative is set out in opposition to the slowed-down dealings of official bureaucracy.

Nothing but Desire

A prevailing feature of noir concerns private actions set against their image in public life; the differential that exists between public exposure and private space. One thinks of Neff in *Double Indemnity* (Wilder, 1942) as an archetypal example. Neff busily organises his work mandate while informing us of his problems, making us suspect Neff's voice as concealing something that is, in time, necessarily revealed. This revelation is what help explains why the noir universe, when depicted in this way, as Joan Copjec points out,

> "Has been perceived as essentially deceptive, though it is, in fact, a world in which nothing is hidden, everything must come to light. This is really the dark truth of film noir" (Copjec: 1994; 192).

Copjec's point runs counter to the dominant critical approach to film noir. The approach in question has underlined secretly repressed pathologies (whose very repression) as the cause of such corruption. For Copjec, this is a way of looking at things which is ultimately askew. Instead, the darkness which constitutes the deception of noir, is only partially embedded: darkness always come to light. When Deitrich's profile is contrasted with the dead body of Quinlan at the end of *Touch of Evil* a non-diegetic piano jangle accompanies Deitrich's surmising on Quinlan's morality; the truth of noir left to a considerably marginalised prostitute. But the contrast between a 'man' lying face up in the water, the body politic as human body, and the 'hooker' with greater access to truth than state officials, is a composed one. It is as if the truth of noir has 'come to the surface,' is there in plain view. There is nothing hidden, nothing concealed for which we must decipher and understand. On the contrary, the physical monster before us accords with the physical monstrosity of the Law. Indeed, Quinlan's floating dead body, when he literally becomes the other he confronted illustrates this; as both a joke on the 'wetback' entering U.S. territory and an illustration that in noir everything comes to light. That Quinlan's body expresses the 'emptying' of desire needed for this coming into view, in a dangerous film, means nothing remains hidden in noir. Or to put this in another way, and by conclusion, the vulgar representative of the law–Quinlan–is vulgar because he *is* a representative of the law.

Conclusion: Desire and Evil

We are now venturing towards a conclusion, coming on the back of a consensus regarding the treatment of evil in these films. The case concerning Beckert's criminality can now be evaluated on the basis of the following comments by F.W.J. Schelling,

> "This universal judgement about a disposition to Evil which is consciousless and even irresistible, a judgement rendering it into an act of freedom, points towards an act and consequently towards a life before this life" (Schelling in Žižek: 1989; 168).

Overlooking the origins of murder means overlooking the very issue Schelling regards as "the life before this life" of the murderer; in modern parlance, 'nature.' Simply put, Nature is. It is absurd to say Beckert is naturally free, while at the same he has no choice to commit his crimes; he must kill. Taking his nature as the conduit of his being, or looking at him as hard-wired biologically to commit the crimes he commits, frequents us from pondering why he kills. And if we cannot ask why Beckert kills, it is a lazy configuration to then refer to him as evil. In doing so, we frequent concepts–autonomy, responsibility, morality–when most needed. If the 'sexual offender' has yet to fully penetrate the semantic field psychiatry, and as Beckert's 'sexual offence' is made to correlate with 'insanity' by the defence, his depravity is suggestive of a stigma 'evil' cannot properly designate. Evil is, paradoxically, both a choice and something which is chosen for him. So, finally, and with this choice recognised, we are in a position to say, as a filmic project *M* ultimately and crucially draws our attention (as moral subjects) to the making of judgments on 'evil' personages when what is most needed is an understanding of the role responsibility plays in relation to evil. The other significant feature of the film is its play on the virtual; the court we 'see' possibily–and probably– the design of another devious criminal, deflecting attention from his own criminality. In this way, diegetic uncertainty plays a major role and its distortion of time is something Lang is suitably concerned with. If an illusion, the 'discourse on evil' may well be an illusion within an illusion.

By contrast, Welles asks us to think of evil in its precise relation to good, so that the good is always in a peculiar almost Miltonic relation to evil. But he also positions us in such a way that we are compelled to think the difference between the immoral, evil and *radical evil*. Because it opposes the law and the Law *Touch of Evil* is a dangerous commentary on the typology of evil. For it demonstrates when it is necessary to be immoral–use a touch of evil–*to do* Good. But it also demonstrates that what can appear to be good can actually mask a systemic and radicalised form of evil.

CHAPTER THREE

PASOLINI AND THE REMNANTS
OF NEOREALISM:
TOWARDS AN IMMEASURABLE EVIL

The Remnants of Neo-Realism

The films of Pier Paolo Pasolini and Liliana Cavani span a period technically removed from what is possibly the defining cinematic movement in twentieth-century Europe: Italian neorealism. Remnants of neorealism are nonetheless apparent in their films. Robert Kolker regards Italian neorealism as the fundamental reference point for the new wave cinema of the 60s; perhaps the development of cinema in general (Kolker: 1983; 16). Kolker believes a renewed way of thinking about 'reality' emerged: an event-defining break with an industry increasingly compromised by vested and commercial interests. In its challenge to the increasingly stagnant filmic conventions of bigger production companies, neorealism brought film back to its initial foundations–grounded in representation and the objective world of 'reality.'

Neorealism emerged when the nation state was being reshaped in the post-war years. The instigators of the movement believed the camera to be a source of objectivity: a vital way of seeing 'reality' (Bondanella: 1983; 15). For Bondanella, a radically new approach to 'reality' (distinct from documentary) becomes discernible in the Italian feature film, as socially divisive issues are brought to the fore in a quasi-documentary fashion. While film historians found a meshing together of 'real life,' pulp fiction and melodrama in the Hollywood film, the inspiration for neorealism is thought to lie in concrete social issues (Bondanella: 1983; 40). A nation scarred by the fight against fascism would turn to cinema as a means of mending this. For many neorealism gathered pace when filmmakers like the Marxist-aristocrat Luchino Visconti began to experiment with the temporalilty of form. In *Ossessione* (Obsession (1942)) for example, time is suitably slowed down, allowing the, "close interrelationship of the protagonists to their surroundings" to be felt (Bondanella: 1983; 21). In a typically realist style, characters are cast as custodians of class interests.

Not surprisingly, Visconti's 'embryonic communist consciousness' is thought to depend,

> "Less on a struggle with nature and between men than on a grand vision of man and nature, of their perceptible and sensual unity, from which the 'rich' are excluded and which constitutes the hope of the revolution, beyond the setbacks of the floating action: a Marxist romanticism" (Deleuze: 1992; 5).

There is a unified if somewhat synthetic form to this kind of Marxist Romanticism, uniting the collective and individual, the movement gives rise to; moving through the landscape, as Deleuze notes, sensual as an experience. That the main reference point for neorealism is, however Roberto Rossellini, meant for Vache, a dedramatised, naturalised aesthetic; from which an awareness of the Italian nation arises,

> "In contrast to the marble heroes of fascist cinema, the body in Rosselini's neorealism is the human organism inhabited by the antithesis of sheer biology, the soul, as if a Christian spirituality had developed next to a pagan attachment to the earth. In representing the impact of official history on daily life and anonymous people, neorealism adopted the microscopic scale of the *commedia dell'arte* and turned away from the monumental setting of opera" (Vache: 1992; 180-181).

"Official history" and "sheer biology" are considered essential to the movement's development. In *Roma, città aperta* (Rome, Open City (1945)), Rossellini's classic wartime drama set during the resistance, the central axis for the movement is located. Its melodramatic purpose contrasts the paradigmatic slowed down nature of neorealist films; *Rome, Open City* a less obvious example than Visconti's *Ossessione*. Fascist Italy is pitted against an unfolding resistance (in *Rome, Open City*), mythologising historical struggle, while at the same time reconstructing national space around good and evil. That film could serve as a platform for "official history" gives a documentary-like status to a considerably social movement. Yet for Brunette, a good (the resistance) and evil (fascist), brought to melodramatic levels in the film, sees a good and evil of almost Manichean proportions face off, generating the suspense lacking in other neorealist films. Hence, the story of a nation warring against a fascist enemy is central to the melodramatic narrative; on which a crucially rarified moral structure can be situated (Brunette; 1987).

Rome, Open City has one of the most celebrated endings in the history of cinema. The barren landscape, so typical of the neorealist visual vocabulary, appears as any landscape, were it not for an empty wooden chair situated at its centre. The shot of the chair eloquently contrasts the shot of the Don stepping out of his carriage accompanied by guards, clasping his hands in prayer. He looks downwards aware that he will die. Has European cinema a more disheartening image of war; when unassailable forms of good front off against the dehumanising forces of evil? Probably not. The next shot is of a guard coolly sucking on a cigarette; just as the casualness of the Nazi death squads are complemented by a group of schoolchildren who come to witness the event. The Don is tied to the chair and shot in the rear; as he turns towards the land and dies the children shudder in fear, scarred by the presence of evil.

If, on this note, the resistance leader Don Pietri's (Aldo Fabrizi) execution is a pivotal ending to the film it is because he embodies the faith needed to defeat fascist 'evils;' with film as myth, as Bondanella notes, vital to the reconstructed nation; set out in a religious and militant alliance against fascist evil. However, *Rome, Open City* was not devoid of criticism. James T. Farrell, lauding Rossellini, outlined the failed political agenda elicited in the film, which he believed ended up giving certain credence to an already fetishised leader (Farrell; 2009). Such a failure is a marker of the difficulties experienced by the movement in the following decades. Yet, even with such obvious difficulties, filmmakers like Pier Paolo Pasolini gathered inspiration from the films; illustrated in his poetry *Gramsci's Ashes* (1982); which made him a household figure. Pasolini's verse stems from a visit to the grave of Marxist luminary, Antonio Gramsci. The book focuses on the intersection of messianic and militant in Gramsci's writing; complementing films of the time. For Viano, Pasolini's art is a significant attempt to synthesize the messianic and militant,

> "Catholicism's messianic fervor prepared the terrain for Marxism, and Pasolini dedicated much time and energy to the reconciliation of the two. From a political perspective, Pasolini's most fertile intuitions came precisely from the combination of a religious outlook with a radical ideology" (Viano: 1993; 6).

Viano's interest in the messianic and Marxist tendencies in Pasolini is stated; an alliance many felt Rosselini had mapped in *Rome, Open City*. Both Pasolini's early films and neorealist classics such as *Rome, Open City* and *Bicycle Thieves* (1948) use, for Viano, 'natural' socio-historical backdrops to frame the characters. The framing–which tends towards alienation–in expressionism and noir, contrasts the real settings in neorealism (Viano: 1993). Framed against a natural landscape, the face of an actor assumes a naturalised bent. Hence, the framing of crowds and "anonymous people" in neorealism contrasts noir's evidently urban doors and windows (Silver and Ursini (eds): 1996; 57). Workers, idle vagrants, the excess of society, permeate these films, giving to the issues Italian intellectuals grappled with after the War a vivid screen presence. Neorealism's affiliation with the then existing Communist Party, as Vache noted earlier, is pinned on humanism communism tended to emasculate if not reject.

Meyer Schapiro would identify the roots of neorealism in the iconographic tradition (Schapiro in Sitney: 1995). Schapiro believed neorealism, looking forward as a film movement, also looked to the past to reconnect with a more holistic notion of cultural life. For P. Adams Sitney iconography (framing of the subject) is a striking feature of the films; with the explicit references to Dante and the Renaissance used to explore the oft considered fracture with the real historical past (Sitney: 1995). Yet, considering its storyline alone, many saw *Rome, Open City* as a film in which Dante's struggle is projected onto the post-war dilemma. With a considerably different concern (to that of historical fascism), my own consideration of *Rome, Open City* notwithstanding, I want to argue that the resistance–whether communist or Catholic–is considerably reduced in 60s films; so that a Christian and Marxist collective as all-embracing struggle against evil is no longer the pivotal concern. In making this claim, I support the view that neorealism foreground the conflict between already established notions of good and evil at the expense of explorations of what the terms mean. As P. Adams Sitney suggests, "concentrating all of the evils in the Germans, Rossellini discovers a safely distant scapegoat that could play no role in the political situation of 1945" (Sitney: 1995; 36).

If the historical images of fascism which permeate neorealist film chime with the pathological, the fascism on which this rests, in all its vibrancy, must be countered in an alternative capacity. The fascism addressed in *Rome, Open City*–with Don Pietri's (Aldo Fabrizi) death a sublime Christian response–is reconfigured in the aftermath of neorealism. Pasolini and Fellini make films which question the 'real' in its manifest substance; by way of confronting the very premise of 'reality.' As such, both would give the subject, as distinct from the objective, a new purpose. As Fellini observes,

"To me neo-realism is a way of seeing reality without prejudice, without convention coming between it and myself–facing without preconceptions, looking at it in an honest way–whatever reality is, not just social reality, metaphysical reality, *all there is without man*" (Fellini: 1996; 52).

For Fellini, neorealism depends on whether 'the real'–in whatever way we perceive it–can be felt without 'subjective' prejudice; that is, whether we can conceive of 'reality' as intrinsically objective. Pasolini, answering this, refers to neorealism as a "vital crisis." For Pasolini found the perpetual revolt against spectacularised entertainment as hinging on a new crisis within neorealism. This chapter addresses this. For this chapter traces the changes in Italian cinema from neorealism to the art-house movement, instigating an analysis of the quite brilliant ending to Pasolini's career. As Miltonic 'excess,' sexuality and evil, have a deep-felt prominence in Pasolini's final film *Salò,* it is necessary to give preceding films–as neorealist context–necessary consideration. For Pasolini, and Cavani, explore evil around reality. In this sense they confront the remnants of neorealism.

"While Fascism," Mark Kermode notes, "has been addressed in the Italian Cinema since the days of 'Rome, Open City' by the end of the 60s directors had begun to examine its legacy in less black and white terms" (Kermode; 2002). Caution is required, nonetheless, in assessing this statement. For in 'Fellini's Voyage to the End of Neorealism' (Bazin: 1971; 60) André Bazin believed evolution necessary for the maintenance of any considered neorealist vocation; to prevent it from becoming a style. Bazin considers 'realism' to flounder (in its impact) in import when its imagery is turned into a 'style.' In other words, realism needs to continually reinvent its methods, otherwise it cannot remain true to the real. For many theorists and historians, Fellini was the first to confront this,

"If Antonioni and Fellini still cling to a semblance of objective realism, they reject entirely any kind of arbitrary dramatic construction, preferring to be guided by the autonomous dictates of the crisis in question…The aim is no longer to construct a plot, but to show people living with their problem" (Leprohon: 1972; 170).

In excavating the basic premise of Fellini's voyage beyond neorealism, 'crises' and indeed their representation in political, cultural or sexual terms are said to prevail, encouraging a newfound reflection on a critically disordered, indeed, global world (Leprohon: 1972; 170). Like Fellini, Pasolini litters his films with characters whose aversion to social normalcy is a prominent moral issue; the poetic dexterity of a Dante, coupled with the aura of an Augustine, notable in the crises identified by Leprohon. Given that Pasolini began working as an assistant scriptwriter to Fellini on his classic *Le notti di Cabiria* (Nights of Cabria (1957)), it is not surprising similarities abound. As Pasolini states,

> "Realism is such an ambiguous and loaded word that it is hard to agree on its meaning. I consider my own films 'realist' compared with neorealist films. In neorealist films day-to-day reality is seen from a crepuscular point of view... Compared with neorealism I think I have introduced a certain realism, but it would be hard to define it exactly" (Pasolini in Viano: 1993; 53).

For others, Pasolini's visision is at loggerheads with realism. In accenuating (what Viano notes as) the mystical-allegorical, 'realism' assumes a more complex, dangerous role (Viano: 1993; 53). Not until *Uccellaci e uccellini* (Hawks and Sparrows (1966)) is the relationship between art and cinema reflected on in a suitably cinematic manner. Critical of '68 (like Godard), he turns away from the modern. In adapting classical texts, such as Sophocles's *Oedipe Re* (Oedipus Rex, (1967)), in a suitably allegorical style, he links the classical/medieval to the modern period.

Oedipe Re positions these concerns in relation to the family in a certain theoretical capacity. *Teorema* (Theorem (1968)) develops these in a more obviously modern direction. Pasolini turns to the semiology of action, with its minutaie concerns writ large,

> "What is necessary therefore is the semiology of the language of action, or, in its simplest terms, of reality. That is to expand the horizons of semiology and of linguistics to such an extent as to lose our heads at the very thought or to smile with irony, as is proper for specialists to do" (Pasolini; 1993; 204).

His paradoxical 'realism' was addressed in *Seque*, with Umberto Eco accusing Pasolini of being closer to the metaphysicians of the medieval age–Scotus Eriugena and Pseudo-Dionysius–than the critical realist of the present in the journal. The contradictions that make Pasolini so fascinating a character himself are evident in the debate with Eco but this is nonetheless endemic of a wider debate in Italy around structuralist studies of language and structuralism's invertent claim for universality. Pasolini envelops the narrative of *Theorem* around the family structure–its closed-in theorem–and poses particular questions to the movement. A messianic

Visitor (Terence Stamp) appears as an Other–from exteriority–causing a crisis to occur. This crisis, as many of the film's critics have pointed out, is one of non-signifying 'signs.' As Viano states, the Visitor's role,

> "Is not one and the same for all the characters, for he simply makes the knowledge of their respective realities possible. The mysterious guest is like an acid test revealing the identity of the signs-in-crisis. He embodies an exceptional force capable of driving the signs in the text to a passionate (pathological) self-revelation. Hence it is less a question of defining him than of understanding his effects" (Viano: 1993; 202).

Is the Visitor's impact surprising? For it is only when Otherness impacts on familial identity, as a totality, that, "language not being the governable instrument of a speaking being" is profoundly felt (Derrida: 1986; 96). As the pan-semiotic dimension, the 'subjective' considered as a cause of action is suitably undermined. In Pasolini, the structural imprint is found in a world defined by language. Milton hovers quietly in the background.

The Beatific Vision and Pasolini's 'Nightmare'

'Reality' (as a phenomenological entity) consumes André Bazin in his (now considered) groundbreaking essay 'Fellini's Voyage towards the End of Neorealism' (1967). Written in the 1950s, the text prophesies *La dolce vita* (The Sweet Life (1960)) and *8½* (1963) and the films' impact on the history of cinema. Bazin uses terms to describe this, 'magic,' 'supersensualism' and 'grace.' Relations of a purely objective nature–as the pivotal realist concern–are precient, in contradistinction to an artistry prioritising the subjective realm. For Bazin, at least in this essay, emphasis on a modern subjectivity is a part of this. Italy's boom may be a reason for changes in Italian life, but Italian film of the 1960s can be considered a significant response to these changes. Opening *La dolce vita* with a statue of Jesus transported by helicopter over Rome signals a dramatic shift in value. As a now dislocated sign–accelerated by the onset of neo-capitalism–the 'crisis' of the Italian project in all its complexity is felt. If Marcello's journey (Marcello Mastroianni) requires re-evaluating signs and their meaning, the spurious 'false guides' of the *Inferno* are evoked,

> "The imagery too is transposed from Dante. The film begins with a huge statue of Christ, its arms ironically extended in benediction, being carried as it seems, away from the city by airplane; it ends with a shocking inversion of a traditional Christ symbol in the monstrous, hideous dead

fish holding in its mouth a swarm of small dead fish–a transposition of the
Satan figure at the pit of Dante's hell" (Lewalski: 1978; 114).

Marcello reveals himself to be a subject like Augustine in the early stages
of the *Confessions*: caught between the excesses of pleasure and the grace
of eternal Truth. In Augustinian terms Marcello is a sinner; attracted by
the burgeoning affluence of the city, born of a naked earth. The many
poetic nuances of the *Inferno* can be felt as heroic Marcello struggles with
personal demons. In the final sequence, as a gang of all-night partygoers
retreat with Marcello to the beach, a hideous sea creature–akin to a
monster–is washed up on the shore. Marcello's vision is interrupted. A
reverse shot captures a young girl waving at the distracted anti-hero.
Tangible grace, marked by the possibility that Marcello can redeem
himself, is felt. A kind of redemption is implied. Dante's inferno begins to
fit with the moral decadence of the new Rome; the film's departing
moment suggestively messianic in the atmosphere evoked. Unlike
neorealist films' at times didactic message, Marcello's redemption is
merely hinted at. Critical of hedonistic Italy, the end of the film never
divulges anything other than human contact, as opposed to the alienated
form Bazin writes of, as a means of change.

None of this is really surprising given that the 'vision' of the Virgin
Mary (by a group of schoolgirls) attracts Marcello and the national media
earlier in the film. Marcello's reporting of the people gathered (as
photographers vie for a shot of the children) is offset by his retreat. When
from a distance in the final scene Paolo waves to Marcello the grace
Bondanella identifies is notably felt. A subtle reference to Beatrice,
Dante's spiritual muse, is explicit in Paolo's wave. Fellini's spectacularly
staged commentary on Dantean themes, *Roma* (Rome (1972)), furthers his
critical concerns about Italy. Multiple bit parts are held together by the
complex 'idea' of Rome as city. These then bleed together in the final
Vatican scene when a papacy gazes upon a brightened catwalk of models.
The costumes are more and more dazzling; a Pope finally held aloft as the
camera cuts to a barely lit Roman street; lights swirling without focus.
Motorcyclists move along streets, signalling the dawn in its vibrancy. The
morally challenging fashion show, with its strategies of adaptation to a
new global order, are invariably countered by the swarming motorcyclists
outside,

"Far from being outmoded, the nation is continually constructed in the
discourse of popular culture, providing a kind of point of stability for the

negotiation of complex, social antagonism inherent in capitalism" (Restivo: 2002; 17).

For Restivo, the construction of a 'national' space is textual in form; a fragmentary *bric-a-brac*. It is notable that Pasolini turns to the sub-proletarian world outside the city in his early films; with the considerable complexity of fragmentary space itself spectacularly staged. Like the opening shot in *La dolce vita*, which serves as a visual pointer to the crises permeating these films–climaxing in *Roma*–the 'real' appears in liminal spaces. The neorealist concern turns on the constitutive margins: Pasolini's fascination with crime a fascination with those activities repudiating centralised urban space. In early Pasolini, such as *Accatone* (1961), these issues are brought to bear on crime: autonomy trumping transgression, as the need to resist standard legal codes becomes the pivotal moral concern.

Accatone (1961) draws on the founding gestures of neorealism but at a time when Pasolini began to see global executives identifying with eachother (across national terrains) before finding communality with their national compatriots (Viano; 1993). Now a filmic path to a 'sub-proletariat' life is forged. With a decadent pimp who seeks redemption, amidst post-War Roman destitution, the dissident repentance of the *Confessions* is all but evoked. The autonomy Accatone (Franco Citti)–the film's protagonist–derives in transgressing the law, takes precedence over desire for a 'clean' life. It may well be that Accatone's dissidence is heroic, in the sense that thieves, petty criminals, outcasts, the emblems of 'realism' steal, "images away from their seemingly natural value/meaning in order to appropriate them to another regime of signification" (Viano: 1993; 79). Accatone is–*au tout*–'real.' The real is a residue of diverse social relations, found in the marginal Roman slums depicted in Pasolini's early forays in film: the status (of a kind) of which assumes a vital authenticity; and one which an Accatone represents in all his dubious morality.

Neorealism's popularity is well noted. The movement had a huge global impact, traces of which can be seen in all other 'realisms' of cinematic movements since. Yet the movement, in order to be substantiated as 'realist,' needed this popularity. The populace needed a mirror of their own–at times–ordinary existence in cinematic representation. The popularity of *Bicycle Thieves,* (De Sica (1948)), is a pertinent example. Antonio Ricci (Maggioani) is a father adamantly seeking work, to feed his family. When his bicycle is stolen he can no longer travel to work. With failure to apprehend the thief, Ricci ends up turning to crime himself. The seeking after good, yet trapped by his socio-economic restrictions, is the real issue the film grapples with. Yet the filmic means of presenting Ricci's desire to better himself, with minimal frills and recognisable real life settings is crucial: the fall into criminality taps into the spectator's desires to do good. Here the Augustinian premise is felt. Like Ricci, the situation we have to realise our desires is often compromised by others.

Hence if neorealism is a people's cinema, offering structural reasons for why people choose to do wrong, Pasolini's decision to make an "Unpopular Cinema" can be viewed as a clear attempt to break with this. Rather than pacify the spectator, by allowing them to see the restrictions they confront in seeking to do good, Pasolini's aim is to unsettle, to make the spectator aware of their own complicity, or indeed responsibility for what is evidentially wrong in the 'real.'

Pasolini's joyously criminal "Unpopular Cinema" is a composite representation of the oppressed classes and the authentic margins. In that his films encourage audiences to engage in a new cinematic mode, a significant development of neorealist strategy around the audience emerges,

> "In "The Unpopular Cinema" Pasolini directly addressed the question of the film spectator and took issue with the socio-political approaches that regarded the spectator as passively constructed by texts (267-275). Suggesting that the relationship between author and spectator resembled the one taking place "between democratically equal individuals," Pasolini concluded that "for the author, the spectator is merely another author," someone who understands, who sympathizes, who loves, who becomes impassioned" (Viano: 1993; 45).

The structuralist movement of the 1960s and 1970s had a significant influence on Pasolini. One of its leading intellectuals, Roland Barthes, stated in 'The Death of the Author' that the language of the text be given precedence over its authorial intent. Barthes would prioritise the reader in the dissemination of the text; by doing so he would diverge from traditional views of texts as having an inner message. Pasolini drew on this idea as inspiration. As an avid follower of intellectual currents, he was attracted to the democracy of such a stance. Rejecting cinema's "passively constructed spectator" (Viano: 1993; 45), the spectator generates meaning: reading the language of film. Not surprisingly, the spectator assumed central status in Pasolini's later films. Pasolini had already began to construct elliptic gaps the spectator had to fill in (even if something more compelling was required to make this visible), calling his dialectical practice "heretical empiricism." He defined his filmic method as contradictory in its aims,

> "The scandal of contradicting myself, of being with you and against you; with you in my heart, but against you in the dark viscera; traitor to my paternal state–in my thoughts, in the shadows of action" (Pasolini: 1975; 49).

In the "dark viscera" of St. Matthew's Gospel, *Il Vangelo secondo Matteo* (The Gospel According to St. Matthew (1964)), Pasolini brought scandal to fruition, astounding those who saw in his previous films essentially unresolved issues. Not so. The film is a paradigm shift, marking the point at which Pasolini's engagement with realism changes. From now on, although his films would vary in success, he would try to expand the neorealist vocation. The *Gospel* is the beginning of this. The film concerns a loving yet militant, even violent Jesus (Enrique Irazoqui). Bringing the divisions in Italy to the bigscreen required a versatile realist vocabulary. Hence freeze frames would give iconic affect to the characterisation. Shot in the Mezziogiornio (rather than in Palestine where the 'story' obviously originates), an Italian space familiar to its inhabitants is evoked. From the Angel impregnating Mary (Marqherita Carnio), to a young Jesus (Enrique Irazoqui) angry at injustice he sees around him, the instrinsically Christian dialectic of love and violence is scandalously emphasised. The scene in the desert, a unique and recurring motif of Pasolini films, is a cursory example of this scandal. Jesus is tested by the Devil, as he summons strength to carry out his duties. Yet the scene materialises with none of the theatrical benefits of high-end design. Jesus confronts a man like himself. Both stand shoulder to shoulder, with Jesus clad in a black veil, in a particularly striking visual metaphor for the stand off between good and evil that Pasolini so crucially complicates here and in the montage which follows. Panoramic shots of the landscape give way to a series of facial profiles–capturing the faces of the men who will follow Jesus–in what, in my opinion at least, constitutes one of the most poetic sequences of film put to celluloid; the camera stops as Jesus turns around and begins to speak–"do not think I have come to bring peace" the infamous line that terrifies in its delivery,

> "Do not suppose that I have come to bring peace on earth. I have not come to bring peace but a sword. I have come to bring division, to set man against his father, a daughter against her mother" (Mattew: 10, 34).

That Pasolini's Jesus is borne of radical "division" verges on the blasphemous. Yet staying true to (the letter of) the gospel was pivotal to the production, "it is the feeling of the gospel according to Matthew as a whole when you first read it which is revolutionary" (Pasolini in Stack: 1969; 95). In the mode of delivery, Christ's message (his indictment to follow him and yet remain faithful to the One master), as Self and Other, has a critical combativeness; his actions assuming a crucially polemical status. Yet, if we begin, from this position, to question whether Jesus's acts–from an Augustinian perspective–are moral? Evil? Questions like this remain ultimately rhetorical in their use-value. Pasolini's *Gospel* maintains its attraction in *failing to answer*. The most popular of his films: Jesus is questionably moral. "If a hypothetical viewer came," Robert Ebert claims to, ""The Passion" with no previous knowledge of Jesus and wondered what all the furor was about, Pasolini's film would argue: Jesus was a radical whose teachings, if taken seriously, would contradict the values of most human societies ever since" (Ebert, 2004).

Collapsing *The Gospel* as an 'analogically' compelling message was crucial to Pasolini's 'beatific vision.' It was a non-compromising vision of the gospel (Viano: 1993; 136). *The Gospel* is radical, precisely because of the faithful rendering of the text. Not surprisingly, the Vatican found little to fault. Jesus may well be devoid of the loving characteristics traditionally attributed to him by others, but a morally complex vision of a society defined by its own considerable divisions is depicted with this. Long takes give iconic status to the characters. And because the film is shot in the slums of the Mezziogiornio rather than in Palestine an authenticity is gained; Christ's Passion is set in a world familiar to Southern Italians. *The Gospel* is a mark of faith. Pasolini believed in modern revolution, emphasised by the fact he aspired to make a feature film on the life of St. Paul,

> "Pasolini's aim was to turn Paul into a contemporary without modifying any of his statements. He wanted to restore, in the most direct, most violent way, the conviction of Paul's intrinsic actuality. It was a question of explicitly telling the spectator that it was possible to imagine Paul among us, here today, in his physical existence" (Badiou: 2003; 37).

Pasolini's may well be a violent Christ: like Paul, his life culminates in revolution. The basic Kantian tenets are found in the 'rebirth' of Jesus, revitalising the subject, while capturing *The Gospel* in Pasolini's unique way. If there is a crucial difference it is in Pasolini's Christ's struggle with division of a divine origin. Using real Italy as the setting for the death and resurrection of Christ meant real violence could be integrated into the Gospel text itself. Jesus's resurrection is, in this instance, that of a modern revolutionary, yet one who believes wholeheartedly in the revolution itself. Whether a moral project, or something different to this, the problem of good and evil set out is exactly that: a problem.

The Messianic Intruder

Between 1962 and 1970 Pasolini's more successfully commercial films were his satire on the family, *Teorem* (Theorem (1968)), and his adaptation of Sophocles's *Oedipe Re* (Oedipus Rex (1967)). The storyline of *Theorem* concerns a 'messianic intervention' in the life of a Northern bourgeois family. In contrast to *Oedipus Re* in which the prohibition against incest (the founding Law) is explored in powerful if somewhat perfunctory terms, its sequel of sorts, *Theorem* takes the 'sexual' as its explicit concern. For Restivo, the theorem, which serves as a clue to unlocking the film's in some ways obtuse message, is based on an encounter, "deducible from the givens of the family situation" (Restivo: 2002; 86). In this sense it is not surprising it is the only film Pasolini has ever made to be classified as melodrama. For while melodrama aims, "to make time stand still, immobilise life, and fix forever domestic property relations as the model of social life" (Elsaesser: 1992) Pasolini takes issues with these ideas. In melodrama, a system is threatened, as Elsaessar notes, before inevitably reverting to type. In *Theorem* a visitor enters a house by almost magical means; threatening the system. He proceeds to entice each family member into sexual relations, and transform their inner being in doing so. English actor Terence Stamp plays the visitor. Stamp is a perfectly deployed Other (his role has taken on cult status since), a character who on first inspection encourages a re-evaluation of his presence.

A careful analysis of the Visitor's emergence reveals the genius of Pasolini; the subtlety of his attack on the 'good' dictum of the Northern Italian bourgeoisie. As a series of guests gather for a party, and the camera assumes an almost pornographic amateurish stance, the withdrawn camera remains voyeuristically concealed in the corner of the domestic space; as a series of glances gives immediate verse to the impertinence of desire. There is something overtly 'sexual' about the arrival of guests and the glances between them. The profile shots, which serve to heighten the sudden appearance of the Visitor, are some of the most beautiful committed to cinema and they serve to brilliantly elucidate the sexuality implicit in Stamp's arrival. The next shot, which captures Stamp reading on the veranda, is a particular instance, performance even of 'the luxury class' Stamp's actions are a particular affront to.

On closer inspection is disarray. The Visitor's *jouissance* 'throws' the family; the "timelessness" theorematically associated with the family threatened (Elsaesar: 1992). Yet the intruder 'doesn't signify' in this. His role can be read as an acting out; a materialisation of excess. In the course of the story the father, Paolo (Massimo Girotti) gives away his factory to his workers, the family maid, Emilia (Laura Bettit), buries herself alive. Pietro (André Soublette), the son, confronts his desires. Each suffers a 'crisis.' In that the sexual is depicted as a "discourse of consensus regarding a wide range of practice" it seems "unless we change our ways of relating to signs," as Viano says, "we will not solve the crisis of signs postulated at the beginning of the film" (Viano: 1993; 202). Viano underlines the reasons why the characters look 'outside' the family theorem when confronted with its signifying matrix: as if to experience a sense of emancipation in it; Pietro turning to art, Emelia moving home. If sex is the primary cause of this, it is a sex, as Copjec states,

> "Produced by the internal limit, the failure of signification. It is only there where discursive practices falter–and not at all where they succeed in producing meaning–that sex comes to be" (Copjec (ed): 1994; 18-19).

Copjec's point is important. Far from 'the meaning of life' sex is more properly thought of as "the failure of signification" (Copjec (ed): 1994; 18-19). A theorem cannot be found to explain the cause of human behaviour, particularly in a mechanistic society such as the one presented. Hence a crisis arises. Not knowing the reasons why they enjoy, "discursive practices falter" (Copjec (ed): 1994; 19): Emilia eventually buries herself alive; Paolo gives his factory to his workers. Paolo running naked in the desert is one of the most poignant endings in Italian cinema; the desert wind blowing away the belief that something pertains to an 'end.' Thus, the opening scene of the film is subtly re-enacted at the end; the evocation of Paolo as Christ critiquing the very idea of revelation associated with him. The long take, in which the profile of the human body comes evermore into line, is one of the most breathtaking scenes of the film. The sudden shift from long shot to close-up, however, helps to accentuate the emotional power in the sudden cry of 'rage.' And of course, rage is another instance of the non-signifying. Yet it evokes, suggests, means something; it is in language yet outside. It is the rage of a body Pasolini saw evermore prey to consumerism, moulded by the globalising forces which overcame Italy. Just as Christ raged on the cross, and the earth shuddered, Paolo rages at the forces that surround, unable to properly 'see' them. This is why the reverse shot of Paolo as he looks over the vast desert, and we look with him, is such a beautiful end: the desert is where human rage is but a whisper.

Unsurprisingly, Pasolini's most prominent concern with reference to the 60s is the sexual revolution's failure to advance intimate forms of human relationships. The "New Power" is the critical term he used to designate a discourse he despised precisely for the kind of microscopic naming of pleasure–or its revelation–touched upon in *Theorem*. The increasing ethico-political discourse surrounding sex, led him to suggest,

> "First: the progressive struggle for democratisation of expression and for sexual liberation has been brutally superseded and cancelled out by the decision of consumerist power to grant a tolerance as vast as it is false. Second: even the "reality" of innocent bodies has been violated, manipulated, enslaved by consumerist power–indeed such violence to human bodies has become the typical feature of our time…what used to be the joy and pain of sexual fantasies, is now suicidal disappointment or utter apathy" (Pasolini in Viano: 1993; 296).

Pasolini's polemical, indeed, confrontational writings are companion pieces to the films of the time. Sex is decried as a mark of 'our' identity, with 'sexual discourse' brought to new levels of specifics. Not until he wrote so despairingly on sexuality did he describe sexual 'liberation' as a product of consumer society. *Salò* advances this critique. A phantasmatic 'nightmare,' based around the nihilism of sexual discourse, it offers a complete vision of the "consumerist power" Pasolini critiques in his writings. For while the documentary *Comizi d'amore* (Love Meetings (1965)), a sensuous excursion in documentary filmmaking, was shot while sourcing locations for *The Gospel According to St. Matthew*, Pasolini came to recognise the increasingly complex intersection of power and sex in Western consumerist societies when making it. Sexual concerns given a more disturbing outlet in *Salò,* are a consequence of adapting de Sade, from which transgressing almost every censor category is expected. Set in the Northern centre of fascism the film is controversial from the outset. Pasolini took it upon himself to explore Christianity in the *Gospel*, but *Salò* takes at its starting point the Nietzschean critique of Christianity. In *The Anti-Christ*, Nietzsche states, "this purely fictitious world distinguishes itself very unfavourably from the world of dreams: the latter reflects reality, whereas the former falsifies, depreciates and denies it" (Nietzsche: 2000; 18). Only in a Nietzschean sense can the dream unravel as its perverse underside. For our understanding of the film, it is not necessarily reality which Pasolini ficticioulsy awakens us to, but our all too vivid nightmares.

Saló and the Ethical Test

"The idea that the world was saved by this young innocence
wasn't sincere. It's not true,"
—*Bernardo Bertolluci.*

For the majority of World War II Mussolini's government had its base in the Northern town of Saló; the town part of the last of Nazi-controlled territory–the *Republic di Saló*–which had been used to resist the Allies progress. The location is historically significant to an Italian. It is the centre of fascism. Set on the outskirts, the film focuses on four fascists: a Duke (Paolo Bonacelli), a Bishop (Giorgio Cataldi) a Chief Magistrate (Umberto Quintavalle) and a President (Aldo Valetti), government dignitaries who envisage defeat and decide to sexually assault their own people. The opening scene of the film focuses on youths herded up and brought to the outskirts of the nearby town of Marzabato, a former palace with newly decorated modernist overtones. With the walls lined with baroque and modern artefacts, four male guards and four middle-aged women, each of whom play a subsidiary role in the development of the terror, accompany the dignitaries as they begin the onslaught. Three of the women 'signories' are prostitutes, employed to recount their perverse encounters with men. The tales are meant to arouse the dignitaries and guards, while eliciting the 'perverse' history within history itself, against the closed-in system they construct. Each is a stimulant to the impaled imagination of the group. The fourth of the party accompanies on piano, yet remains silent until deciding to kill herself in a moment of rare clarity late on.

Pasolini's 'Circles,' inspired by Sade's hell and Dante's *Inferno*, structure the film. The first, 'Circle of Mania,' focuses on manic perversions such as sadism and masochism. The second 'Circle of Shit' is based around the theme of coprophagy (climaxing in a dinner of the victims' excrement to celebrate the President's marriage to one of the boy victims). In the final circle, the 'Circle of Blood,' those who disobeyed the dignitaries' rules are tortured. The signories play an active role in the performances, as each 'specialises' in a particular 'Circle;' the tales are only interrupted when the dignitaries demonstrate how certain acts should be performed. Science is concentrated in the act. Repulsive, in parts dangerous, Pasolini's nightmare is not devoid of the comic moment. Gary Indiana states, "there is something absurdly winning about Pasolini's explanation of the shit-eating in *Salò* as a commentary on processed foods, and the fact that Pasolini was being sincere when he said it" (Indiana: 2000; 13). The final Circle consists of a series of comic acts literally 'discharged;' in questing after absolutes the fascists brutally torture their victims. Each, though, takes time out to view the torture at hand, as each is framed peering through a pair of binoculars from an elevated room when doing so. As they focus on the atrocities, as cabaret music plays in the background, the view from the binoculars takes over the whole of the screen. This is an extreme subjective shot; it intensifies the acceptance of the events *morally*. As a classic cinematic moment unfolds before us, the camera shifts from the 'inside'–the officers' looking–to a self-reflexive 'outside,' thus making it apparent that the 'real' is not necessarily on screen, but "primarily the screen itself" (Žižek: 1992; 221). As spectators of the carnage, the dignataries' position mirrors the viewer-position,

> "The intensified presence of the image of assassination, remarked by Pasolini, is paralleled in *Salò* by a suffocating nearness. Indeed, as one of the libertines turns the binoculars the wrong end around before looking through them, the spectator vainly hopes that resulting reduction of the image will distance it and thus bring some relief from its overwhelming presence" (Copjec: 2002; 203).

Copjec's is a hard-hitting point; based on a spectator positioned so that they see themselves as a libertine, and evil they look upon, feel responsibility for. Fascism is within us all. Aligning the gaze of evil with our gaze, the binoculars turn around. Michael Apter has written extensively on manifestations of 'danger' in various spectacles like the film experience. Central to his theoretical framework is the "detachment frame;" a mechanism which makes those things, "which cause displeasure when confronted in reality.... cause pleasure when considered through a protective frame" (Apter: 2007; 70). Film is one of the cultural fields in which the "detachment frame" is most clearly felt. The audience retreats into a space, detached from real danger, and confront things that, if they were to threaten them in real life, they would flee; impelled by anxiety. In many cases, Apter notes, spectators flee from the space, faint, or are overwhelmed by the emotional experience at hand. Yet what makes the end of *Salò* so specifically unique in this sense, and from which the qualification dangerous is required, is the audience is made to confront why they *haven't* fled. It is not the danger on screen that overwhelms them but the danger experienced when the "detachment frame" vanishes without

overwhelming emotions being felt. It is the feeling of displeasure when
pleasure reverts to real displeasure. All of this then–in essence–is like a
suffocating nearness; the spectator in sync with the dignitaries on screen.
As Mark Rappaport adds,

> "Pasolini says, regarding *Teorema*, *Porcile* and, undoubtedly, *Saló*, that he
> wanted to make a cinema that was "unconsumable"–certainly a witty pun,
> since *Porcile*, among other things, concerns itself with that which ought
> not be consumed" (Rappaport: 2002; 2).

Godard believed the cinema failed in forseeing the horrors of the
Holocaust camps yet these are set by Pasolini in the power oriented
domain of 'sex.' This is felt in the final scene, when Pasolini's aim is to
make the look of the spectator complicit with the horrors on-screen;
making us, Kermode notes, "party to what we've just seen" (Kermode,
2002). If *Theorem* has an emancipatory aim, in the sense that a project is
fashioned around elucidating the transgression of semiotics, it is the
opposite which is the case here. As Viano notes, closing the semiotic, the
sexual impulse is encoded, 'textualising' the victims' bodies (Viano:
1993; 204). Mesmerised by the object, while demanding that the victims'
beauty remain constant when tortured, the dignataries seek an impossible
end. Inspired by de Sade's account of sexuality, Pasolini drew on a
vibrant strain of criticism concerning the Enlightenment's dark underside
(Adorno and Horkheimer in Rabaté: 2003; 102). Pasolini came to espouse
views not dissimiliar to those of Jean-Michel Rabaté,

> "Kantian reason leads ineluctably to the calculating rationality of a
> totalitarian order. Its counterpart is the systematic mechanisation of
> pleasure in Sade's perverse utopias. *The Critique of Practical Reason*
> stresses the autonomy and self-determination of the moral subject, and
> thereby defines the pure form of ethical action" (Rabaté: 2003; 102).

Rabaté condemns the "perverse utopias" generated in Kantian morality,
identifying a "systematic mechanisation of pleasure" in its discourse
(Rabaté: 2003; 102). Graphically, the imperative to enjoy, invoked,
revoked, and comically presented in *Saló* is parodied *in extremus*. The
Duke, perhaps the most despicable character, states categorically "all
things taken to excess are good" (*Saló*: 1975). The "excess" (integral to
'language' and meaning) of Miltonic evil is posited as the terrain of an
experiential good. It is a transvaluation of morals which is reigning
untowards and which,

> "Accentuates the visionary mood, the unreal nightmare quality of the film.
> This film is a mad dream which does not explain what happened in the

world during the forties. A dream which has an awful logic in its entirety
but chaos in its details" (*Salò:* 1975).

If the neorealist objective can be defined as the cultivation of unmediated
reality, yet rather paradoxically as moving images, the totalising impulse
around this is the concern here. Pasolini constructs a system in the film
which compels us to think that certain forms of pleasure resist meaning.
Pleasure cannot materialise, since its lack holds the system together and
this is the pertinent point; hence, the torture. Pasolini's 'nightmare,' to
coin the film's title within the *topos* of a perverse evil, is like having to
hold sand: slipping at every grasp. The dignitaries' failure to grasp the
'singular impulse' yearned for constitutes a failure to objectify the real. It
is a failure to objectify pleasure. Pasolini's film is about the failure of
neorealism in general. That is, its failure to capture the reality it based
itself on in a totalising manner. In his final film, terror increases until
murder is the only option. As Gary Indiana puts it "Pasolini's heroes
appear to experience their own depravity as an unassaugable irritant, no
less than their victims' experience of submission. This has to do with the
stiff way the actors have been directed, the stifling lack of exuberance in
their evil" (Indiana: 2000; 59). Trying to domesticate enjoyment Lacan
called *jouissance*, simply compounds its evil. An excess corrupts those
who seek to domesticate the real. *Salò* is what happens when we lose sight
of this.

    The ending again serves to perfectly illustrate this. The anguish on the
faces of the dignitaries is not unlike Paolo at the end of *Theorem*. Yet this
time, 'rage' cannot be contextualised as an instance of failure; failure to
seal off the real from the Real; or rather a failure to encapture the unsaid
of sexuality. Beginning in pastiche of old-style pornographic films, with
their poor level of acting out a 'performative' sex, the carnage quickly
follows. The blurring of the image, reminding us that we are looking
through the same binocolaurs a character is also looking through, is a kind
of subtle hint that getting at the 'real'–in its filmic as well as sexual guise–
is more difficult than imagined. As the carnage begins, we sit repulsed,
yet, as Indiana has stated, slowly begin to see the clues that all is not what
it seems. The enlarged 'cocks' are one clue, the eye popping out a direct
intertextual reference to *Un chien andalou* (The Andalusian Dog (1928))
another; as if to suggest in dreams we sleep with all sorts of 'horror.'

    It is in this sense that *Salò* is about the aftermath of neorealism as
much as fascism, sex and the new power. As a commentary it explores the
fascist impulse which lays claim to the totalising objectivity of the 'real.'

It's not that the film tells us not to believe in 'reality' but that attempts are continually made to reduce the diversity of human experience to the preordained, telling us what the 'real' is and can be. In an age when the eccentricities of human behaviour are exploited in reality TV in more objectified ways, *Salò* is a warning that 'feeling' doesn't always have a reason.

The idea that perversion is a wrong action is codified by the implication that any such attempt to align perversion with good, as Augustine tried and the dignitaries follow, albeit in their own perverse way, leads only to ineluctable forms of horror, the kind outlined by Pasolini with such panache and which serves as the weird moral undercurrent to the film. In Pasolini's world, Augustine has little room to maneuver. The attempt to define True reality as God's reality (and its failure to take into account the totalising impulse that lies behind this) is mirrored in the horrific world that Pasolini presents before his death. In other words, believing in a 'perfect' real overlooks the fact the 'real' contains the excess of a non-truth within it. Pasolini's world contains the shadow of Milton and Lacan, where totalising impulses, attempts to impose the 'real' at the behest of an other, has the perverse effect of turning good to evil.

Conclusion: 'Til Death Do Us Part

"I couldn't seperate the photograph of Pasolini's corpse, covered in blood from the film I was seeing,"
—Bernarado Bertolucci.

"Pasolini is me,"
—Morrissey, *You Have Killed Me.*

In a documentary on Pasolini's life, *Whoever Says the Truth Shall Die* (Bergstein, 1981), *Salò* was called a manifest mistreatment of his philosophy. Yet writers, such as Naomi Greene, claimed the hymn to life of his previous three: *The Trilogy of Life* is balanced by such a doom-laden vision. If an all-consuming 'unreality' is the reward for such unsavoury vision, *Salò* is a considerably epochal event; one on which Pasolini's New Fascism rests,

"Pasolini filmed Fascism in its sexual dimension, in its sexual repression and perversion to show the perversions of our society which sees itself as free but which is dominated by dark hidden forces" (Macciochi in *Whoever Says the Truth Shall Die*; 1995).

'Dark forces' circulated during the making, and four months after *Salò* a sexual encounter of an equally dark kind would lead to Pasolini's murder. The death of this now famous celebrity captured the nation's imagination. Even today, conspiracy theories abound as to who killed Pasolini. Was it a lone rent boy? An avatar of darkness? A political conspiracy against a perceived national threat? Critics have pointed to Pasolini's brutal death in relation to the sexual depravity of his last film. Dangerous in its capacity to transgress, those who saw it as the last straw in liberal credibility questioned how such a hideous, odious piece of entertainment could satisfy. The backlash led philosopher and champion of freedom, Jean-Paul Sartre, to ask, "not to put Pasolini on trial." Sartre rejected opinions in the right wing media that death was a just reward for evil. That Pasolini portrayed evil in such an untoward way led some to suggest his life perversely imitated his art. For others his film fulfils Roland Barthes's assertion that,

> "The social intervention of a text is not measured by its popularity…. or by its faithfulness to the economic-social order it reflects….but rather by the violence which permits it to *exceed* the laws that a society, an ideology, a philosophy, give themselves in order to appropriate…historical intelligibility. This excess has a meaning: writing" (Barthes: 1971; 16).

Critical of his filmic adaptation of Sade, Barthes would nonetheless point to the subversion of the "economic-social order" at the heart of Sade's writing as the inspiration; a writing this chapter has argued, Pasolini twists respectfully into his own (Barthes: 1971; 16). The Italian writer Franco Cordelli has–in his own way–echoed Barthes's opinions. Cordelli identifies the film's power in its denunciation of power,

> "The desire for power–and isn't this what Pasolini is denouncing? Isn't the claustrophobic, sumptuous funereal interior of the villa the aseptic and Lacanian white space of representation, where everything is reduced to a sign, where everyone is equal in the ass, in a "hole," in a "lack"? Aren't the violence and sex above all indifference, distance, a pure spectacle, that is the epiphany of capitalism (Cordelli in Greene: 1990; 214)?"

Salò, for Cordelli is a meta-cinematic commentary on the "epiphany of capitalism." For Cordelli the lack in the *Other* constitutes the experience of an enjoyment which needs to be filled. At times the 'hole' is the 'ass' the dignitaries see as 'divine;' at other times the 'real.' But if there is a moral to Pasolini's final film it can be discerned in the following terms. The dignataries seek to quantify what, by its nature, is unquantifiable. They want something to signify which doesn't signify. To find a set of rules to experience the same pleasure each time they engage with someone sexually they must harness excess which, by nature, resists being harnessed. Call it 'excess' Milton found surging through language, or *jouissance*, the void Lacan believed the premise on which the Law is founded, any attempt to master it will lead only to the destruction of those who seek.

Strangely, we now take a step back in time, to explore a companion piece to *Salò*. This time however, fascism is depicted in the guise of a Nazi legacy, one which haunts Europe and shadows its subjects. If the victims of *Salò* are implicated in the horror they experience, in some cases desiring their own terrorisation, this desire is explored in a quite significantly different guise by one of Europe's most insightful, yet also most controversial, female directors: Liliana Cavani.

CHAPTER FOUR

'STRIKE DEAR MISTRESS AND CURE HIS HEART': EVIL AND THE LAW IN LILIANA CAVANI'S *THE NIGHT PORTER* (1974)

Introduction

"You said I came close,
As anybody's come,
To live underwater,
For more than a month
You said it was not inside my heart, it was
You said it should tear a kid apart, it does,
Didn't wanna be your ghost
Didn't wanna be anyone's ghost,"
—The National, *Anyone's Ghost.*

Jean-Luc Godard's *Weekend* (1968) presents us with a cannibalistic society; one in which the ruling class feast on bodies of those below them. It is a defining moment of the carnivalesque. Given the filmic vision of man striking out against the rulers of modern France, it is little surprise *Weekend* is considered–by many–Godard's most radical film, "it is clearly made by someone who has reached a position of total disgust and rejection of his own society. The revolutionary leader announces at the end of the film, 'our guts throb long after making love. Because of man's immense horror at his fellows'" (MacCabe: 2003; 200). In modernity, cannibalism is a bourgeois pastime. Pasolini serves up his own cannibalistic orgy in *Porcile* (Pigsty (1969)), bridging the politically aggressive *Weekend* and Italian art-house.

Sitney, a critic for whom the enemy-status depicted in neorealism is all too easily attributed to Fascism, points to the enemy fashioned by filmmakers in this period as overtly focused on figureheads, instead of a capitalist ideology advocating participation by all (Sitney; 1995). In the late 50s and 60s new Italian filmmakers turned away from the direct politics of the neorealist period and began to explore the intersection of politics and ethics, found in Pasolini and Liliana Cavani. Pasolini believed in a new kind of moral discourse which could encourage greater criticality,

> "It is useless to delude oneself about it: neorealism was not a regeneration; it was only a vital crisis, however excessively optimistic and enthusiastic at the beginning. Thus poetic action outran thought, formal renewal preceded the reorganization of the culture through its vitality (let's not forget the year '45)" (Pasolini in Rhodes: 2007; 59).

By the late 60s and early 70s Pasolini and Godard had diverged from the crime narratives of their earlier careers, more politically involved in films such as *Le chinoise* (The Chinese (1967)) and *Salò*. The Italian director Liliana Cavani also came to prominence around this time. In Cavani's television drama, *Francesco d'Assiso* (Francis of Assisi (1966)) the hallmarks of an art-house allegory are all too readily visible; in a film concerned with issues of an unfashionably moral kind. Cavani's film was regarded as an explicit rejection of the "clichéd hagiography" Gaettone Marrone identified in tributes to the Saint (Marrone: 2000). At the film's centre is the depiction of a revolutionary militant. Indeed, Cavani's Francis is a significant contribution to 70s films inspired by the iconic Saint. While Rossellini's *Francesco guillare di Dio* (The Little Flower of Francis (1950)) had used Francis to explore the ascetic Saint politically, *Uccellaci e uccellini* (Hawks and Sparrows (1966)) explored Francis's break with the Church as a way of exploring Pasolini's own break with neorealism. In reductive terms, poverty was now a spiritual force, a way of resisting materialism. The undermining of a destructive affluence, in these films, was felt to challenge self-rewarding ideologies. For Cavani, Francis was a guard to the impoverished masses, those felt betrayed by the trenchant moralism of the Church and the secularism of the Left. Cavani's second film, *I cannibali* (The Cannibals (1970)), has a similar premise, and can be viewed as a significant complement to Godard's and Pasolini's films. Controversially reworking the story of Antigone, the film uses the cannibalistic thematic in order to probe totalitarian indifference to human life.

Cavani's first feature length film, *Portier di notte* (The Night Porter (1974)), is similarly controversial. Set amidst the moral debris of the 20th century's most public issue: the Holocaust, a survivor returns to her *former* captor, an exiled SS officer. The film centres on the meeting of

Max (Dirk Bogarde), an SS officer in hiding after the War, and Lucia (Charlotte Rampling), his former victim in the camps, in 1957 Vienna. On being reacquainted, the couple begin to re-enact a relationship formed years prior to this; with the remainder of the film a suspenseful insight into the mindset of former officers and survivors. The plot itself climaxes with Max's former SS colleagues, put out by Lucia's appearance, shooting the couple dead; a point at which Max is dressed as an SS officer and Lucia has decided to dress herself up as a little girl. Not surprisingly, given the charged nature of the material, the film caused explicit outrage, propelling Cavani and the film into the international realm. Alain Giroux greeted, "a thinly disguised Fascist propaganda film…. a high point in social, cultural and political barbarism" (Giroux in Bondanella: 1983; 349). Giroux's outrage finds expression in Primo Levi's *The Drowned and The Saved* (1988). For Levi, the film is a "moral disease" (Levi: 1988). Few, such as Peter Bondanella resisted the tide. Bondanella saw the film as a heartfelt response to the Holocaust. In its unorthodox depiction of 'evil,' victimhood elicited in more nuanced terms (than usually the case), the film is thought to have moral worth in confronting the Holocaust–*ex post facto*–distinct from affirming Nazi values. Of course, the Holocaust requires sensitivity; particularly around a relationship between executioner and victim,

"The portrayal of evil nevertheless does not imply praise of it, and the superficial attack on the film's supposed 'Fascist' character entirely misses the point" (Bondanella: 1983; 349).

Either way, Cavani confronted the discourse on evil. Rather than simply solicit 'fascist evil,' Bondanella notes, a unique re-evaluation of the executioner/ victim relationship in films concerning evil is given (Bondanella: 1983; 349). Pasolini rarely alludes to the guilt of the victims in *Salò*, to the extent that Mark Kermode described the film as, "making willing victims of us all" (Kermode: 2002), but victimhood is the nuanced concern of *The Night Porter*. In *The Night Porter*, the "incommensurability of…trauma and present survival" (Wilson: 2000; 49), that which Emma Wilson identifies as central to Kryzysztof Kieślowski's *Bleu* (Blue (1993)) is equally harrowing in its expression. *The Night Porter* is, as I will contend, a significant contribution to the idea, as Wilson suggests, "trauma and survival must necessarily be rethought in the context of the post-war era" (Wilson: 2000; 44). Commissioned by the government to shoot a documentary on victimhood, Cavani began probing the less noted forms of the experience; centering on the gut wrenching guilt (as expressed by Levi) experienced by survivors of the Holocaust. Films exploring bonds between victim and oppressor are rare. Yet it is crucial that reference to a contractual bond between them is made by Max in *The Night Porter*. Lucia returns to Max, as the victim/executioner contract is hinted at. The Austrian settings, and the contract, are significant features of Leopold Von Sacher-Masoch novels, the novels from which the term masochism originates. This therefore requires inspection. For the contract needs to be considered around alliances between oppressors and oppressed. The contract is an alliance. But it is one which feigns laws binding subjects in institutional settings. Personal, secretive even, it is defined by the feigned subservience to institutions (Nazi terror the most blatant form of institutionalised evil). Couples form pacts to feign institutional allegiance; the Historical institutions of the time. Yet, most crucially, feigning allegiance is considered a more precursory means of resisting symbolic power.

It is noteworthy then that Max talks about contracts; as the contract is hinted at as Lucia's reason to stay in Vienna. On meeting, Lucia quickly requests her husband travel ahead. Max had already appeared dressed in his Nazi regalia, in what is conceived as a kind of anger towards Nazism's demise. Yet the opposition between law, expressed by the uniform, and the contract, expressed by Lucia, is prominent here. Max's SS allegiance is set against spectacular cultural displays, from ballet to opera, from which an ongoing desire to reinstall Nazism seems a significant aim; the umbrage taken with Lucia's return an avid response to her contesting of this. Lucia is that part of history which cannot be contained as history; a ghost from the past who resists institutional capture. At the time of the film's release, Cavani referred to the "false divinity" of Nazism (Cavani in Marrone: 2000; 142). Max's and Lucia's relationship helps explore this. On one level, subservience to a leader constitutes the divine per se. On another, the officers' leader Hans (Gabrielle Ferzetti), and his 'neurosis,' generate links–auspiciously–between guilt and the law. For as Hans argues,

> "We have decided to delve together to the very bottom of our personal histories. We have decided to confront them speaking without reserve, without fear. Remember, we must try to understand if we are victims of guilt complexes or not. If so, we must be freed of them. *A guilt complex is a disturbance of the psyche, a neurosis*" (*The Night Porter*: 1972).

Hans and the other exiles use a mock trial to locate and destroy the files of possible witnesses, the implication being that guilt–which Max experiences– is pathological in its origins. Believing the trial will 'free' the officers from their guilt coincides with a belief in overcoming guilt as the way to revive the institutions of the Third Reich. Guilt (towards the Nazi regime) is said to derive from its demise. Moreover, as Hans and the exiles want to account for possible witnesses to their crimes, emphasised by Hans observing, "let's not delude ourselves; memory is not made of shadows, but of eyes which stare straight at you" (*The Night Porter*: 1972), guilt is felt. Yet guilt is also a significant emotion of both sides. As much of the film's criticism concerned Lucia's perceived 'allegiance' to Nazism as a perceived value system, as this is set out in flashbacks to her time in the camps, those from which the term "Nazi chic" was coined (Lucia, dressed in Nazi uniform, singing Marlene Dietrich inspired cabaret), this is set against the ongoing mock trial and the contract which shadows it. Her 'support' of Nazi values, I argue, 'appears' as support; contractually required. Irony is at the behest of seriousness; 'obedience' a mocking of Nazi Law in its authoritarian form. If morality (on which the coming analysis rests) is addressed around the appearance of 'evil,' the film can be read, as I will show, as more subversive in its 'evil' than Giroux and Levi insist.

The end of the film helps the analysis to begin. A medium shot of Max and Lucia holding hands sharply contrasts the looming bridge in the background. Symbolically, the bridge serves to remind us that Max and Lucia are travelling a moral path. That they fail to cross this bridge is one way of suggesting–in a kind of spurious Augustinian moment–the failure of moral action. For the film tragically ends in mutual death. Gaettone Marrone observes a, "perceptual kind of realism" in the end (Marrone: 2000; 81), in that death overcomes life. With Max and Lucia's hands in profile, the relationship formed earlier is renegotiated in new symbolic terms,

> "Max … ultimately asserts his sanity and accepts his own guilt. And in so doing, he removes Lucia's burden of guilt from her conscience. This explains why he dresses her in the little girl's uniform at the end of the film. He has freed her from her past, and in a certain sense his is an act of selfless love" (Bondanella: 1993; 348).

In rejecting the trial–prior to the above-mentioned selfless act–the evil impacted upon Lucia is undermined; and in a suitably cathartic manner (what we see in flashbacks). Re-engaging the past makes it easier to navigate the present. Parody is central to this, as it allows for the subordination of power: Lucia pretends *to be* subordinate. An example of this is Lucia's assumption of 'roles,' like in the scene when she assumes Max's clothing and takes on the masculine 'role' in the relationship, in the process pretending to assume the symbolic role of patriarch or Law. Such pretence is crucially experienced as a playful engagement with fixed identities; identities such as 'victim' and 'executioner.' If the contract is dismissed as irrelevant, Lucia's playful actions too easily offend. The 'role,' as such, is missed. And if a playful assumption of roles is overlooked, so too is the place of the contract in the relationship; for the contract's value amounts to a series of intended performances. In this sense, Gilles Deleuze's critique of masochism is a beginning for the analysis,

> "We are no longer in the presence of a torturer seizing upon a victim and enjoying her all the more because she is unconsenting and unpersuaded. We are dealing instead with a victim in search of a torturer and *who needs to educate, persuade and conclude an alliance*. This is why advertisements are part of the language of masochism and have no place in true sadism. And why the masochist draws up contracts while the sadist abominates and destroys them" (Deleuze: 1989; 20).

It is pretty clear that an "alliance" like Deleuze speaks of is found in *The Night Porter*; a particular form of behaviour is consented to; a kind of advert which will secure the alliance, to make sure it is open–like all adverts–to interpretation. We find this in the way Max and Lucia interact, switch identities, basically perform; all of which celebrates the non-substantialist nature of the performative act. The contract, it seems, is the bond that brings this into play, consolidates the performative as such. In performance, significant 'issues' emerge, all of which impinge on the problem of evil as it readily pertains to the film. One such issue is executioner and victim; considered as performed 'roles.' Bondanella's suggestion that 'evil' is performed–irrespective of the will to do evil–sheds light on Lucia's desire to re-educate (the executioner) Max in moral terms (Bondanella: 1983; 348). It allows an alliance to be identified; yet one which calls for its own critical evaluation. And far from making 'evil' clearer in meaning, Cavani's characters, in deft silence, summon us to inquire.

One such summons occurs midway through the film. Max sits dressing Lucia. As he puts a shoe on, she suddenly stands up and removes herself to the bathroom. She then smashes a bottle of perfume, before locking the key. The image of Lucia crunched in profile, her dress matching the tiles of the bathroom, has diegetic sound as mere accompaniment. As Max cuts his hands in the glass, and Lucia bends to comfort him, her hands are crunched in the glass debris by the cruel and unforgiving Max. Yet, far from crying, shamed by his cruelty, she smiles and returns the smile of his gaze. It is as if this display of violence is part of a 'bond' the basis of which we can only imagine.

Critics found in the silent game playing in *The Night Porter* a perverse adulation of Nazi Law. Yet although the terms of the contract between Max and Lucia are never set out, that sexual gratification (evoking the principles of courtly love) is kept at a distance makes the contractual element, condemned by Giroux, subtle in its power. An example of this subtlety can be seen as the film nears conclusion. Max and Lucia are in hiding, Max having quit his position as night porter, with both inverting gender roles: Lucia smoking a pipe in Max's clothes, while Max appears feminised, wearing make-up. As Lucia toys with a jar of jam, smearing it across her face, its sexualised properties given emphasis, the sexualised element of 'play,' with the qualitative equation of jam and sperm, comically underpins the sex itself: Max and Lucia having sex in the aftermath of this play. If the contract stipulates this behaviour in order to parody the law, it involves the comic undermining of its function; Lucia must feign conformity to it. Hence, in the cabaret scene (set in flashback), like in the scene just mentioned, Lucia appears in drag. She thus assumes an SS officer 'role,' erotically teasing the officers who sit in a smoke filled room. Yet far from espousing an allegiance, the performance is a feigning of submission. Lucia's and Max's secretive, non-historical pact requires this. That is, something evades the capture of the Nazi's objectifying historical machine. That the Nazi's want to 'account' for this, integrate it into the files, is indicative of their need to objectify and historicise an 'alliance' which, for Masoch at least, must evade the historical. The alliance cannot overturn the law. For the law is all-powerful. But it can resist.

That Max notes, "when all seems lost, something unexpected happens. Ghosts take shape in the mind. How can one pull away from this, this phantom with a voice and a body....this part of the self" (*The Night Porter*: 1973) is telling. For in adding, "I always honour my contract" (*The Night Porter*: 1973), he underlines the vital function of the contract in the relationship. In bonding those lacking a bond, the contract brings an essential element of play to the masochistic enterprise. If the *contract* is felt in mimicking the actual properties of the regulated sexual act (as law), expressed in the flashback scene when Lucia dances, or in Lucia's 'beatings' by Max, something bonds the couple. Yet it is not difficult to see why this bond would be so contentious. We cannot blame Giroux and Levi for taking offence here. Pockets of resistance which cannot be codified as part of the Nazi machine, must remain as so to evade capture. Hence, it is easy to think of Stockholm Syndrome, or Nazi sympathy around the performance. Feigning seriousness can appear all too serious. There is no concrete means for distinguishing play from serious behaviour.

The cabaret scene is an example here. One of the most powerful scenes in post-War cinema *tout court* the ambiguity of appearance is vibrantly expressed. As mentioned, dressed in Nazi regalia, Lucia dances and sings to masked officers, entranced by her power over them. Military roles are seen as fixed; consolidating the division between victim and victimiser. Yet another assessment of this scene sees a 'performance' of victim/victimiser. What many critics of the film considered disrespectful towards the victims of the Holocaust, a significantly controversial charge (especially so, if Lucia is contractually obligated to Max) against Cavani may well 'be' something else? If Lucia's roleplaying serves as a resistance, as those schooled in resistance would testify, mimicry, the performative act par excellence, has intrinsic power. In this sense, it helps resist symbolic Nazism. "To distinguish ontologically between "guiltless victims" and "murderers,"" as Marquerite Waller so ruefully observes, "is to try to cement the moral purity of these categories" (Peitropaolo and Testaferri (eds): 1995; 210). Distinguishing one, as Giroux does, *is* itself potentially fascist. For it suggests resistance requires a certain type of behaviour,

> "The bodies and faces of both figures become the site of a dissonant and denaturalised visual language that, across the disturbing story of their past and present relationship denaturalises the legibility of sex and gender" (Waller in Peitropaolo and Testaferri (eds): 1995; 210).

The paradigm of similarity is subverted. But it is subverted when identity is displaced; and that which Waller finds dissonant in its power can be discerned. Cast as a displaced Other to the officers, Lucia is able to mock (rather than effectuate) assimilation (Peitropaolo and Testaferri (ed): 1995; 210). Indeed, her strategic use of masochism works as a parody of assimilation. For Lucia's dance/ performance can be read as a mocking of the law's capacity to assimilate the otherness of gender roles. Mockery triumphs when transgression is a 'transgression' of Nazism in its capacity to oppress.

Masochism and the Law

In his opus magnus *Being and Nothingness* (1954), an intriguing insight into the desire for punishment, which Lucia appears to evidently display in the film, is given by Jean-Paul Sartre (indeed, the guilt from feeling this same desire is explored by Cavani),

> "Masochism, like sadism, is the assumption of guilt. I am guilty due to the very fact that I am an object. I am guilty towards myself since I consent to my absolute alienation. I am guilty towards the Other, for him with the occasion of being guilty–that is, radically missing my freedom as such" (Sartre: 1954; 378).

The guilt expressed "towards the Other" serves here as an object position craved–whether consciously or not–by the masochist (Sartre: 1954; 378). We can go further by suggesting that if the very desire for objecthood is a cry for security, to be an other for *the* other, then Lucia's role says a lot about the the aftermath of captivity. The Sartrean position on masochism would also appear to find a curious support in Lucia's submission to Max, allowing herself to be tied, beaten, and locked in the apartment; precisely because she enforces the 'object' victim role upon herself. If the decision to stay in Vienna is based on assauging the guilt caused by surviving the camps, Lucia's role complies with Sartre's reading. This would suggest that she is compelled by this same guilt. Or as a masochist she cannot "freely" decide (Sartre: 1954; 378). However, this way of looking at things is complicated by the act of deception at the beginning; when Lucia deceives her husband. It is more likely that in some shape or other, Lucia's way of cathartically dealing with her survival guilt is to re-engage the relationship; doing so through a certain engagement with parody. The finale can be said to offer a certain support to this reading of the film: Lucia appears in a little girl's dress with Max dressed in uniform. Both return to their original roles. In one sense objectification comes to an end; performance is no longer required when it has already worked its power; particularly over those seeking to stabilise power-relations. Yet, in another sense, the capacity for power-relations to enforce object status on their victims is found reinforced in a regressive manner. Indeed, for Giroux, regressing to original roles at the end is viewed as a sick support to Nazism: the apparent disease of this corrupt art. I will argue against this view. I believe the end is more nuanced: the intersubjective performance expressed in Max adorning his uniform indicating the journey from evil to good.

Max and Lucia never travel across the bridge. But the crossing itself serves as a projective 'end' to guilt. Important (and this is Cavani's point) is the *will* to cross. Judging the film in the context of the will, albeit, 'differently,' allows certain conclusions to be drawn. If Deleuze's view, "THE LAW, as defined by its pure form, without substance or object or any determination whatsoever, is such that no one can know what it is" (Deleuze: 1989; 85) helps ascertain the manner in which the law "operates without making itself known" (Deleuze: 1989; 83) and ostensibly, the law as "a realm of transgression where one is already guilty" (Deleuze: 1989; 83-84), then the subject doesn't necessarily feel a greater sense of righteousness the more (s)he submits to the law. Rather, as Deleuze says, the "more strict his obedience, the greater his guilt" (Deleuze: 1989; 85). Significant issues are indeed raised by this assertion. Firstly, when considering the symbolic-patriarchal law of the Third Reich as cause for the *neurosis* the officers experience in the film, the experience itself can be given more precise clarification. For the greater a submission to a law (which no longer exists yet) haunting them in non-existence, the guiltier the officers feel. The law is a sadist force, bullying them into submission. Only in contractual resistance to this can the bond from sadism break; offering us a reason for why Lucia feels compelled to stay in Vienna and reignite her ('cruel') relationship with Max. Secondly, if the contract's peculiar rationale alleviates a guilt burdened by the law, it is important then, when looking at the finale through this lens, that the contract, as Deleuze outlines it, as 'that' which is without an abiding and legal sanction, is considered, as it helps morally reconcile the death of Max and Lucia at the end of *The Night Porter*. Death, a metaphor for the death of the contract, indicates, paradoxically, a triumph over the law. As Deleuze states,

> "It is already apparent that in his attempt to derive the law from the contract, the masochist aims not to mitigate the law but on the contrary to emphasize its extreme severity. For while the contract implies in principle certain conditions like the free acceptance of the parties, a limited duration and preservation of inalienable rights, the law that it generates always tends to forget its own origins and annul these restrictive conditions" (Deleuze: 1989; 91-2).

Two points arise in response to Deleuze. First of all, Lucia's and Max's relationship is of "limited duration," the "free acceptance of the parties" of which is a means to transgress the extreme severity of the law (Deleuze: 1989; 92). The law is not–in this case–an internal freedom to be tapped into. Rather it is an externally endowed punishment. Secondly, Lucia is obligated to assume the role she does within the confines of the contract. It is not that Max beats Lucia, but that he 'beats' her as part of a contractual enterprise. Hence, Max admitting his love for Lucia doubles as rejection of the law. Deleuze's theorisation of masochistic "humor" is a way to explore this,

> "The essence of masochistic humor lies in this, that the very law which forbids the satisfaction of a desire under threat of subsequent punishment is converted into one which demands the punishment first and then orders that the satisfaction of the desire should necessarily follow" (Deleuze: 1989; 88-89).

The scene discussed earlier, when Max chases Lucia into the bathroom, and then cuts his hand on the broken glass, before smiling wryly at the 'punishment' given to him is pertinent here. Only after being punished for his sexual advance can enjoyment ensue. It is in this context that the humour involved in masochism can be understood in *The Night Porter*. Feigning authority subverts its intrinsically systematic power. What we see is not evil as such, but rather 'evil' stemming the guilt evil has begot. In Deleuzian terms, only in feigning the 'severity of the law' is its subsequent subversion felt. As Cavani says,

> "I felt the need to analyse the limits of human nature at the limit of credibility, to lead things to the extreme, because there is nothing more fantastic than reality" (Cavani: 1973).

Inquiries can be made into such a rich fantasy base around evil. One of these concerns the roles Max assumes. With Lucia as Salomé and Christ, given the head of the prisoner Johan who abused her and whom Max beheaded in an act of 'love,' Max can then assume the minoritarian role of Jew, as persecuting other, displacing that of Nazi executioner to the Jews. Identities, now shown rather than said, hover above the surface. It is in this second sense that attention is drawn to Lucia's arrival in the camps (Marrone: 2000). For it is easy to overlook when she is asked to state her religion–as Max frames victims in a documentary he has charge over in the camps–as she looks up, awry, and states 'Catholic.'

Christology and Moral Crisis

"It's a story from the Bible,"
—Max, *The Night Porter*.

"Shiny, shiny, shiny boots of leather,
Whiplash girlchild in the dark,

> Comes in bells, your servant, don't forsake him,
> Strike dear mistress, and cure his heart,"
> —The Velvet Underground, *Venus in Furs*.

Performance plays such an important role in *The Night Porter* that it is difficult not to see the film as itself a commentary on the power of performance to distill symbolic displays of power. Throughout, ballet, cabaret, song and dance play a significant role. But this is true of Max and Lucia's relationship as much as it is the Nazi exiles that resist them. But there is also a strong religious theme running through the film, so that religiosity in the guise of performance can also be said to play a significant role. As such, violence, and in particular that which is peculiar to religious myth, can be discerned in numerous instances of the film, a number of which are elemental to the performance. Most theorists of masochism emphasise the role violence has come to play in the related activities. And indeed the sexual charge of *The Night Porter,* when Max ties Lucia to his bed and locks her in his bedroom, negotiating her 'trial' with his fellow exiles, gives vent to this. But if we assume, as Marguerite Waller observes,

> "That everything is as it seems when we see a close-up of Lucia, with her hands chained above and behind her head, approached by Max, who grasps her torso, we may as many do, find the images unbearable" (Waller in Peitropaolo and Testaferri (eds): 1995; 210).

Those who find these images "unbearable" may well miss the performative substratum underpinning Max's and Lucia's relationship (Peitropaolo and Testaferri (eds): 1995; 210). The masochistic substratum, as derived from Deleuze's reading of Leopold Von Sacher-Masoch's novels, allows significant parallels to be drawn with Lucia's and Max's masochism. For masochism, as Deleuze argues, is,

> "A phenomenon of the senses (ie., a certain combination of pain and pleasure); in its moral aspects it is a function of feeling or sentiment. But beyond all superpersonal elements that animates the masochist: this is the story in which he relates the triumph of the oral mother, the abolition of the father's likeness and the consequent birth of the new man" (Deleuze: 1989; 101).

Deleuze goes on to observe the 'male' position in masochism in crucially ethical terms, "Man on the cross, who knows no sexual love, no property, no fatherland, no cause, no work" (Masoch in Deleuze: 1989; 100). In Masoch's *The Mother of God*, the character of Mardona assumes the role of Mother of God. Lucia's role–as a feminine enactment of Christ–can be seen as a rendition of this. At one point Mardona states, "it is the love of the Mother of God that brings redemption and gives birth to man" (Masoch in Deleuze: 1989; 98). It is not too difficult to see in Lucia's role redemptive Christian overtones; the feminisation of the patriarchal one of its implicit aims. Indeed, like the Virgin Mary, it might be Vienna she returns to to immaculately 'conceive.' Her mission is to birth a new man from the ashes of Nazi horror, and in so doing resurrect the moral; with its ethical implications for Max. In one sense, Lucia is the projected Virgin Mary. In another sense Max is the projected scandalous Christ; thus suspending the ethical. For we know Christ dies at the hands of the Jews and Romans. But in tying Lucia to his bed, to place Lucia in the role of Christ, Max assumes the role of 'scandalous' persecutor. The Biblical tale is re-*presented*. Reversing the historical trajectory of the Holocaust, with the wholescale destruction of Judaism, Max *becomes* a Jew persecuting Christ. The point not to be overlooked is Max and Lucia die but their relationship is played out around the suspension of an all-punishing law. It might be said that Max becomes a 'new man' in his old uniform: the ultimate paradox. His catharsis is more complex than common sense equations; the purging of guilt more dangerous than we know. Like the Cathar perfect, ritual, distinct in using the symbolic, allows Max and Lucia to cathartically redefine their past: resist evil in 'evil.'

All of this is subtle in a way that the relationship is subtle. There is no direct mention of Christianity (as defining the roles). However, if the evil of the crucifixion is performed, with Christ's resurrection heralding Good's triumph over Evil, Max is positioned as symbolic Jew. He inverts his role of sacrificial victim to the Romans. When he attempts to cross the bridge at the end Max has become a new man, even if the bridge is never crossed. As microhistory bears down on "operatic macro history" (Vache: 1992; 191), performing what Vache sees as a "transubstantiation of interiority into social identity" (Vache: 1992; 187), Max–in SS uniform– responds to the otherness in Lucia and asserts his own guilt. Now, the past colludes with the present: the dangerous proposition. Suddenly, the camera turns to those trying to kill Max and Lucia, as they lurk dangerously in the shadows. Left to consider the death of the principle agents, and the obliteration of a microhistorical 'alliance' (between Max and Lucia), which has changed the *realpolitic* of neorealist objectives in ethical terms, we find that 'objective' history is transformed by microhistoric storytelling.

Conclusion: The Fascist Within

Nazism, and indeed its representative allure, Saul Frielānder suggests, "lay less in any explicit ideology than in the *power of emotions, images and phantasms*" (Freilander: 1984; 14). In *Saló*, the sexual and political phantasmatically align. For Pasolini, the pathology of absolute power emerges with the search for absolutes on the world political stage; questing for absolutes allows for the apotheosis of absolution.

In contrast, critics were quick to recognise *The Night Porter* as an ideological consolidation of Nazism rather than a concern with the *fascist within*; the luring impulse of fascism as a political ontology. By reducing its overall message to one of propaganda, and seeing it as a support to Nazism, Giroux, among others, overlooks the use of parody and performance as a way of subverting the manifestation of the fascist impulse. Cavani's vision of evil needs to be understood in this sense; otherwise *The Night Porter* simply disturbs. Offering redemption to the sinner: in this case Max, only occurs when responsibility *for* evil–in this case the greatest of the 20th century–is recognised.

Epilogue: Cavani and Evil

From *The Night Porter* Liliana Cavani films have continued to address the problem of evil. Cavani's adaptation of Frederic Nietzsche's *Beyond Good and Evil, Al di là del benne e de male* (Beyond Good and Evil (1977)) is a fictional account of a *ménage-à-trois* relationship between the philosopher (Erland Josephson), Lou Salomé (a female Russian émigré Jew) (Dominique Sanda) and Nietzsche's friend Paul Reé (Robert Powell). The narrative concerns the appearance of Doctor Dulcamara (Amedeo Amodio) as the Devil in disguise who–having visited Venice–encounters Nietzsche in a macabre ballet: the ballet of Good and Evil (a fictional account of Nietzsche's descent into madness in the years prior to his death). Obsessively Kafkaesque, for Gaettone Marrone, "the enchantment of the dance stem(s) out of its inherent ambiguity between resemblance and illusion, as in a play of mirrors reflecting dreams and visions" (Marrone: 2000; 136). The performance on which Nietzsche gazes comprises two dancers, one of whom is given the name Good, the other Evil. The dance develops to a point at which the dancers are indiscernible. Set in a sparsely decorated room, animated by shadows and chiaroscuro lighting, the doctor engages the dance as he is joined by a figure that resembles Christ. A battle then ensues between the dancers and climaxes with Good strangling Evil (Marrone: 2000; 145). Nietzsche's gaze meets the devil in close-up; his startled expression capturing his descent into madness.

'Documenting' Nietzsche's genius and madness is a considerable high point in the Cavani aesthetic. Cavani's later films, *Interno Berlinese* (The Berlin Affair (1985)) and *Ripley's Game* (2002), are more directly concerned with the "foul criminal deed." Like the Coen Brothers or Welles, such a deed is shown to differ from its "passionate" other (Bataille: 1973; 31). Calculated, planned evil, as it exists in the criminal underworld of modern societies, is a more explicit concern of Cavani's as she delves deeper in her exploration of genre. The last of the German trilogy, *The Berlin Affair*, is an adaptation of the novel by Junichiro Tanizaki, *The Buddhist Cross: 1928-30*. The film is set in years leading up to World War Two and concerns the wife of a German diplomat, Louise von Hollendorf (Gudrun Landgrebe), who develops an erotic obsession with the daughter of the Japanese ambassador to Germany, Mitzuko Matsugae (Mio Takaki). Von Hollendorf's husband (Kevin McNally) becomes involved in an affair which–following from key erotic events–spirals out of control. In the final stages of the film all three characters drink from a deadly potion, leading to the death of Mitzuko and Louise's husband; Louise realises Mitzuko has spared her death. Cavani describes the film as "the story of an idol and her adepts" (Cavani in Marrone: 2000; 142), referring here to the iconic status of Mitzuko. In *The Gaze and the Labyrinth: The Cinema of Liliana Cavani* (2000), Gaettone Marrone echoes this point,

"As the source of Louise's initiation into the sacred mysteries of Eros, the Japanese woman retains an instinctive alliance with the erotic through the sublimated transgressive sexual act. Copulation recaptures its ancient pathos. Death takes on a special dimension, which is urgent, essential, religious and mythical" (Marrone: 2000; 147).

Mitzuko helps Louise deal with the kind of divinity Cavani believes is invariably "false" (Cavani in Mattone: 2000; 142). The divine contrasts with the iconic status of Mitzuko, distinguishing the Buddhist Cross from the Nazi Swastika. The film is a profound investigation of the iconographic tradition; using significant profiles to capture the Eastern aesthetic resonance. Having described the period in which the film is set as the most irreligious in German history, due no doubt to its leaders taking the place of a transcendental divinity (while they themselves are a caricature), a collective group ceding their desires to an Eastern Goddess is given similar fertile expression, with Mitzuko as Goddess and 'visual icon.' As a standalone film *The Berlin Affair* is Cavani's most expansive. Her next film, *Ripley's Game,* is unapologetically concerned with cold-blooded criminality: the "foul crime" given precedence over the "passionate." Adapted from the prestigious crime writing of Patricia Highsmith, author of the Ripley novels, the plot concerns a sociopath and American criminal, Tom Ripley (John Malkovich), who relocates to Europe and sets up a criminal empire. Ripley is a cold-blooded killer whose evil dealings are fascinating and ruthless in orchestration.

Jonathan Trevanny (Dougray Scott), Ripley's neighbour, describes him as lacking the refinement of a true European, and this remark leads Ripley to seduce him into a life of crime and murder. Trevanny already suffers from leukaemia and lives in the knowledge that his death is imminent. Ripley nonetheless uses his low-life associate, Reeves (Ray Winstone), a cockney living in Germany, to attract Trevanny. When he asks Trevanny whether he would consider murdering a member of the mafia in order to financially secure his family's needs after his death, Trevanny is left to consider the financial gains of intentional murder and homicide. Highsmith's novel and the transferential displacement of evil onto another party–emphasised by Riply's manipulation of Trevanny, has been discussed at length in *Looking Awry: An Introduction to Jacques Lacan through Popular Culture* (1991), where Slavoj Žižek observes,

> "Even in her first novel *Strangers on a Train*, she established her elementary matrix: that of a transferential relationship between a psychotic murderer capable of performing the act and a hysteric who organises his desire by means of a reference to the psychotic, i.e., who literally *desires by proxy*" (Žižek: 1991; 176).

Of course, the transferential relationship that develops between Ripley and Trevanny is emphasised after Trevanny has finished his second bout of murder, helped by the evil Ripley. After choking three members of a Ukrainian mafia Trevanny becomes violently ill and is unable to carry out his further duty. The serene Ripley points out,

> "I like your conscience and when I was young it troubled me, it no longer does. I don't believe in being caught because I don't believe anyone is watching… You were brave today" (*Ripley's Game*: 2002).

A pan-shot of Ripley as he picks his teeth follows the close-up of Trevanny staring emotionally into the mirror; the image masking the moral horror evoked in this scene. Ripley's response, "the only thing I know is that we're constantly being born" (Ripley's Game: 2002) countenances Žižek's suggestion that Ripley's is,

> "A contradictory sentiment according to which the evil person is wholly responsible for his wickedness, although it is integral to his nature–that is, although 'he was born like that:'"to be evil' is not the same as to be stupid, irascible, and other similar features pertaining to our psychic nature, Evil is always experienced as something pertaining to a free choice, to a decision for which the subject has to assume all responsibility" (Žižek: 1989; 166).

Ripley may assume some responsibility for his actions. But he fails to see them as "integral to his nature." In this sense he illustrates the autonomy in doing evil (Žižek: 1989; 66). Far from "stupid" and "irascible" Cavani's Ripley is cultured and intelligent: attractive even. Žižek, in his emphasis on this, allows us to assess Cavani's portrayal in certain Augustinian terms, concerning both responsibility and moral action. For when presented through the autonomous transgressive act Ripley appears to revel in in the film, his capacity to assume responsibility for evil gives him a perverted moral authority over the fearful Trevanny. The hysteric dwelling endlessly on the evil act, Trevanny, is by contrast, "stupid" and "irascible;" his only redeeming act in the film is his death when shielding a bullet for Ripley. At this point, he has become–in a moment of high cynicism–the saviour to his evil executioner. In marrying popular crime genres and astute moral issues in a more direct film form *Ripley's Game* opens up two new cinematic pathways to the mature Cavani. The first is the attraction to evidently evil characters (although the film is set in northern Italy, none of the characters are Italian). The moral point of the film concerns pursuits, in this case Ripley, of goals without consideration for the cost in achieving them. But also, and secondly, normality. Just as Ripley's murders appear normal, 'necessary' even, Trevanny's perverse reasons for murder are hideous. We cannot but enjoy the wickedness Ripley emits precisely because it mimics, in terms of its structural features, the very qualities that we regard as good. When murder *is* capital gain; the logical extension of the market into the moral life; everything seems normal.

The Night Porter is Cavani's most significantly 'dangerous' film. It is dangerous in the sense that it plays 'evil' against evil, using performance as a vital means of resistance to its grasps. But it is also dangerous as a potentially career ending film for a modern day filmmaker. For the idea that a woman would wilfully return to her bondage, a Holocaust survivor would deceive her husband in order to relive the horror of the camps, seems so ridiculously absurd that it surpasses even the most expansive boundaries of fiction. If there is truth to the myth that criminals always return to the scene of the crime, can the same not be said for the victims? Why wouldn't victims, who have been subjected to a law bound by the State in which they were reared, not want to find some form of resistance to that law, other then through simply fleeing it?

CHAPTER FIVE

'BARBARISM BEGINS AT HOME': AUGUSTINIAN EVIL IN HANEKE'S *BENNY'S VIDEO* (1992)

"Unruly boys,
Who will not grow up,
Must be taken in hand,
Unruly girls,
Who will not grow up,
Must be taken in hand,"
—The Smiths, *Barbarism Begins at Home.*

"Kill the Pig! Cut his Throat! Kill the Pig! Bash him in!"
—William Golding, *Lord of the Flies.*

Literature devoted to Austrian director Michael Haneke, the concern of the next three chapters, is limited. Haneke is widely researched as an auteur, as is the role of violence in his films. However, influenced by the 60s and 70s Italian art film (and most particularly the films of Michelangelo Antonioni), his films can be perceived as diagnostic interventions in a broader and contemporary Europe. Haneke is therefore considered a profoundly intellectual filmmaker. As Rosalin Galt insists, "Haneke not only owns a particular aesthetic and geopolitical identity…he speaks as an auteur, an artist, an inheritor of the European cultural and intellectual heritage" (Galt in Price and Rhodes (eds): 2010; 222). In Haneke films, the moving image–or indeed the ontology of the image–has a profoundly ethical status. The commercially successful *Caché* is one such example. Reflexive strategies are used to complement probing moral content; taking to task the responsibility of adults for childhood acts. Equally fascinating is *Funny Games* (1995 & 2006), a film made in German and in English. Goading the audience (as if we too are an accomplice to the crimes committed) in a Pasoliniesque manner, the employed tactics left a nasty taste; particularly for those critical of Haneke's moralising; his audience looked upon with moral superiority. *Das weisse Bande* (The White Ribbon

(2009)), a recent production, is both a morality tale and an unashamed whodunit. Yet, with an ironic twist, it fails to reveal who done it.

Much has been written about Haneke's explorations of the violence in contemporary society, yet my real interest in Haneke stems from his consideration of evil. It would be an oversimplification to say that Haneke is at the vanguard of the media violence debate, replacing the variables of scientific research with the ambiguities of film. Haneke's films are certainly confrontational in the sense that they often deliberate on the impulse to violate others. But to say that Haneke's confrontational reflexivity gives support to the view media violence equals child violence, and those that support this, would be wrong. David Trend argues that, "nowhere in the literature or science of media violence has there been any documentation that children are naturally disposed to violence." But he goes on to state, "despite this paucity of evidence, children remain at the center of the media violence debate" (Trend: 2007; 37). Now, children are also central to the violence depicted in Haneke films; especially those addressed in what follows. But, as Haneke's films are less directly concerned, I would like to argue, with the idea children are predisposed to violence, and more concerned with a possible predisposition to evil, Haneke, as we'll see, finds children particularly interesting subjects. This is not because they are naïve or innocent, but because they are the purveyors of the ontological, in its most distilled form. If there is such a thing as nature, it is in children its rawest, most unaltered form of expression, can be found.

Children are interesting for other reasons. One reason is the debate about evil in Augustine and after, can be contextualised quite readily in relation to child violence or 'evil.' When we think of perversion as a deviation from a higher reality, we can consider children who perform evil acts are thinkable within these terms. One way of looking at this is to say children who act in this way have simply swerved in the wrong direction, and with proper tutelage will swerve back in line. To use Augustine's terms, the performed evil is simply a privation, a lack which requires filling in. Now, taking this as a starting point, is interesting, because, Augustine, as we discussed, deliberated also on the other possibility or possibilities of positive evil. Far from a lack, evil might be a positive force. Such evil gathers subjects in its sway. It can thus manifest in children. Augustine's interest, generally but not exclusively, lies in the will. Two men can look upon a woman, with one deciding to rape the woman in lust, the other deciding to dwell on her beauty. It is pointless to seek a cause for the evil choice, the orthodox Augustine suggests; unless, that is, we believe evil is also a substance. For the orthodox Augustine, the rapist is weak of will. Trying to find a cause, as mentioned earlier, is like trying to see darkness: the absence of light. For the unorthodox Augustine, the cause in question is evil.

Whether this evil is extended outwards, in acts of cruelty or dehumanization, or whether it takes the form of auto-aggression, as excellently theorized by Oliver C. Speck, Haneke has displayed a particular fascination with the child's propensity to harm. His films, and the ones I give particular focus to, are most evidently concerned with the relationship between children and adults, perhaps exploring the ontology of the child. Yet, as I want to make clear, this ontology is intricately bound to an ethics. It is an ethics which surmises on whether harming others is, as some believe, a 'natural impulse.' In fact, in films that explore evil, those which take central prominence in the remainder of this book, the theoretical composition of the 'child' or what is socially constructed as 'childhood' takes on an explicit ethical form of investigation. For it is in this curiously shape-shifting concept, which is ingrained in the popular consciousness as the wording for innate goodness, that the propensity for evil shocks us most. Conservatives and liberals agree that the media violence children see, "has become part of a toxic mix that has now turned some of them into killers" (Lieberman; 2006). In addition, books such as *Stop Teaching Our Kids to Kill* (1999) by David Grossman and Gloria deGaetanno, confirm the popular consensus. So, in what follows, Haneke films are discussed as inquiries into this particular moral consensus. This is not to say that Haneke thinks children can be evil, but that the problem of evil as it pertains to human nature is far more complex than we might admit.

Discussion of 'evil' is surprisingly lacking in criticism of Haneke, but in the three chosen films it is a significant and, I believe, obvious concern. It is central to *The White Ribbon*, continuing longstanding interest from *Benny's Video* to *Caché*. If there is a gradation to Haneke's oeuvre as identified at the beginning of this book, it can be traced in these films. *Benny's Video* concerns a girl killed by a teenager Benny (Arno Frisch), followed by the parents' 'cover-up' on discovering the body. Evil and the psychology of a remorseless murderer are the pivotal concerns. Detached and avuncular, Benny, like the protagonist in *Caché* Georges, has a strained relationship with the 'image.' In Georges's case, he feels an Algerian immigrant his parents had once considered adopting (only for

Georges to put a spanner in the works) has returned to harass him: sending him video images and related drawings of his home (and childhood events). Someone watching him is matched by the thought of him returning to terrorise. That the sons of the estranged men appear, hinting at an involvement, at the end, has a disturbing edge. The end, I will argue, with echoes of Edgar Allan Poe, on which the next chapter focuses, presses the familiar, interminably present on us. If the evil (young) men do is pressed upon us (in no uncertain terms), terrorists of a sort must also be confronted. Peter Dews's point that, "forces deeper than the familiar repertoire of unappealing human motives, such as greed, lust, or naked ambition" are generally considered evil (Dews: 2010; 4) has a renewed pertinence in this regard; one which I believe is necessary to respond to. Haneke films are situated around these vices. Greed, lust, naked ambitions are some. But these are subservient to something greater and more harmful.

Rather than dabble in didactics around these vices and what they mean, Haneke's films initiate reactions in us. And so, react we must. But in reacting we navigate a hybrid space between the art film–with narrative uncertainty of import–and the crime, with good guys and bad; a space in which the peculiar realm for such reaction is emotionally fuelled. In the realm of emotional navigation we are able to assert, along with Wheatley, that,

> "Formally, modernism is reflected, for example, in the early films through the withholding of narrative information and of psychology, ellipsis, fragmentation and foregrounding of the medium, all of which conspire to provide a 'clarifying distance' that will transform the viewer from 'simple consumer' to active evaluator" (Wheatley: 2009; 22).

Hence, the characters of Haneke films can often appear detached, lacking in emotion and its expression. Psychological explanation is rarely provided. Haneke doesn't want his audience to identify in overt terms with his protagonist. He therefore includes a kind of fragmentary aesthetic, often reminding us of the fact we are evaluating a story: a set of actions that could belong to us. Of course, an "active evaluator" assumes responsibility. But if it is demanding to evaluate the images in a film like *Funny Games* with it aggressive reflexivity, films like *The White Ribbon* use subtler means to trouble the interpreter. In both, the problem of evil can be overlooked; precisely because the more immediate challenge of piecing together the filmic is taken up. Yet the problem of evil takes centre stage in *The White Ribbon,* as moral agency is foreground in a pertinent sense regarding the problem of *radical evil*. Questioned about what inspired him to turn a script initially written for television into a feature-length film about evil, Haneke referred to the German Nazi, Adolf Eichmann, and his trial. Haneke thus spoke about the trial's impact on 20th century ethics and his desire to respond to it in a more direct capacity than the lengthy television format. For Haneke, Eichmann's capacity to obey an obviously criminal law was as shocking as the crimes which he later committed. Unable to fall back, as Arendt said in her trial report,

> "On an unequivocal voice of conscience–or, in the even vaguer language of the jurists, on a "general sentiment of humanity" (Oppenheim-Lauterpacht in *International Law*, 1952)–not only begs the question, it signifies a deliberate refusal to take notice of the central moral, legal, and politicial phenomena of our century" (Arendt: 1994; 148).

Failing to register the slaughter of Jews as 'wrong' is in itself shocking if the moral collapse on which it hinged wasn't so clear. Eichmann's claim to be a Kantian, undermining the Kantian 'ought,' renders the consideration of *radical evil* necessary when exploring the perversion of the will exhibited. Eichmann's behaviour, and the many war criminals that were oblivious to the singularity of *their* crime, can be traced–in a socio-historical context–to a political and ethical nexus. Yet because this is not necessarily a cause, but a partial one, the longstanding concern with evil lingers. In his exploration of this, Haneke will focus on the kind of behaviour Max Horkheimer notes is, "inclined to submit blindly to power and authority" (Horkeimer and Flowerman; 1950; ix). In these terms, Haneke's concern with the fascist impulse becomes a more readily apparent issue. His film focuses on the origins of Nazism. But in confronting the film as a study of evil, as I do, its uniquely filmic treatment also needs to be assessed.

Extending the traditional auteur work of previous greats–such as Bresson, Antonioni and Pasolini–Haneke has nonetheless gained a notorious reputation across the Atlantic. Not surprisingly, his stated aim to combat the, "cinema of distraction" he associates with a dominant Hollywood realist model (felt to echo the dominant hegemonic political system of its origin), does little to suggest a forthcoming meeting of minds with 'the opposition.' As stated in *71 Fragmente,*

> "I attempt to provide an alternative to the totalising productions that are typical of the entertainment cinema of American provenance. My approach provides an alternative to the hermetically sealed-off illusion which in effect pretends at an intact reality and thereby deprives the

spectator of the possibility of participation. In the mainstream scenario spectators are right off herded in mere consumerism" (Haneke: 2000; 172).

Dismissing "entertainment cinema" is coterminous with dismissing the hegemony of Western film distribution. The recent publication of Peter Brunette's Haneke monograph, by its very appearance, suggests a more welcoming U.S. profile (more recently Oliver C. Speck has published a book on Haneke in the U.S.), particularly in the wake of critics of widely distributed broadsheets proving more than hostile to the Austrian's film work. Bestowing an audience (more often than not) with retrospective punishment for pleasure taken in the films he makes makes Haneke's boorishness the most prominent complaint against him. Punishment for taking pleasure is, as we'll see, a concern of the more confrontational films, but not the only concern. For as many critics would argue, the spectator of a narrative film doesn't necessarily experience the director's intentions as such–but often the opposite. A.O. Scott, film critic with the *New York Times*, has proved particularly hostile to Haneke's output. Scott has been offended by most of the films. Indeed, such offence is taken to *US Funny Games*, it is seen as a verile attack on "American" audiences,

> "The conceit of "Funny Games" is that it offers a harsh and exacting critique of violent, vulgar amusements, a kind of homeopathic treatment for a public numbed and besotted by the casual consumption of images of suffering. That the new version takes place in America is part of the point since Americans–to a European intellectual this almost goes without saying–are especially deserving of the kind of moral correction Mr. Haneke takes it upon himself to mete out" (Scott; 2008).

Scott's point (with potentially reverse discriminatory impulses) is contentious in every possible sense, especially as a didacticism about cinematic violence, coupled with Brechtian alienation, can allow for a more direct ethical experience *of* the films. Yet, with reduced moralising in *The White Ribbon,* and reduced to a substantial degree, Scott still finds the film troublingly offensive,

> "Anyone who has seen Mr. Haneke's "Caché" or his twin versions of "Funny Games" will be aware that he does not believe in the blamelessness of youth. Quite the contrary: children, in his world, carry the sins of their parents in concentrated, highly toxic form and are also capable of pure, motiveless, experimental evil. What will become of these particular blond children? Do the math: it's 1914. In 20 or 30 years, what you suppose these children will be up to? Our narrator, well into old age, is telling us he is revisiting the strange events in the village to "clarify

things that happened in our country" afterward. But "The White Ribbon" does the opposite, mystifying the historical phenomena it purports to investigate. Forget about Weimar inflation and the Treaty of Versailles and whatever else you may have learned at school: for Nazism was caused by child abuse. Or maybe the intrinsic sinfulness of human nature? "The White Ribbon" is a whodunit that offers a philosophically and aesthetically unsatisfying answer: everyone. Which is also: noone" (Scott; 2009).

Scott's visceral response to historical investigation of a uniquely philosophical-ethical persuasion is warranted. For caution is required when engaging with the film. For the "historical phenomena" Scott purports to investigate is evil, and evil on a grand stage. Scott's belief that evil presented in terms of the collective guilt it begets is considerable: when everyone is guilty noone really is. Collective guilt, when collective means everybody, is thus a duly problematic notion. When evil is committed in a systematic State applauded fashion, like Nazism, the law integrated into officialdom, the perpetrators–of such heinous crimes–end up hiding behind the dictates of a Law while claiming to be its honourable citizens. Carrying their actions out as dutiful Kantians, in the way of a certain Adolf Eichmann, makes a collective index of individual action; hence, no one subject assumes a personal guilt-relation.

So there are good reasons to consider Scott's observations on Haneke just as there are good reasons to consider the mindset of the protagonists in *Benny's Video* and *Caché* from the perspective of evil. For Scott considers child abuse as a cause of fascism–and dismisses the film–even if the power of *The White Ribbon* lies in confronting the numerous guises of evil. The Doctor who abuses his daughter is just one representative of evil in the film. To think he is the only one misses the point. Conventional in his monstrousness, typical of older notions of evil in method, the Doctor (Rainer Bock) is too obsessed with his own unsavoury desires to be callously evil in the mode of say, an Anton Chigurh. A monster in his own twisted way, believing he is doing good by others, others are essential rather than superfluous to his perversions. The character open to most disdain is the Pastor (Burgart Klaußner). In laudably affirming his own righteousness, the Pastor shames others. But the moral of the Pastor, I believe, concerns the evil involved in allowing evil to take place.[1] In

---

[1] Amy Berg's outstanding *Deliver Us From Evil* (2007) is an exemplary study of this phenomenon. The film focuses on the paedophile sex abuser, Father Oliver O'Grady, and the litany of abuse cases he left in his stead, and uses first-hand interviews with O'Grady as part of the footage. Yet as much as O'Grady appears as a villainous criminal, a deranged abuser of children, the network which shields

abuse cases, the culprit, like Beckert in *M*, is vilified. But the network surrounding the culprit, allowing abuse to take place is a different form of evil. We will explore what 'form' this evil takes in *The White Ribbon* later.

Haneke has never been afraid to define the ideological position from which his films are made. His background in both Germany and Austria, and indeed his move to France, have meant his cultural affinity is with those countries that participated most directly in World War Two; and perhaps suffered the most in the process. His inquiry into human fascination with violence, and indeed cruelty (as Speck points out), is coupled with an abiding interest in relaying the ethical deliberation on violence onto an increasingly uneasy audience. Catherine Wheatley has written an exemplary study of this particular strategy (and therefore I'll refrain from overt analysis of this here), while others have explored the critique of violence in *using* violence. However, what makes Haneke such an interesting filmmaker for me is the reflexive means in doing so; masking a concern with evil. Just as the question of how violence is critiqued by Haneke is at the forefront of Haneke studies, for good reason, the question of how evil is critiqued, and ultimately what Haneke has to say about it, should be at the forefront as well. Defensive when asked about evil, Haneke, I contest, prefers to relay any such deliberation onto the spectator.

Given his profile as a leading art-house filmmaker in Europe, there is a need to ask what Haneke has to say in his films about evil. And this is the aim of what will follow in this last third of the book. Inquiring into what Haneke says shouldn't, at least from my perspective, necessitate a lateral position on his films, for as Haneke himself says, he's not a philosopher. But his films do philosophise for him. And therefore, as much as he'd like to relinquish responsibility for what his films say about evil, the semiotic position, I believe he has a responsibility to them; the moral one. Therefore, in comparison to earlier, what follows is quite personal about 'Haneke.'

An extrapolation of evil in early Haneke, using *Benny's Video* as a genealogical marker, will now be undertaken with Augustine's help. For if

---

and protects him, emerges, over the course of the documentary, as a force of evil greater than the evil agent. Those who turned away from confronting O'Grady are just as evil, if not more, than the person, who abused the children in the film. For they fail to confront his abuse of others.

the main concern is responsibility for evil, subsequent chapters address how this pertains to later Haneke; complementing this chapter. We begin, however, with a story about a boy; a boy who, whether he intends to or not, kills.

The Evil That Young Men Do

Michael Haneke's *Benny's Video* bears all the hallmarks of a masterpiece. Each frame is meticulously planned, leaving an impression long after it ends. The second installment in *The Cinema of Glaciation*, the name for the first three of Haneke's Austrian films, set in his native land, *Benny's Video* is Haneke's most controversial. The plot is multi-layered, the main one about Benny, left alone in his apartment for a weekend, inviting a girl home, and then videoing the killing. Benny hardly conceals the murder. His parents return to find a video of the killing. Yet rather than consult the authorities, they dispense with the body; brushing murder under the proverbial carpet and hiding the evidence.

The murder, like the murder of Marion (Janet Leigh) in Hitchcock's *Psycho* (1960) is one of the more disturbing features of a very disturbing film. Benny is a minor, living with his parents in a suburban Viennese apartment. But he kills his victim with cold precision. He does so from a space marginally off screen, with the murder exposed on a monitor at the centre of the frame. Benny films himself killing. As the girl cries out for help, Benny appears intent on framing the murder with almost clinical precision. With its wincingly ritual killing (the voyeuristic spectacle folded onto the audience) controversy courted the film. The occurrence of high profile child murders brought the debate on film related violence to boiling point around the time of Haneke's film. The most notorious of these murders was James Bulger (in Liverpool). Ten-year-old boys Jon Venables and Robert Thompson abducted Bulger from a shopping centre, before killing him in a ritualistic-type fashion. That Bulger was abducted from New Strand Shopping Centre in Bootle before being walked for over three and half kilometres to the Walton and Anfield Railway Station (where he was bludgeoned to death (by ten yr old children)) magnified the question of what would motivate such a crime; especially in children acting collaboratively. Why would children, sanctified by the populist media as innately innocent, commit such a heinous crime? Surely there was a reason? The failure to find an extentuating factor, and indeed the scapegoating of the children as irrevocably 'evil' in their criminal intent, was taken up by Blake Morrison,

"Inadmissable evidence. Wasted knowledge. What's known but can't be said. All those experts, not allowed to use their expertise. Inadmissable because a court must investigate only Whether: did these boys kill James Bulger, or not? Pure judgement: clean and clear as mountain lake. The river Why runs underneath but can't be permitted to muddy the waters. A child has been killed and a verdict's wanted. The nation must be purged and cleansed" (Morrison: 1998; 94).

Media Studies experts across the UK were quick to blame TV and the slackening of censorship laws. Others decried the effects of screen violence, whether in televisual or video gaming. *Child Play 3* (1991), a gorefest of shlock horror, was just one film cited. Ultimately, like the defence attorney in *M*, evil is found to be both suitable and unsuitable as a cause. For what justifies the murder of a child by another child, horrifying in the Bulger case, is more difficult to answer morally than why adults do the same. In fact, ethical deliberation needs to ask what would make the murder of a human being itself desirable other than in gain. And subsequently, when does a murderer become a responsible adult?

Teenage murder will of course raise issues similar if not the same as those Morrison raises. Clinical psychologist Dr Alison White has spent a lifetime working with child perpetrators of crime. When she is asked to respond to children, and indeed their 'evil,' she states, "I am firmly on the nurture side" (Allison in Laurance; 2010). In other words, White believes children who perform horrendous acts of violence are badly reared. In the context of cognitivism, environment and rearing taking precedence over neurological determinants in pathological crime, it is now generally believed that a neurological predisposition, call it nature, to certain conditions can generate the type of psychopathological behaviour elicited by serious criminals. Yet in seeking to understand *Benny's Video* should we not begin by asking whether, like White, Haneke believes the same? And whether or not a justifiable rationale can be given for intentional murder. While there is a certain need to seek answers for these kind of questions, in that Haneke films can be encountered as attempts to answer questions relating to evil, just as Augustine explored an evil existing in 'us' as a positive force, it may well be that the Bulger case had a resoundingly strong impact across the media because we are living through the shockwaves it sent to a Western populace schooled in the orthodox view on evil: evil as a privation. And because children are considered innately innocent, the image of Bulger hand in hand with his child killers would, in the context of the past twenty years, smash this view. It smashes it because, as much as we are compelled to reject the privation argument, we are, in a society where justice reigns, compelled to assume it.

I will address these points in more detail over the next three chapters. Analysis of evil (as distinct from immoral, or in some cases immoral/evil borderline cases) acts, along with the rationale for committing them will take the form of a moral analysis of Haneke films. What makes Benny such a compelling case is the fading line between reality and its mediatised appearance, which, by congregating around his actions, we are invited to explore. When contextualised in relation to the Bulger case, the debate around the film hinges on views of mediated violence instilling the feeling that another world exists–removed from reality–where things are 'playable' for the child. Taking this view, Peter Brunette asserts, "*nonordinary* reality is presented in such a tantalising way that people want to experience it" (Brunette: 2010; 37).

Brunette's is a merited reading: Benny seeks to replicate the *nonordinary*; experience what is *not* actual experience as experience. Unsure as to why he kills, the *point de capiton* on which the film hinges is, for Brunette and Speck, the Egyptian holiday sequence. As with the subtle ending of *La dolce vita*, a moral purpose can be discerned in this: Benny comes to realise the destructiveness of his earlier behaviour; assumes a moral disposition. Yet the film's success lies in the diametrically opposed readings it engenders. A less optimistic reading is that Benny clinically murders–and to avoid argument let us assume that the act of murdering an innocent girl is *evil*–because he is evil. Benny is simpy bad: a kind of 'evil for evil's sake.' While both are morally challenging, neither is fully conclusive. After the cover-up, having shown little concern in concealing things, the moral problem expands to consideration of Benny's parents' status as the evildoers. The issue of second-degree murder, or manslaughter, is foreground. We know Benny invited a girl home, and playacting with a stun gun killed her, but whether intentional in his activities is relatively unclear. The cover-up is, however, intentional. Equally, whether we can consider manslaughter a more suitable descriptor for *the* murder is difficult to judge, as it is the actions of a boy not an adult. Asked "why did you do it?" Benny replies, "I don't know, I wanted probably to see what it was like" (*Benny's Video*; 1992). Intentions, and the will as something knowable in the properly epistemological sense, is problematised.

In *The Psychopath Test: A Journey Through the Madness Industry*, Jon Ronson has explored how the desire to experience what something is like, irrespective of the emotions of those affected, is a rote response given by psychopaths. The multiple-child killer Peter Woodcock, when asked why he murdered, responded glibly, "I just wanted to know what it would feel like to kill somebody" (Ronson: 2011; 91). Yet, even though he responds in a similar way, a reading of Benny as a psychopath runs counter to his characterisation in the film; where intent is difficult to read. Indeed, anti-psychologcial characterisation in the films of Robert Bresson, which Haneke has written on, champions eschewing conventional psychological expression; in this sense Benny is typical of anti-psychological form.

Committed within the bedroom space (using a live feed to record the encounter), the murder has noteworthy parallels with Marion's death in Hitchcock's *Psycho* (1960). Close-ups of the shower used to wash away blood bring to mind the most famous of scenes (Marion's murder) in *Psycho*. The cold silence, however, gives greater realism. The cover-up, nonetheless, nodding to Hitchcock, is arguably more disturbing. Benny–possibly a psychopath undertaking his first murder–and Norman are similarly detached. Both are awkward in demeanour and both seem lacking in empathy; hence Benny executes his murder in a not dissimilar way to the way Norman greets and then murders Marion. Yet, even with such similarity in before and after, the murder of the girl shocks (a friend of mine who is also a filmmaker has attested that *Benny's Video* is the most disturbing film he has ever seen), for having witnessed him killing animals and recording them at the beginning, an example of his superiority over the powerless, killing humans seems to follow *from this*. A grandiose point about human malevolence towards others is made. But of course, this is far from Haneke's main point. For following the murder, the narrative takes an unexpected turn with Benny's parents' decision that it is in everyone's interests, fearing Benny will be criminalised for the remainder of his life, to dispense with the body and life to carry on as normal. When Benny and his mother go on holidays to Egypt Benny continues working on a video travelogue crucial to his exoneration. The time in Egypt has added importance, for as Speck notes,

> "The week that mother and son spend in a holiday resort in Egypt is important because the audience must retroactively locate Benny's change of mind in this short vacation that primarily serves to give the father enough time to accomplish the gruesome task of cutting up the body into small enough parts to flush them down the toilet" (Speck: 2010; 133).

Is there a change of mind? And is an overtly positive assessment of the scene in question one which locates a "change of mind" as such? We will return to this issue at a later point. For it is enough to note that Benny's parents become accessories. Whether this serves a personal or public Good is a central dilemma of the film. If their response to the murder gives a green light to murders committed behind closed doors, without recrimination, it is surely a greater evil than Benny's. But wanting to protect a minor from the threat of the criminal justice system is more recognisably immoral than evil. That is, shielding a child from the extremity of criminal charges is wrong, even if a human element can be discerned in parents seeking to protect children in this way. It is therefore of more than passing interest to recall the treatment of children like Benny–child murderers–and the vigilante attacks against them, for the Bulger case stands as notice. Jon Venables was returned to prison for possessing images of child pornography, leading journalists to explore the difficulty he experienced when living under false premises (Venables was released under a witness protection programme), in fear of his true identity being revealed at every moment. Venables, speaking through video link so as not to be identified, spoke about his relief in returning to jail. Mark Hughes observed at the time, "while his identity remains hidden, the snippets of insight provide a glimpse into a life consumed by fear that his new identity would become known, burdened with the pressure of living a lie and ultimately defined by depravity" (Hughes in Laurance; 2010).

The life of David Smith and Maureen Hindley, chief witnesses to the prosecution in the Moors Murders, also stands as notice. Even though Smith was the main witness, having gone to the police to report the killing of Edward Evans by Ian Brady and Myra Hindley, his life in the immediate aftermath was one of persecution and shame; unable to find employment and accused on a daily basis of being a 'child murderer.' The irony was deep-felt. A public in shock at the horrors of Hindley's and Brady's crime, nonetheless believed the accusations both murderers made against Smith during the trial. Hindley and Brady famously accused David Smith of planning the murders. As a result, tarnished by the guilt of association, yet proven innocent by the courts, Smith lived for years in Manchester as a social pariah, beaten on a regular basis. As Smith was only a teenager at the time, his treatment by the public is telling.

If the point of all this is the 'depravity' Benny, like Smith would experience–irrespective of whether he intended to murder the girl or not–there may well be some remnant of good behind the decision to cover up the crime. In the context of the protection foregrounded as such, one of the key issues at stake concerns the question of who is ultimately culpable? And how do we assess this in specifically moral terms? Who is the criminal and the baddie in this terrible equation? Is this simply a tale of parental woe in a society where children are increasingly cut off from their parents? Or is it a story about a boy programmed to murder and kill his peers; which nothing can alter? Is it possible that Benny finds an inferior 'animal' in a girl from the lower social classes, similar in status to the pig he videos being killed at the beginning. If this is the case, *Benny's Video* is as much about class violence, as it is about boy kills girl; Benny believing he is simply carrying out the goals of the social strata in which he thrives: the social design he actively pursues based on his warped middle-class consciousness. Just as Fritzl believed and defended himself on the basis he was a good 'family man,' set on protecting his family against all the dangers of the modern world, perhaps Benny believes the designs of the class in which he belongs are being championed; wilfully building a better world. If so, the film is a serious indictment of Austrian society.

The main sequence to look for answers is Benny and his mother's holiday in Egypt. Both intend to return after the cover-up. Before this Benny had visited a barber to have his head shaven, making him resemble a prisoner of war or a skinhead, depending on the point of view. His image, nonetheless, seems out of step in Egypt. With this rural and largely agricultural backdrop, Benny and his mother are free of the trappings of Western consumer societies. When Benny sets about recording local life, one of the few scenes of genuine emotion–when the immensity of the crime crashes through the wall of denial erected by the family–takes place. As mother and son watch Egyptian TV, anaesthetised to their surroundings outside of the hotel, Anna breaks into a barrage of tears. The moment is unheralded; that is by any obvious narrative trigger. Rather, it's as if the emotion that has been blocked out by the murder has come crashing through. In Lacanian terms, it's as if the Real has suddenly penetrated the symbolic barriers on which it acts as the encompassing 'background noise.'

Far from incriminating Anna, making her appear all too aware of her crime, the moment in Egypt makes explicit the crime after *the crime* itself. With his gesture towards his mother, reminiscent of the gesture which ends Bresson's masterpiece, *Pickpocket* (1959), a story of evil turns into a story of significant remorse and guilt. But whether the trigger Speck among other readers identifies, as an integral feature of the sequence, constitutes a "change of mind" is open to question. For Haneke shows us, if he doesn't necessarily tell, what this touch means. In Bresson's film, Michel reaches out through the prison bars to touch Jeanne (Marike Greene), who has finally visited him; the implication that something has changed Michel all too palatable. Benny reaches towards the mother, affected by her outward show of emotion, but whether his symbolic universe has been properly penetrated by guilt is never clarified. Keith Reader's work on Bresson is interesting here. In his analysis of the final scene of *Pickpocket*, Reader points to the infamously moving yet generally unconventional ending. For Reader, the ending is less, "a restoration of the imaginary plenitude of the relationship with the (pre-Oedipal) mother" than one diminishing, "the border between the human affection of Eros and the divine reach of Agape;" a bond of spirtual grace felt between his characters (Reader: 2000: 60-61). Whether a similar bond can be discerned in Benny's experience, a grace of sorts expressed in the touch, is never clarified.

Of course, as simply an interpretation of the events, we should remember that criminals–such as Anna–are capable of remorse; especially with their getaway intact. Anna's tears are cast in a lesser light, however, when we consider her guilt-ridden and aware that protecting her son is immoral. Nonetheless, our ability to come to a definite conclusion as to whether Benny intentionally kills the girl and is now showing genuine remorse for doing so is clouded by the fact that he never talks about it with any kind of emotion. There are few pointers as to the motivation for the crime. On the one hand, Benny goes about his day as if nothing has changed; significantly unpertubed by the death of the girl he brought home. On the other, his behaviour is typically teenagerly; the carelessness of which is notably overcome in Egypt as the boy matures and becomes aware of his crime. If his Austrian oppression is captured in framing–echoing Antonioni in this light–of Benny's silhouette, against doorways, windows or, most often his bed–the alienation that he suggestively overcomes in Egypt is shaped by open far away climes. It is, as if, contact with Otherness in some shape, has regenerative effects for a maturing Benny.

The Egyptian holiday sequence has, for scholars like Oliver C. Speck, an allegorical thrust; such is the significance of Egypt as the destination of choice for the family. As Speck notes,

> "The obvious irony here is that the Biblical holy family flees into Egypt to avoid Herod's murdering troops, while Benny's "Flight into Egypt" happens after an innocent has been murdered" (Speck: 2010; 133).

Speck offers a caveat. He states this "appears to trigger Benny's flight from his "un-holy" family" (Speck: 2010; 133). There is a certain truth to be discerned in this analysis; but whether it accrues from a reading of what happens–as distinct from it being a self-evident truth-is perhaps crucial. Indeed, it could be that Speck–and he's not the only one–is duped by 'Benny,' wanting to believe he goes to the police for the betterment of everyone. While it would be nice to think he prevents his parents reasserting a perverse 'normality,' so that they pay the price for manslaughter, the fact that the video recordings taken in Egypt are part of an edit which is more than simply recreational, part of Benny's video, makes for a disturbing proposition: Benny's 'holiness' is inferior to its other.

With this in mind, should we still consider, as the majority of critics do, Anna's tears–set in the banal confines of a hotel room–as a trigger for Benny decision to go to the police? And even, in the context of Augustine's following refrain,

> "Evil is contrary to nature; in fact it can only do harm to nature; and it would not be a fault to withdraw from God were it not that it is more natural to adhere to him....God, who is supremely good in his creation of natures that are good, is also completely just in his employment of evil choices in his design, so that whereas such evil choices make a wrong use of good natures, God turns evil choices to good use" (Augustine: 1984; 448-449).

That Benny is *the* real victim. His 'good nature' triumphs in the end. We might never know if he is incriminated for the murder yet it appears his parents attempt to cover it up, is. Because they are framed on surveillance monitors (in the final scene), as well as being framed as subject in Benny's videos, there is a certain hint given that the parents, *ex post facto,* constitute *the* crime. In one sense, *Benny's Video* has a moral purpose, in the sense of reaffirming Augustinian privation. On another, Benny's video has purpose–like the video–incriminating the parents. In the first sense it is a reminder that children are incapable of perversion and that evil is a socially generated deviation. Yet, in the second, and the film is notoriously slow to make either interperation the dominant one, the power to frame the other–Benny's video evidence of his parents' involvement in *his* crime–is an evil one. So in reading Haneke's position as sceptical of the representative image as image, Speck reminds us of the way in which Benny "frames" his parents, if only to show us the social capital invested in representative strategies and the uses of them (Speck: 2010).

Mea Culpa (and I Don't Care)/ or: Haneke's Cosmology

At the end the viewer must consider the boy leaving the police station being on the path to redemption. Two main interpretations are left open, the first of which suggests Benny is redeemed, the second that he is evil. Yet the filmic treatment of these encourages the spectator to decide. The first interpretation (and Haneke's films are notoriously open to interpretation) contrasts with less ethically rewarding interpretations of Benny's actions. A "*prise de conscience*" (Brunette: 2010; 36) may well have led Benny to the police. But that Haneke has painted the world in dualistic terms, Benny is evil from birth, lingers as a real possibility. Taking this latter position, Benny saves his skin when, in the final scene, he goes to the police. It is possible Benny is the subject of a pervasive, "power that emanates from within, between and beyond human nature" (Molloy; 2010). Here is a criminal who, from filming the killing of a pig in the opening scene of the film, demonstrates an, "innate human propensity to evil" (Bernstein: 2002; 5); the slaughter endemic of his fascination with evil. Speck notes the "moment of death when the bullet enters the pig" as "aestheticising the killing, and thereby raising ethical questions" (Speck: 2010; 82). He therefore points to a central ethical concern; the ethical within the aesthetic realm; that a video of a killing begins the film can test our resolve; that is, when confronting killing per se. We can ask: to what extent aestheticising killing is linked to the evil act?

It would seem then that the animal slaughter, shown at the beginning, invokes a fascination–Cathar-like–with non-human flesh, which will–hinted at here–*eventually* become a fascination with flesh per se. Over the course of the film, killing will become the ultimate expression of this perverse fascination. If Benny, a recipient of parental care perverse in its logic, is a psychopathic murderer–a killer in all but name–killing animals may well be a psychopathological trait. Moreover, the murdered girl's presence in the video raises similar issues. That is, the fact the girl is shown in the video; 'shown' to Georg, is significant. For her presence in the video suggests Benny's main concern is likely to be the aestheticising of killing; and that he mistakenly confuses killing with the aesthetics of killing. In fact, when first watching *Benny's Video*, I was led to believe that Benny's actions constituted, using the distinction between immoral and evil acts, an act of extreme immorality; manslaughter based on Benny using the girl for significant aesethetic purposes. Unlike Chigurh, who dehumanises others by killing them with a stun gun, the fact that Benny kills the girl with a stun gun while videotaping the act raises questions about the representation and intentionality behind the murder. If replaying his actions in wicked delight consumes Benny he is surely disturbed. But if he replays what he videos because he is making a film about killing, failing to realise the difference between killing and representing killing, then he is more than qualitively unwell.

If videoing the murder is pathological, in addition to the killing of animals, Benny's video is equally disturbing. Purpose is given to the recreational video that seemed to simply pass time: it incriminates his parents. Yet, while considering the videos are edited for a malevolent purpose is disturbing, other equally disturbing features to the film require attention. When viewing the video of the murder, Benny's father responds in a disturbing manner by questioning Benny about the girl's background; an accusation based not on his determining some perverse justice but on whether Benny has told anybody about what he has done. That Benny responds by saying he thumped a boy at school and is presently being reprimanded for doing so has an ironic ring; the public display of justice at odds with the now private masquerade. In the knowledge that Benny has concealed things, Georg then sends him to bed, asking him to open his door. However, Benny's door–from which a ray of light filters through– has an alluring significance; a metaphor for a Benny caught in the maelstrom of opposing forces. In the dark, Benny is a prisoner of evil.

It is, of course, within this 'disturbed' context that Anna's burst of laughter on hearing that Georg is considering dispensing with the body– fearing Benny will be committed to a psychiatric institution otherwise–is one of the more disturbing moments in a very disturbing film. At a precise moment when laughing is most inappropriate, its manifestation serves to underline the absurdity of the situation. Dispensing with the body has both a rational purpose–on the basis of the reasons put forward by Georg–and an absurd one: downplaying Benny's crime. It is absurd because, incriminating everyone, Georg and Ann become accessories to murder. By diverting attention from Benny's actions, with the decision to brush Benny's crime under the carpet, far more in assessing criminality appears to be at stake; that is, than simply judging the criminal. For the fact that Benny is a minor and that neither parent has actually committed the murder of the girl muddies the significant moral problem. It is only in the aftermath of returning from Egypt that the image of Benny's room reappears out of context. Anna and Georg are discussing 'parental neglect' and dispensing with the body of the girl. With neither speaker situated in the frame, and only the their words audible, we can only surmise the point-of-view is from Benny's bed. As the discussion turns to dispensing with the girl's body, an image–uncanny in its repetition–(of the door ajar) appears to be strangely out of joint. For, in this shot, a close-up of Benny in the process of being interviewed by policemen comes into focus, retrospectively realising that all of this, Benny's video, is documentary evidence of his parents' involvement. As Brigitte Peucker puts it,

> "The parents' conversation will serve to indict them as accessories after the fact for the murder that their son has committed. As Benny turns himself in, the videotape becomes not only a document of violence, but its instrument as well. In keeping with the film's trenchant critique of contemporary mores, it remains unclear whether Benny's act is a moral one–a Bressonian assumption of guilt, with religious overtones–or merely an act of violence against his parents, the flipside of the utopian space suggested in Egypt" (Peucker; 2004).

As Peucker states, the film ends as Benny leaves the interview room to confront his parents, to whom he simply says 'sorry.' The camera focuses on the parents waiting on their son, as a monitor hangs from the ceiling recording their live presence. In the background the news is documenting the possibility of intervention in the Balkan War; but also the refusal to designate ethnic zones around this. It is no doubt an allegory on the nature of Benny's evil and his refusal to countenance others involvement in his evil doings. The parents sit and wait: all the while awating their fate. Meanwhile, their child walks out of the main office, staring nonchalantly at his feet.

Benny confesses–through the video that he innocently plays with–but it is difficult not to see some kind of calculated evil at play. Indeed, were it not such an outdated 'methodology,' it is difficult not to identify a prefunctory dualism here; Benny an avatar of the dark, a cosmos consisting of a battle between two opposing forces. Because of this the signature image–taken from Benny's point-of-view–of a door ajar where light struggles to penetrate darkness is an apt image for this overriding theme. The image incriminates parents who, despite their detachment from the brutality of the crime, strive to protect their son. With this reading, as pessimism cuts into the orthodox rendering of evil as privation, Benny's evil is not simply a deviation from a higher form of good, as Augustine's

Neo-Platonic reworking of Christian doctrine sought to maintain, but *part of* human nature. Benny, with his penchant for fabrication, is more than a suitable candidate for its expression. For, given the chance to redeem himself, he decides not to. In an interview about the inspiration for making *Benny's Video*, Haneke spoke about collecting stories concerning types of violence similar to that which Benny performs. Haneke was particularly taken with the response given by violent youngsters that the motivation derived from wanting to feel what it was like to maim somebody in this way.

Haneke offers a curiously metaphysical appraisal of the media and its capacity to detach its users from the mainstay of ordinary reality, wondering if kids such as Benny lack the ability to distinguish between ordinary reality and its nonordinary other. There is a sense reality and its defamations–certainly when considered in this way–can detract from the moral issue at hand; that detachment from reality–whatever reality should mean in this sense, is left for the interlocutor to divulge–has deep lying immoral consequences. It means for Haneke an obsession with images–representations as such–is not just bad, but potentially evil. There is a sense that Haneke would want to believe this, rather than admit that what really concerns him is the link between human contact and goodness. For if televisual violence in all its vitality makes violence all the more attractive, activating a dormant principle for doing it, must this principle first of all exist? And is this principle, hovering in the wings of Haneke's films, Evil?

Haneke the Augustinian

Augustine's journey into the miasmic theoretical field from which evil is borne takes many different turns, from the Manichees through to the Neo-Platonists and Christianity. His position on evil, as argued earlier, binds theoretical strands into a powerful if somewhat shape-shifting edifice. It is a position which can leave little room for the moral. In his early Christian faze morality requires grace. Later dualism returns; Augustine's enthral to the spiritual is to the detriment of the world being aligned with evil; similar to the Cathars. Analysis of Augustinian thought brought a rather alarming concern with the Good to light. Striving to maintain the Good from mutable imperfection, it was argued, has an adverse effect: positing evil in absolutist terms.

Benny's Video is a film which propositions us to consider absolute evil. In fact, this proposition constitutes what I argue is the danger of the film. It is quite possible that in asking us to consider, Haneke is able to mask his *own* indecision on what evil is. For on the one hand Benny using video to incriminate his parents, tell the truth, is crucial in illustrating newfound awareness of lived reality as other to its representation in TV. Only when his mother cries out; when a certain dispensation appears to have been given; can we identify Benny as having made a pact with the good by repositioning himself as a moral subject. An alternative is to 'see' Benny shopping his parents in order to carry on his evil existence unhindered by any parental control; Benny, presented and furnished by Haneke as Evil's agent. Building images of murder, used for pleaure and to incriminate, Benny, like a modern day Dorian Gray, is seduced. On the one hand the film is about a teenage boy becoming a moral subject, aware of what is right and wrong. On the other hand the film is about a sick child, without the empathy to care for those who have sought to help him, however perverted their attempt at helping has been. The film is, therefore, on these terms,

> "Prompting us to assume a position of moral spectatorship, in which we are able to consider the content of his films and the cinematic situation (and the relationship of the two) in accordance with our existing moral principles…His cinema is not didactic but educational" (Wheatley: 2009; 46).

We can add to this: Haneke unsettles his viewers in educating them about evil. And this education, with its moral prompts, is *itself* unsettling. It is unsettling because the dominant Western audience doesn't want to think that evil exists. And they certainly don't want to think that, like Augustine, the only autonomous act is an evil act. So in response to Scott and other critics of Haneke, who denigrate his work's failure to commit to a moral position, relaying this onto his viewers, we are now in a position to argue that Haneke is an Augustinian. He wants to believe that evil young men do is of a corrupted will, the net result of a bourgeois neglect, and in a society of spectacles as distinct from real values, but the more he tries to commit to this view *absolutely*, the more he begins to be seduced by its obscene underside. *Absolute* evil exists, and it it is played out in those most vulnerable to it. It is not that the subject wills a lower form of good, Benny seeking to make a film that has 'realist' pretension and thereby has little understanding of what he is actually doing, but that the subject, in this case Benny–and this can include children of all shapes and sizes–can actually enjoy evil. If the canonical Augustinian in Haneke is concerned with the idea that, on the one hand, Benny's decision to save his skin, literally demonstrates his commitment to his own twisted good, the less orthodox Augustine in Haneke maintains scepticism towards this view. Even in a society which venerates children's innate goodness, we cannot avoid the fact children do evil. For Haneke is, for the large part, a filmmaker after Bulger. And it is this fact, which hovers in the background of all he does.

It is for this precise reason that the end is such a typically Hanekean one; lacking closure and dangerously placing images within images; as if to remind us again that the representation of evil in the film is in reality a representation of a representation. What makes this such a significant ending within the context of treating evil filmically is that in content alone we are encouraged to think of the problem of evil as relating solely to Benny's actions and the cover-up, while the ending complicates this by making it apparent that the imagery which carries this content is itself a series of images. The problem of evil, treated filmically, is for Haneke, a problem itself; hence Benny's perverse preoccupation with imagery is something mirrored by our own; the dangerous truth of what we must confront. If, in terms of reading this content we can say that Haneke is an Augustinian, then his particular brand of Augustinianism has a Neo-Platonic resonance: we should be just as sceptical about images as we are about evil.

CHAPTER SIX

DOLI INCAPAX?
RE-EVALUATING EVIL AND ITS ORIGINS
IN MICHAEL HANEKE'S *CACHÉ* (2005)

"I heard the word. Wonderful thing! A children's song.
A children's song - have you listened as they play?
Their song is love and the children know the way,"
—Brian Wilson and Van Dyke Parks, *Surfs Up.*

"Woe to the land that's governed by a child,"
—William Shakespeare, *Richard III.*

Michael Haneke's *Caché* is a film generally classified as controversial in its allegorisation of France's past. Few regard the film as being about evil. Few indeed have located the problem of evil as a feature of Haneke's film. Brian Price notes, "the closer the representation of violence moves towards its occurrence in the world, the more we can learn from it; the farther the violence gets from the world the more it contributes to our moral degeneration" (Price in Price and Rhodes (eds): 2010; 36). Price's is an attempt to address the causes of violence in *Caché*. This chapter redresses this, proposing that the focus of Price's critique is misdirected; violence at the expense of evil. As such, the chapter diagnoses the mischievousness (a term often used to describe children) in *Caché*, as something which inevitably turns sour.

Murder, and indeed its agents, generates moral issues. One of these is whether the instigating agent is outside the legal age, *doli incapax* (which literally means incapable of doing wrong); that is whether old enough to intentionally murder others (*mens rea*). In a significant number of European states murderers below the age of eighteen are the considered produce of dysfunctionality; the young, as Augustine states, are those essentially borne of the good. Few recent films have concerned themselves with the abiding issue of *doli incapax* as *Caché* does. It can even be argued that the finale of the film is haunted by the presence of an indominatible evil (in the young); the matrixal and postcolonial expression of self and other, which many reviewers focused on, tending to dominate the ensuing debate about its presence. Yet, given the variable forms of this presence, there is, I would argue, little doubt of the reification of a need to consider evil; making us as an audience judge what we consider it to be. In this sense moral panic, experienced by the diegetic protagonist, finds its own emotional mirror in the spectator. More succinctly, as Oliver C. Speck notes,

> "In *Caché*, however, the implied viewer finds the spectatorial position strangely vague and undefined. The event to which the tape bears witness does not concern the content of the clip (a possible blackmail scenario comes to mind), but the very fact of being under surveillance. The narrator/camera-operator is never revealed and, most importantly, the narrator's ontological position remains unclear" (Speck: 2010; 38).

For the ontological, read moral. Moral panic is felt by protagonist and audience. The dénouement is more complex. Haneke wants us to experience ethical unease in relation to this. He wants this to have value and form. To experience 'terror'–the limits of tolerance–identification must be registered with a friend who perpetrates it. I therefore propose in the following that the 'friend and enemy' duality structures the film in its constitutive whole: the opposition between 'us' and 'them,' protagonist and its other a significant ruse. It could be that a "campaign of terror" arises (Ezra and Siller: 2007; 220); or one which certainly appears terrorising; and that all these issues bleed into an overriding one. For, the very mention of such a heavily invested term as terror draws attention to intentionality. If A is terrorising B, should we then assume A is aware of what they do? Do they intend harm? Is terror always the object of intent? Is it always intentional? While the semantic impacts on this discussion, it is necessary to say that terror (as an attack of specific pre-meditated intent) bears upon the problem of evil (in equally direct terms). As Marcus G. Singer notes in 'The Concept of Evil,' "evil is an action so horrendously bad that one cannot conceive of oneself as performing it, or conceive of any reasonable person doing it, and if the action is done deliberately and intentionally, in knowledge of what one is doing, that action is evil" (Singer: 2004; 196). This chapter considers, along with intentionality regarding *doli incapax*, the basic concern set out by Singer; around, that is, the idea of conceiving of terror as something antithetical to reason. In this sense intention is addressed. For if evil is hard-wired biologically, is there a point to *doli incapax* as a rational concept? And is this the implicit concern, relayed in so many different ways, of the Augustinian Haneke?

The following is a somewhat congested discussion: multiple topics of discussion combine. I think the reason for this is due to the significant layers that make up *Caché*. The film can be seen as a study of so many things. And indeed, the level of research into the layers of the film is astounding. One of the things that has tended to be overlooked is the idea of revelation; that the end reveals something we don't want to be revealed. Thus, when the term terror is used I see this as a particular instance of revelation; the terrorist is revealed. I contextualise this in relation to other Haneke films. Reading the film as an allegory on terrorism, the War on Terror, in that the victim confronts the terrorist as of their own making, and confront their own responsibility in the terrorist's emergence, is an enticing one. And in some ways this reading lies at the surface of what follows.

Friends and Enemies

The "friend/enemy" opposition is quintessential to Carl Schmitt's infamous study of political life *The Concept of the Political* (2007). The need for 'enemies,' a major focal point of the study, is considered by Schmitt to be universal in scope, with the text giving emphasis to oppositional structures, such as the ugly and beautiful (of the aesthetic), Good and Evil (of the ethical) as bridges to the political. Because, for Schmitt, the political consists of friends and enemies, good and evil spring–in a kind of cultural variant–from this. "Political antagonism," Schmitt writes, "is the most intense and extreme antagonism, and every concrete antagonism becomes that much more political the closer it approaches the most extreme point, that of the friend-enemy grouping" (Schmitt: 1996; 139). Schmitt prioritises the political,

> "Every religious, moral, economic, ethical, or other antithesis transforms into a political one if it is sufficiently strong to group human beings effectively according to friend and enemy. The political does not reside in the battle itself, which possesses its own technical, psychological, and military laws, but in the mode of behaviour which is determined by this possibility" (Schmitt: 1996; 37).

Protagonists fronting off in films structured around starkly oppositional behaviour can take on a political dimension. In the sense that it feeds off polarisations and permutations of this type, Béla Tarr's seven-hour odyssey, *Sátántangó* (Satan's Tango (1995)) is an obvious example. In Tarr the friend has a messianic purpose, granting on those unbecoming an impulse for social change. In the course of the narrative, however, the friend appears in an antithetical relation to its friendly disposition: an undercover agent working for the State. In this way Tarr's opus, by drawing on the Schmittian axis, positions enemies as friends; only for the narrative trajectory to reverse this process. At the end the insidious corruption of the regime reveals itself. In a retrospective exposé of bureaucratic Hungary, the idea of a messiah returning from the dead to save the community, parodied by Tarr in its interminably Christian dimension, encroaches upon Schmitt's matrix when this same presence emerges as the distinguished enemy. Suspense consists of not knowing who a friend and who an enemy is, a structural ploy mirrored in other mainstream films: Mark Pellington's U.S. suspense drama *Arlington Road* (1999) a particular case in point. Both films, markedly different, concern a 'neighbour' and 'friend,' masking their real motives. The end sees responsibility for the defined activities deferred onto another (in the latter onto a specialist who works in anti-terrorism) as the 'friend' now reverts to that of enemy.

That permutations of the Schmittian axis are discerned in films of a loosely political nature suggests its pervasive flexibility: its infinite possibilities. The pairing opens up on further examination to an array of possible and indeed evocative variations: neighbour, foreigner, immigrant, and adversary, revealed in *Caché*. Politicisation can be considered the net effect of an enemy whose role is to penetrate the life of former 'friend,' Georges, centered around an event which occurred more than forty years ago, the police massacre of October 17, 1961, when Arab protestors were subsequently drowned in the Seine. Chat show host Georges Laurent, the 'friend' in question, leads a sanguine intellectual 'lifestyle.' When videos are sent in the post, depicting the outside of his apartment, childlike representations of bloodied acts follow. Soon the tapes focus on the estate on which Georges was reared. The deafening silence of the images unnerves Georges. At this point Georges and wife Anne (Juliet Binoche) dismiss the possibility Pierrot (Lester Makedonsky), their only son, is involved in a prank. Georges then, without telling Anne, identifies Majid, an Algerian his parents had considered adopting when he was six years old as his adversary.

Haneke's trademark intertext, the text within text–videos within film–without the extradiegetic spectator given a safe distance to 'see' that these are intertexts, finds its most penetrative exposure in *Caché*. Indeed, the use of video again, as the 'evil' twin to the cinematic, has a malevolent presence; even if the tapes are benign surveillance tapes. As some of the videos appear to have been shot at Georges's childhood home, Georges's and Majid's antagonistic past resurfaces. The intertexual resurfaces in a series of images, some of which appear as videos, others flashbacks of Georges's youth. With the suspicion of Majid plotting against him gathering pace, Georges's belief in his own 'victimisation' gradually increases. "Blaming others (instead of the self)," as Catherine Wheatley observes, "serves as an ego-protective function: a shamed person may find it much less objectionable to think that the problem is the other" (Wheatley: 2009; 166). For Wheatley, Georges apportions his 'enemy'– Majid–with certain blame, in a precarious indication of the detachment he experiences from the Other (Majid). Just as feelings of familial alienation appear to stem from his apparent sense of detachment, two significant things of note can be discerned. Firstly, in failing to consider alternatives to his reading of events, he fails to confront the enemy he projects as other; immunising Georges to the dialectic he is held within. Secondly, with this immunisation intact, he accuses "Majid of "terrorizing" his family. ….asked by Majid whether he is threatening him, Georges answers, "Yes, I am threatening you!"" (Speck: 2010; 222).

Georges experiences, in a post 9/11 context, the discernible elements of a *terror*: Majid's name even resonates with the Islamic term Jihad. At a crucial point in the film Majid is located and quizzed by Georges. Yet the story is further complicated when Majid takes his own life (in one of the harrowing scenes of the film). Majid vehemently denied making the tapes (at all). The suicide is repeated–shown this time from a lower angle–in a tape Georges receives when he returns home; complicating the whodunit. That this information is presented in intertextual form poses two significant questions of concern. The first is why Majid, an elderly reclusive man, would go to such length to unsettle Georges only to then kill himself? As a whodunit it simply doesn't add up. And could there really have been a camera concealed, capturing the action in what appears to be a high definition format? Some critics have argued that Haneke's film, with its use of such intertextual trickery, is actually a kind of postmodern experiment in the god-like status of the authorial director, cruelly manipulating his (*sic*) audience to think that he has planted 'hidden' answers to diegetic problems. Others, such as Wheatley, read the project as a renewed engagement with the countercinematic, when any comfortable assumption on the part of the extradiegetic spectator as to what is happening is negated in advance (Wheatley; 2009). But it is also possible Haneke is practicing a kind of filmic illusion, in the sense that he is asking us to consider 'evil,' a problem hovering on the surface of the narrative action, in the guise of an attack with cruelty as its goal.

Confusion, if this is the effect of such intertextual trickery, is amplified in a later scene when Majid's son (Walid Afkir), (who is never named and who appears for the first time at this point), appearing for the first time, confronts Georges, in such a way the friend/enemy is chrystalised in another generational form. Rejecting the son's claims, a son who dispels the notion he and his father are responsible, Georges returns to his bedroom and pulls the blinds. Just as he seems to be sleeping there is a cut to Majid taken away as a child. We then see Georges gaze from the barn in which he confronted Majid as a child. The only sound is that of morning birds singing. The school Georges had collected Pierrot from earlier appears in long shot, changing the temporal status to what appears to be the present, with Peirrot and Majid's son occupying the left-hand side of the frame. Although credits roll, no explanation is given for how the boys know each other, or indeed why they are talking. For Brianne Gallagher, "France's colonialist guilt and violence is left to France's future generations" (Gallagher: 2009; 23). Gallagher's emphasis on the next generation makes his a relatively positive response. And yet it is a noteworthy one; it offers a considerable support to critics such as Max Silverman,

> "Although we do no know what the conversation between the two young men is about in the final scene, one possible interpretation is that the colonial barriers and atavistic reflexes of previous generations may be loosening through dialogue and a new attitude to difference" (Silverman: 2007; 249).

Catherine Wheatley is less enthusiastic in her response. Wheatley believes it likely the two boys have been, "...in cahoots" (Wheatley: 2009; 163). This insight isn't developed to any great length, except in a footnote, yet we can, however, elaborate on it. Did the boys target their parents? Did a 'joke' get out of hand? Have we been lulled into thinking the world of crime and evil presented here is reigned over by adults, when a propensity to evil, as neuroscientists and experts in psychopathology have shown, is just as likely to manifest in children. Peter Brunette's is a telling support to this, "does this, looking to the past, mean that Pierrot and Majid's son, each for his own reasons, have been a partner in the making of the disturbing tapes?" (Brunette 2010; 129), contrasting with a consideration of the tapes as meta-reflexive in stature; postmodern trickery Speck believes is not unlike the tapes used in Lynch's *Lost Highway* (1997)

(Speck; 2010). Other critics, such as Robin Wood, have been less obsequious, noting "the pessimism of the film.... qualified by that last shot echoing the end of *Benny's Video* (in which the boy betrays his own father, an act that Haneke courageously sees as justified) and suggesting the possibility of collaboration, revolution and renewal within the younger generation" (Wood; 2006); using earlier films as a possible springboard for understanding later ones.

The end demands our attention. With the audience expected to 'miss' the culprits being the point of concern, parallels with Edgar Allen Poe's novella *The Purloined Letter* are recognisably discerned. Poe's text is about a 'letter' stolen from the quarters of the Queen by the illusive Minister D, who proceeds to hide the letter in his domestic quarters. In pursuit of the original document the police encroach on the Minister's quarters, beginning a search of unparalleled detail.[1] Having failed to locate the 'letter'–for which the police are positively convinced the Minister has hidden in his quarters–the intervention of the detective Dupin is required. Dupin proceeds to illustrate the intentions of the criminal, locate the hidden 'letter' hanging from the fireplace, and replace it with a duplicate 'letter.' In the process the eminent detective explains to his interlocutor the premise on which the masquerade is achieved,

> "But the more I reflected upon the daring, dashing, and discriminating ingenuity of D–; upon the fact that the document must always have been *at hand*, if he intended to use it to good purpose; and upon the decisive evidence, obtained by the Prefect, that it was not hidden within the limits of that dignitary's ordinary search–the more satisfied I became that, to conceal this letter, the Minister had resorted to the comprehensive and sagacious expedient of not attempting to conceal it at all" (Poe: 1994; 353).

The masquerade is not a masquerade. Well, not at least in the conventional sense. It is not that the letter is hidden in the nether regions of the ministerial quarters. It is rather that the 'letter' is hidden on the paradoxical premise that it's not concealed at all. By locating it above the fireplace a willfully perspicuous account of the need to look beyond the abstract mathematical considerations–scientific reasoning–is given. The "pure signifier" doubles as the key character in Poe's narrative. It situates each recipient in a triadic structure. A series of glances, between the

---

[1] The use of Poe's tale is indirectly inspired by commentaries on the text itself in psychoanalytic contexts. My own reading draws from the textual explication offered by Jacques Lacan in his seminar on the short story.

family members, forms a similar structure in *Caché*. In the early stages of the film Georges and Anne peruse the video surveillance of their home, from which they gaze at Pierrot. Georges suspects Pierrot. Yet in the process his gaze enacts a double repression, firstly in rejecting the claim his son is guilty, secondly by refuting the guilt he himself imposes.

For long periods of the film, Pierrot hovers in the background. The fact that he goes missing at one stage, or cannot be located, with his parents 'terrorised' in the process, is an interesting way of concealing the fact that his going missing has purpose. If, that is, his presence is, like the 'letter,' there, but missed by the insensitive viewer. Hidden in the family bosom, perceptive of the fracture between his parents, he is also remarkably poised, never letting his emotions get the better of him. Originally a suspect, Pierrot, is last seen in his bedroom, until the end when shown outside the school in discussion with Majid's son. He is never concealed from view; never hidden in a conventional sense. In fact, he is, like the letter in Poe, all too visible. Hence, when he is 'revealed' as the credits role, the largely political friend/enemy opposition, central at this point, reverts to a moral one. It is enticing to see an enemy returning to enact revenge; Majid as the embodiment of a certain return of the repressed. But the very idea that something in front of the gaze has been qualitively missed *quo* Poe's letter allows for a more disturbing realisation. Teenagers a few years older than those who attacked James Bulger have been overlooked as culprits. Frightening elders–a prank–may have been these teenagers' intention. But they may also have collaborated with the sole intention of doing harm. Within this context, it is of more than passing interest to recall the murder as performed by Benny in *Benny's Video*. Benny's bedroom is all but a lab in name. It contains all the paraphernalia required to make the videos used in *Caché*. That the murder of the girl is recorded live–with Benny's cool demeanour–is testament to the role of video in Benny's life. Yet considered further, is it beyond the scope of argument to suggest that the same video used to record murder by Benny, is used to instigate murder by Pierrot and Majid's son? Such are the similarities. Although the end suggests a wickedness of sorts, it is failure to see this in relation to the narrative action earlier which counts as failure to 'see' evil. It is not that the boys are 'hidden.' Is is rather that we, as spectators, hide from the fact children can terrorise. That is, missing this, fail to confront the malevolent impulses in children as well as adults. Hence, the film is like an experiment in moral understanding. The question is, will we recoil in horror or hide from the fact the boys have instigated terror?

The fact that so few reviewers of the film have addressed the issue of evil so directly positioned at the end is interesting. That Haneke leads us on a merry dance regarding postcolonial stand-offs, interracial multiculturalism and other topical issues, only to confront us with what we have evidentially 'hidden' from our investigative journals, is something few reviewers and subsequent scholars have dwelled on. Many, preferred to dwell on the bait given by Haneke rather than analyse the 'catch.' But if there is a real sense that the end is the ultimate affront to those who would hide from thinking that their own children are capable of cruelty, violence, murder even, then how can moral problems that we face regarding child crime ever be truly understood. If we always see the beam in the other's eye, never in our own, are the problems that we face destined to remain 'hidden;' concealed from thought and exposition.

Given this difficulty, it is not surprising *US Funny Games*, Haneke's next film, makes *doli incapax* a central issue. For the film is unquestionably about two teenagers performing evil acts with intent. Two teenagers interrupt a holidaying family, who have just checked into a waterside villa, asking to borrow eggs. They then go on to beat the father with a golf club, terrorise the family over a number of days, before the family are eventually murdered. No precise reason is offered for why they do any of this. That is, other than a possible game being played between attacker and victim. Hence, as Catherine Wheatley has suggested, "the spectator is never given a psychological explanation for the actions of the film's antagonists" (Wheatley: 2009; 83). Nonetheless, it is possible to conclude that the crime *is* intentional: the attackers revel in 'evil.' The attack has a specific trajectory.

What's most interesting about the fact that *US Funny Games* comes after *Caché* is the *obvious* pleasure the boys of the former film take in terrorising a bourgeois family. What is *hidden* in *Caché* jumps out at us. The evil of *US Funny Games* may well be the family guilt externalised; the film a 'funny' play on the sublimated violence instrinsic to the 'family' projected on to Others (not unlike Pasolini's *Theorem*). That the preppy attackers have a class distinction gives sustenance to this reading. That they speak to the audience, in a theatrical exposition of their filmic status, makes their evil, in my view, less disturbing. This is because the teenagers maintain a significantly self-reflexive status throughout. Nonetheless, the final 'unmasking' makes *Caché*, ironically since it is far less violent in its narrative action, a more disturbing film. The fact that two boys, from essentially polarised class backgrounds, could 'connect' in the form of collaboration–on the internet or whatever–and then orchestrate the hi-tech manipulation of their fathers, disturbs more than most horror films disturb. It disturbs because it is far from beyond the bounds of possibility.

Eyes Wide Shut?

"We stand like shoolboys as the judge rises for lunch, and peer at Thompson and Venables returning below. They look like brothers: Cain and Abel, little love lost between them, but joining together to murder," Seth, Blake Morrison, *As If.*

Blake Morrison issued these words when stood in the court at the James Bulger murder trial. For Morrison, the great big Why is synonymous with trying to understand evil. For if Venables and Thompson murdered Bulger in the knowledge of what they were doing, Morrison would need to acknowledge that the children understood what they did was wrong. Brave and compassionate, Morrison's is an elegiac pang to understanding. Whether his words are a response to evil collaboration by children remains. For, collaboration, when two people, not to mind children, act together, is morally difficult to assess. It is much easier to castigate the singular activities of an adult. Now, the end of *Caché* divulges this difficulty to us. The ending intimates that Georges, in our position, having awoken from sleep, is gazing at Majid's and his son in conversation; without revealing the point-of-view. It recalls earlier in the film when Georges is waiting for Pierrot to finish school, and greets him entering the car. If, like before, the point-of-view is Georges, seeing Majid's son talking with Pierrot surely makes him consider the boys as culprits. Georges may well pretend he is privy to a chance meeting. In this sense, like the 'letter' missed in plain view, Georges can miss what he sees.

In the climactic scene of Haneke's *Das weisse Band* the village Pastor (Burghart Klaußner) is confronted by the Schoolteacher (Christian Freiedel), concerning his children as those collaboratively terrorising the townsfolk. The Pastor tells off the Schoolteacher and asks him to withdraw his allegations. The film ends by suggesting the perpetrators walk freely among the others, attending church and keeping up appearances. Like the choir singing in *Benny's Video* the end of *Das weisse Band* draws on the image of choral singing to evoke the cradling of evil in the most nefarious bosoms of society. Leading the service, the Pastor's incapacity to 'see' evil he seemingly spends his life working against is striking. Instead of discerning the truth by following up on the charges, he buries it and blames others. It is unsurprising, given that he does this, that Haneke should remake his earlier Austrian production, *Funny Games* for his debut in English speaking film (following the financial success of *Caché*). For while the perpetrator of an incendiary violence can be considered 'hidden' in *Caché* (like the letter in Poe bypassing conscious approbation to be effectuated at a more subliminal one) the violent intruders on contended suburban life in *Funny Games* are *too* visible. Like protagonists in a video game acting out their evil, these children are symptomatic of the blurring of appearance and reality to apocalyptic levels. Now the latent content of *Caché* bursts into life.

On a conclusionary note, *The New York Times* film critic A. O. Scott criticised Haneke for what he felt was an attempt to educate viewers on the orgiastic violence in contemporary multi-media settings (in *US Funny Games*). Haneke responded to applause when the robbers in the film were apprehended and brutally impeded (at its New York screening, only for this applause to be drowned out by the film rewinding and offering a totally opposite ending) by stating that the applause amounted to a sanctioning of the violence used to avenge the tormentors and a consequential fulfilment of intoxicated desires. Haneke was asking the audience to confront their desire to *see* violence used to expel violence, to confront their conviction in seeing as believing. But we shouldn't conclude that Haneke is an educator in the traditional sense–a teacher who wants to draw attention to such convictions–because of this. By addressing the potential uses of the tools he uses to tell his story he is offering ways of exploring the age-old problem of doubt in our supposed knowledge economy.

CHAPTER SEVEN

SEEING AND FAILING TO SEE AGAIN: ON THE EVIL OF MICHAEL HANEKE'S *THE WHITE RIBBON* (2009)

9/11 has seen a proliferation of films concerning evil and its metaphysical conundrums. Two films immediately come to mind. The first is the Coen Brothers' adaptation of Colm McCarthy's award-winning novel *No Country for Old Men*. In a film in which genre conventions are so openly problematised, an ordinary Joe escapes with a dollop of cash, only to be hunted and in the process killed. All the while the hunter maintains his corrupt ways. During all this the audience is left hostage to a philosophising marshal whose days are numbered; informing us that policing is in itself part of the very problem it seeks to resolve. Part-noir, part-American gothic, the conventions *No Country for Old Men* successfully evokes are, in the process, positively rejected. All in all, a new reflex is given to the noir demeanour.

Across the continent, the Dardenne Brothers' gritty realism, seems–at least in form and setting–worlds apart from that of the Coen Brothers. Both, however take the specificities of criminal behaviour as a point of examination. The Brothers' *Le fils* (The Son (2002)) is an uncompromising study of the coincidental meeting of a woodwork teacher and the adolescent teenager who murdered his son. In some way inspired by the James Bulger affair and the subsequent trial, with its emphasis on evil performed by children against children, *Le fils* is a compelling response. The Brothers state,

> "We were deeply shocked by the incident in England when two boys kidnapped a boy and later killed him. We started thinking about the parents of the two murderers. We wanted to look into the reason why kids would murder a child. What role do the parents play? How does it come to that? How is it possible for a child to become a murderer" (Dardennes Bros., 2002).

Le fils seeks, ultimately, to widen the Hanekean terrain and the subtle line between mischievous play, terror and evil. Typically Bressonian in its capacity to estrange the audience, the film draws its intrinsic power from substantial information being withheld; engendering a sense of strained familiarity with the characters. Handheld cameras follow closely, enhancing the physical bearing of the point-of-view position. But while the Manichean universe in *No Country for Old Men* can be read allegorically as a certain political projection of evil in its time, in contrast, the reconciliation of 'son' and father at the end is a more forthright extropolation on ultimately Christian notions of humanity; that is, in a nominally corrupt universe the power of love to defeat sin. The aforementioned 'celebrated,' acclaimed filmmakers, and the issues relating to the evil problematic in their films, briefly discussed here, are complemented by Haneke's approach in his recent film *Das weisse Band* (The White Ribbon (2009)). Haneke invokes evil–direct and indirectly–in subject matter concerned with criminality. In this sense Haneke and the Coen Brothers are close.

Haneke issues a warrant to explore evil in adolescent behaviour. It is now time to explore this warrant further. My first aim in this chapter is to contextualise Haneke's period drama *The White Ribbon*, his first film to win the coveted or (not so) *Palme D'or*, around what might better be termed the 'perversity at the heart of nature.' In other words, Haneke's vision of 'evil' in the film is addressed in specific terms. For Dews, "a proper reckoning with our history, as well as due regard for the phenomenology of the moral life" has led to "a return to the idea of evil" in recent times (Dews: 2008; 10). Haneke can be said to problematise this reckoning; his concern the phenomenology of evil in film. For Dews, the very term evil can inhibit engagement with conditions that produce the behaviour associated with it. With this in mind (secondly), social conditions are addressed. If *The White Ribbon* is a film concerned above all with Nazism, I argue, this not just a uniquely German problem. It is *our* problem.

After *Salò*

In saying that Haneke's project really begins after *Salò*, we are saying that, with all its brutality, *Salò* paves the way for such an oeuvre. Haneke has recently cited Pasolini's masterpiece among the films he favours, and perhaps his own film can be considered a project continuing its hyper-reflexive vein. Thus, the dignitaries who turn the binoculars on the viewer is a beginning of sorts; an uncomfortable liaison fashioned between them and those who watch. In this sense, "*Salò* engages voyeurism rather than empathy, and attempts to turn voyeurism back on itself with various distancing devices" (Indiana: 2000; 57). One of these distancing devices in the film is "the beautiful ass contest," a contest the dignitaries conduct midway through. Like scientists obsessing with minutiae of the body, the dignitaries emerge as more than characters; no doubt the role they occupy the net effect of Pasolini satirising an audience who gaze with impunity on the actions on screen; the disinterestedness expressed towards the on screen violation of the body,

> "The act of aesthetic judgment is isolated and parodied in a darkly humorous sequence where the four libertine-executioners devise what they call "the beautiful ass contest" in order to determine which of their victims possesses the finest example of this nearly featureless feature. In a dimly lit scene, the judges soberly scrutinize rows of virtually indistinguishable bare bottoms before delivering their final judgment.... the radical act of judgment tears this one ass from the relations of equivalency that would otherwise link it (through resemblance) not only to all others on display, but to the sadists (through sympathy) as well" (Copjec: 2002; 226-227).

Scenes like this provoke those striving to master the situation. Indeed, the parody of disinterested judgment Copjec refers to is felt directly as a test. By detaching the spectator from the action, using various distancing mechanisms to do so, the shock of the final sequence is all the greater in impact: sober scrutinisation all the more disturbing in suffocating proximity. The use of reflexive strategies, aggressive in their emotive shock value, have no doubt diminished with the self-consciously stylised violence of Tarantino and Peckinpah, but some would argue that violence depicted *off-screen* is more subversive. As critics have noted, Haneke rarely represents violence on screen. Instead, deployed on televisions, or just out of frame, its presence is intimated for us. If *Salò* ends with an all-too-suffocating violence, up-close, it intimates a sense of danger in the demand Haneke films make: to imagine the violent act. Like (the CCTV image of) Bulger hand in hand with his killers, the details of what happens are more horrifying when left to the imagination. Violence, murder, torture etc., as Oliver C. Speck notes, "are always simultaneously present via the sound of gunshots and the victims' cries" (Speck: 2010; 9). In this context, the Schoolteacher (Christian Freidel) in *The White Ribbon* imagines the violence we cannot see. He looks upon–whether nostalgically or realistically–a period prior to the outbreak of World War I, as a prophesy of fascism.

Breaking with the setting of his earlier films and using a first person voice-over, Haneke reverts to monochrome. Haneke's first period drama has a reduced palette, mirroring the values the Schoolteacher comes to explore. Looking back on his romance with an emotionally fragile nanny (Leonie Benesch), the Schoolteacher/Narrator tells of attacks on village life; beginning with the village Doctor shunted from his horse (by someone who laid a steel wire) and waylaid in hospitable for almost a month. Later, two village boys are kidnapped, the farmer's wife dies, as a malevolent energy grips the town. Like a medieval morality tale, the agent's truth used to confront evil, the Narrator seeks a seemingly undelivered truth; at least from the point of view of a Pastor the children of whom are suspected of the crime. Momentum builds as the Narrator looks to confront the Pastor with his suspected 'truth.' The plot climaxes as the protagonist confronts the Pastor in the belief his children–some of who are his students–have been terrorising the town's representatives. If he is to acknowledge evil which he has been instrumental in seeking to abolish in his children–the white ribbon of the film's title referring to a ribbon he forces his children to wear when they commit common 'sins'– the Pastor must confront the very phenomena he denounces. Failing to do so however will mean a failure to combine espoused morals with the real life moral challenges faced. Ending in long shot, a dénouement of defineable proportions fails to materialise. The reason, or at least as Haneke intimates to Geoff Andrew of *Sight and Sound,* is,

> "It's pretty clear the children act as a group, rather than one particular person being responsible. As to who might be taking the lead…well, that might change, of course. But when you are working on a film like this, you have to construct the story in such a way that there are several possible explanations for what happens. If no logical explanation is feasible, then the viewer feels frustrated and discouraged from reflecting more deeply on the film" (Haneke: 2009).

To turn a television script into a feature-length film of justice, required calling on the expertise of well-known Buñuel collaborator Jean-Claude Carrière. It is likely the veteran is responsible for the subtlety of plot, the generative development of the off-screen as a preoccupation (we never see the violence imposed on the victims of this violence), but the "aggression towards the audience" (Wheatley: 2009), in a director with a penchant for the macabre, is notably reduced. Set prior to World War I, the plot hinges on a reign of terror against a German towns folk; even if plot is difficult to talk about around a film that never really ends. Critics quickly identified a moral impetus; what Donald Clarke, in *The Irish Times,* saw as an inquiry into 'the origins of fascism.' New Fascism was the term coined by

Pasolini for a power accredited to an emerging global source, but the specifically Northern German setting of *The White Ribbon* led to the accusation that Haneke had rooted the fascist ontology *in* Germany, or Lutheran Germany. *Sight and Sound*'s Geoff Andrew is less accusatory in this sense. But Haneke responds to his probes by identifying,

> "A particular form of Lutheran Protestantism that's there in northern Germany. When I was first thinking about the project, I kept asking myself why so many Nazis, in explaining their actions, would reply–like Eichmann, with no apparent sense of guilt or conscience–that it had been their duty as loyal servants of the Reich. I felt this way of thinking about one's responsibilities to a superior was closely linked to the Prostestantism of Luther" (Haneke: 2009).

Haneke's interest in Eichmann is by proxy an interest in Lutheran morals. His concern is with behaviour: but with that kind of behaviour appearing to be one thing, possibly servile action, yet is actually another. Hence an overlooked historical period or timeframe; when criminals like Eichmann were children; is the specific focus of a film exploring evil. We can only surmise Haneke is less concerned with the conduct (he maintains humankind is itself stained by corruption) of the village children as disorderly, disruptive, corrupt even, than the manner in which behaviour, thought to derive from the 'reasonableness' of the Law ends up legitimising its dialectic opposite. Eichmann, as Arendt knew, believed in a law analogous to reason. Believing himself to be obeying superiors within the Reich as a Kantian, he claimed to act–formally at least–*morally*; the content to his actions of a wholly different order. If monsters should appear *monstrous*, Eichmann's (to all extent and purposes *banal*) demeanour alone bucked this trend, sparking the 'banality of evil' comment which was so controversial on Arendt's return from Israel. Arendt's commentary is worth recalling,

> "They knew, of course, that it would have been very comforting indeed to believe that Eichmann was a monster, even though if he had been Israel's case against him would have collapsed or, at the very least, lost all interest. Surely, one can hardly call upon the whole world and gather correspondents from the four corners of the whole world in order to display Bluebeard in the dock. The trouble with Eichmann was precisely that so many were like him, and many were neither perverted or sadistic, that they were, and still are, terribly and terrifyingly normal" (Arendt: 1994; 276).

The controversy consisted of Arendt being accused of bracketing off Eichmann's wickedness. Arendt claimed a desultory horror at the nullifying of conscience–and moral responsibility with it–in the name of some abstract notion of duty. Looked at from this perspective, the fictional pre-War village of Haneke's film, in which rural innocence exposes itself as a masquerade, seems a strange place to explore these origins. In addition to the rural (as distinct from urban setting), the monochromatic alters the mood indicative of earlier Haneke films. Haneke's first foray away from present-day European settings makes the charge of having Germanised the fascism elicited through crimes identified by the Schoolteacher (as linked to the loose group of children) one which will remain of interest, even if the voice-over, which narrates the story for us, gives the film a somewhat documentary overtone; one which, I believe, makes the issue of truth central to the film. The Schoolteacher's story is of course about children and what they truthfully do. It nonetheless culminates at a point in which the Pastor is confronted (and the charges made against *his* children). Yet the Schoolteacher/Narrator is a goofy figure who could be using his story to deflect from his feelings about the past. Blaming others, as we saw in the previous chapter, can serve as defence against disgust at one's responsibilities. Haneke's comments are therefore pertinent, especially when considering his accounts of pre-War life as part of a strategy probing the roots of real horrific crime–to explore the roots of a duty perverted by criminals such as Eichmann.

Familiar, nonetheless, as a device pioneered in the early 40s, the voice-over/flashback narration is recognisably unstable. As a format it,

> "Can undermine the apparent objectivity of the images as they can question the reliability of the narrator whose flashbacks try to make sense of a past that is rendered as strange, threatening and unfinished" (Spicer: 2002; 76).

The idea that the Narrator is in control of the events, paralleling a love story that should have materialised but never did, is suspect; the events could easily be controlling him instead. The idea that a period drama will paint a truthful picture of an historical period is of course ideological. The fact that the Narrator tells this story shouldn't deflect from the possibility that his 'story' is simply that: 'his story' and not objective historical fact. For it is possible that Haneke is challenging his audience, but this time within the context of his film conforming to a more apparently traditional cinematic style; one which records the movements of historical agents in time without offering, at the same time, the spectator the necessary data to make an 'ethical judgment.' Perhaps the film comments on the filmic treatment of evil as itself problematic.

Voice-over narration is characteristic of film noir. Noirs such as *Double Indemnity* (Wilder, 1942) use the confessional flashback as a form of voice-over. *Citizen Kane* (Welles, 1941) uses a detection-based voice-over as its main narrative trope. But while the narrative voice is used to such effect in films like *Citizen Kane*, the criteria required for a detective voice-over can also be discerned in the Schoolteacher's narration. If his attempt to find the culprits constitutes his detective activity, his subsequent failure to do anything other than consider the crime as historically prefiguring future war crimes means his reasons for telling the story are unclear. On the one hand, he seems to feel 'infinite responsibility' for the past. On the other, the opportunity to redistribute the generational guilt he himself has experienced in the aftermath of the War may be presenting itself. If the narration is mysterious in this sense, so too is the subtitle "A German Children's Story." The story of an abused child has a significant purpose in the greater scheme of things. But its inclusion complicates, rather than simplifies, the historical point. Many have found the linking of child abuse and fascism (among others), hinted in the subtitle, offensive. Asked about this, Haneke remarked,

> "In fact I didn't want that to be explicit for the English and French versions because I didn't want people around the world to think the film was about a specifically German problem (*laughs*). The subtitle was for the Germans, because I was quite happy for them to think it was about them" (Haneke: 2009).

With an explicitly German fascism evoked (hence the somewhat insidious laugh), Haneke's subtitle has a contentious ring to it. It directs the audience towards the children's story while indelibly suggesting the *real story* concerns events around this. By directing the audience towards the children and the white ribbon which lends the film its title (used by the Pastor to shamefully remind his children of their minor transgressions (masturbation, bullying and so on)), the communitarian nature of such a gesture adds a metaphysical punch to the revenge the crimes suitably evoke. One way of reading the semiotics of the 'ribbon' is to see it as a moral emblem for repelling communitarian moralists who argue in favour of shaming children and criminals to copper-fasten threatened moral codes; the ribbon Haneke's moralising on the insipid nature of these methods. In this way the ribbon is part of the morality the Pastor exemplifies. For those who terrorise without any clear motive must surely contrast those who experience guilt because of it; even if either are influenced by the Pastor's measures. It is in this latter sense that the one redeeming character, the Farmer's son (Sebastian Hülk), seeks revenge from relative exclusion. The son, as we've seen a dangerous Hanekean character, sets out to revenge his mother's death. In Haneke's world, revenge is a vice easily discerned. But others are not so easily so.

Apart from its use in shaming others, the 'ribbon' has an interesting semiotic purpose. The 'white' ribbon evokes the unimpeachably Good in those free to choose. The ribbon's unintended outcomes, which ends up laying the ground for the Schoolteacher's narration, is sprung from the shame generated by the ribbon imposed on young adolescents. Hence, when theorists of shame focus on the generative moral awakening it incites in those effected by it–one thinks of the shame experienced by Georges in *Caché* when he retreats to his bedroom or Beckert in Lang's *M* when confronted by the mob–or when private experiences (such as masturbation) become public, they confront a particular manifestation of emotion as a response to being shamed.

Shaming the child should make them reflect on an earlier incarnation of the self, from a new position. Shame, Martha C. Nussbaum implies, is structured in this way. "To put things more generally," Nussbaum writes, "shame, as I understand it here is a painful emotion responding to a sense of failure to obtain some ideal state……in shame one feels inadequate, lacking some desired type of completeness or perfection" (Nussbaum: 2004; 184). The shamed child is a considered warning to those who saw the perpetrators of shame concentrated in the Nazi regime; Haneke's ribbon drawing our attention to the relationship between the shamed and the illusory ideal on which fascism rested. By generating the experience of moral inadequacy the self-generated desire to make the other feel morally inadequate can be felt. In this way, the process of reflecting on being shamed indeliably generates its opposite, a basic inability to connect with the conceptual edifice of an ideal (and thereby *unshameable*). "It is only when one expects oneself to have control or even perfection in some respect," Nussbaum adds, "that one will shrink from or cover the evidence of one's lack of control and imperfection" (Nussbaum: 2004; 191). Shaming others by adorning them with a white ribbon, as the film dwells on regarding the children, may well derive from the expedient belief that it will generate a subject around such lack, as expressed in the Pastor's relationship with his children. However, this is only one reading of shame.

Haneke has already explored shame as the base result of an allurement to evil. Recall Benny shopping his parents to the Law, his shameful look towards his feet when he meets them leaving the police. The rural setting for *The White Ribbon* strips the modern world of its nebulous distractions; the media saturated prison in which children such as Benny exist. For the shame returned to in each confrontation the Pastor has with his children is emblazoned in the ribbon and its reminder of the authoritarian/disciplinary society, meticulously set out in texts such as Michel Foucault's *Discipline and Punish* and Adorno's *The Authoritarian Personality*. Cold, austere, polarised, the world furnished by Haneke is, like Foucault's, 'disciplinary' to its core. Indeed, the most emotionally fraught scenes of Haneke's film concern the visitation of the children to their disciplinary Pastor father. With fear and loathing, the child, adhering to the Patriarch, motions violence destructive in its intent.

Banal or Radical Evil?

To what extent is *The White Ribbon* about 'evil?' More precisely, is it about the problem of evil? On its release, extreme malice (by subjects claiming to do being doing one's duty) was a recurrent topic of conversation for Haneke. By mentioning the infamous Arendt report, a discourse arose that defined the film as a journey into the origins of fascism, and an inquiry into violence of an extreme nature. Yet, extreme violence is never explicitly *shown* in *The White Ribbon*. Without an obviously violent ringleader, it is difficult, if not impossible, to say the film is about fascism. Unlike, for example, *Salò*, which *is* so obviously about fascism, *The White Ribbon* is a film set prior to the birth of the National Socialist movement. It might deal with the fascist impulse but real history is another issue.

And yet, for Haneke the film is also about Lutheranism, Eichmann, the mentality needed to engender totalitarianism; and 'evil' precisely *because* a culprit for the crimes is lacking. By making such an explicit reference to such an explicit criminal as Eichmann, Haneke reveals, yet also misleads. He reveals in the sense that attention is drawn to Arendt's report; Haneke's concern with something other to evil monstrousness; a power which gathers precisely because of its communal nature. He misleads in that 'duty' and normality, concepts used by Eichmann in his defence, are not those which can be strictly applied to a 'children's story.' The duty required of children doesn't always pertain to the categorical imperative. Yet by referencing Eichmann as an influence, Haneke is referring to a real historical subject; even if his emphasis on the personalisation of history thus runs hollow. It is difficult not to find in these kinds of references a sense of bad faith unnecessary to the great auteur. Referencing a murderer on the scale of an Eichmann is controversial. Particularly, when accompanied by a lack of information regarding the nature of Eichmann's evil–something which has caused immense debate in moral circles. Haneke wouldn't be the first to find in Eichmann's crime a curious manifestation of the modern, with its cold bureaucracy and depersonalised relations. But even so, it is *too much* to say a film about children is about Eichmann without this remark given the context it deserves. If only because the Lutheran Church he also references deserves better. It is ironic then that the great émigré philosopher Hannah Arendt spent most of her life overshadowed by her comments about Eichmann but an Austrian director can make a film stating that Eichmann's case is an inspiration, without anywhere near the same level of scrutiny. That the modern, something Haneke films explore in a way that marks him out as a special filmmaker, is a central facet of Arendt's comments, qualifies Haneke's statement in some capacity.

So, when asked to imagine the 'evil' culprit, from which the whodunit plot is formed, the audience is primed for a film about monstrous evil in a conventional sense. This is all the more important when we come to consider the *lack* of monstrousness shown (in a Wittgensteinian sense) in the film, other than the Doctor's paedophiliac relationship with his daughter Anni (Roxane Duran). To *imagine* the 'evil' depicted in the film relies on imagining the people *suspected*. Unlike Benny, or Pierrot, the children *in general* are suspected of the crime–emerging over the course of the film as a kind of monstrous communal ego–rendering them evil in a more radical sense than those depicted in earlier Haneke films. It is perhaps easier to imagine children perverted by self-love, harassing others than it is well adjusted, shame-induced (*mea culpa*) children, engaging in greater and greater feats of dehumanising behaviour.

We must assume then that murder, cruelty, and injury, the acts which concern the Schoolteacher's perspicuous investigation in the film, *are* evil. And this is because a group commit crimes of a suspiciously radical nature. Hannah Arendt's investigation of evil (one which took many turns throughout an illustrious and controversial career), focuses on the intention to do evil, most notably in the debate surrounding the term 'banality of evil.' Her use of absolute and radical evil as specific concepts can help engage with evil in the film. As mentioned earlier, Arendt recovers radical evil from *Religion Within The Limits of Reason Alone* and its original Kantian expression. Her most famous work *The Origins of*

Totalitarianism (1973) broadens the term from its original use. Concerned (as she would become in the post-War years) with evil as ""thought-defying," as I said, because thought tries to reach some depth, to go to the roots, and the moment it concerns itself with evil, it is frustrated because there is nothing. That is its banality" (Arendt: 1978; 240-255), evil (not surprisingly) is both radical and banal, in Arendt's analysis, when the rights of human life are destroyed on mass.

Arendt's concern, and the concern of those (of which there are many) who attacked her, is whether there is only subjective evil. Whether evil can perpetrate communally, systemically as law, is indeed questionable. For how do we legislate for evil prone to materialise in a system? It is worth remembering that the Eichmann controversy hinged on the apparent lack of responsibility Eichmann displayed. Subsequently Arendt was said to have displayed insensitivity to the monstrosity of the acts committed by Eichmann. Arendt was accused of rendering Eichmann a cog in a much greater wheel, ultimately and insensitively downplaying his monstrosity. And yet in devoting most of her life to exploring totalitarianism in all its brutality this was possibly the furthest thing from Arendt's mind. Just as Haneke's response to Eichmann's trial focuses on 'duty,' Arendt found in Eichmann's normality a more offensive malignancy than seen before; 'good' and 'duty' a mask for a greater disease than the selfishness of traditional evil acts. Moving beyond the Kantian definition of *radical evil* to confront this tradition, her thoughts on evil now concerned assaults on humanity considered as an end in itself. In 1951, receiving a copy of *The Origins of Totalitarianism* she had earlier sent to Karl Jaspers, Arendt realised the copy withheld a cryptic note "Hasn't Jahwe faded too far from sight?" She replied,

> "Evil has proved to be more radical than expected. In objective terms, modern crimes are not provided for in the Ten Commandments. Or: The Western Tradition is suffering from the preconception that the most evil things human beings can do arise from the vice of selfishness. Yet we know that the greatest evils or radical evil has nothing to do anymore with such humanly understandable, sinful motives. *What radical evil really is I don't know but it seems to me it somehow has to do with the following phenomenon: making human beings as human beings superfluous (not using them as means to an end, which leaves their essence as humans untouched and impinges only on their human dignity; rather, making them superfluous as human beings)* (Arendt: 1958; 7).

To formulate her position Arendt returned to Kant and *radical evil* (and its corruption of all maxims). She drew on Kantian concepts. But she did this to engage (to formulate her position) with crimes against humanity. Arendt found the rendering of others superfluous as a unique manifestation of evil. Rendering others superfluous is an evil radical in all its horror. Yet the disassociation he displayed towards this was something Arendt found unique to Eichmann's behaviour. Some believed this (when looked at through the lens of the categorical imperative) to be a state-sanctioned means of evil; the 'systematic' 'cog in a machine' theory when perpetrators argued they rigidly followed protocol to offset personal guilt utitlised. As such Eichmann claimed he himself was a victim, unable to differentiate duty from morality. In *Hitler's Willing Executioners* (1997) Daniel Goldhagen accused Arendt of defending this view. Goldhagen argued that thinkers like Arendt are, "positivistically inclined social scientists who seek to reduce all phenomena, no matter how complex or unprecedented, to a fixed set of "economically rational" motivations" (Goldhagen in Villa: 1999; 40). Goldstein attacks American liberalism (inspired by Arendt) in its attempt to downplay the existence of extreme evil, believing, "the person most responsible for this image (is)... Hannah Arendt" (Goldhagen: 1997; 379).

The philosopher Richard J. Bernstein has defended Arendt from these accusations, complementing others, such as Dana R. Villa. Villa offers a rounded view of Eichmann, considering the 'cog in a machine theory' and the horrifying failure of conscience Arendt confronted in Eichmann. "All the controversy surrounding the Eichmann book has served to obscure what it is, in fact, about: the fate of conscience as a moral faculty in the midst of a generalised 'moral collapse'...,'" as Villa writes, and so "Eichmann's case demonstrated how conscience, in such a context, is perverted: it no longer tells individuals what is right and what is wrong. But neither is it totally silenced, for it continues to tell people like Eichman what their "duty" is" (Villa: 1999; 45). As she came to believe that the failure of conscience elicited by Eichmann in his now notorious defence was the result of a new form of evil, Arendt found in activities of this unheralded type a banal criminal if not a banal crime (Villa: 1999; 45). Of course, someone so brazenly unaffected by the Final Solution as Eichmann–coupled with the acts integral to its functioning–horrified Arendt in a purely moral sense. But Arendt was horrified also by the perversion of genuine thought Eichmann's *insights* so clearly revealed. The failure of independent thought was, for Arendt, horrifyingly banal *and* evil.

It is important to consider the relationship between radical *and* banal evil in Arendt's analysis. In respect to Bernstein, his approach to such a controversially theorised evil requires certain points of analysis given to considering the vital attributes of human life: spontaneity, plurality and natality. When humans become superfluous to life, he argues, the eradication of these attributes is felt (Bernstein: 2002; 65). *Quo* Arendt, he states the, "fundamental question of post-war intellectual life in Europe" (Arendt: 1994; 134) is evil. It is not surprising Bernstein considers the responses to Kant in *Radical Evil: A Philosophical Investigation* (2002). The opening chapter has a fundamental stress, the paradoxical elements of *radical evil* taken to task (one which Arendt circumvents by transferring emphasis in her later writing from radical to extreme evil),

> "On the one hand, he never wants to compromise the basic claim of his moral philosophy: that human beings as finite rational agents are free…On the other hand, Kant also wants to affirm that all human beings have an innate propensity for evil" (Bernstein: 2002; 33).

Bernstein finds an insolvable moral bind around the fact that, "we can explain something that we simply cannot explain" (Bernstein: 2002; 35). *Radical evil*, as a chimera of dark in flashing light, intensifies the struggle to define criminality just as it struggles to lay bare the responsibility for its existence. Human beings possess an innate propensity to intuit something wrong, and a similarly innate ability to repress this intuition.

The remainder of this chapter addresses the manner in which Haneke responds to this kind of evil, particularly when the question of intuiting something as wrong but lacking the moral awareness to intervene to stop it, is of issue. This means exploring the film in relation to a systematic evil. My contention is, however, the problem of 'evil' operates on three specific levels in *The White Ribbon*, the first of which relates to the Narrator. All of the crimes over the period of time in which the story is told–the assault on the Doctor which leaves him hospitalised, the attack on Sigi (Fion Mutert) and the burning of the barn–and which he traces chronologically–culminate in the attack on Karli (Eddi Grahl); the disabled child who is left partially blind. As the crimes become increasingly vindictive, yet at the same apparently more systematic in their choice of victim, and as the Baron's wife flees the village in fear, the Narrator begins to suspect a ring spearheaded by the Pastor's children: the aim being to make the victims superfluous to the village. His investigation culminates in his confrontation with the Pastor (in one of the more exciting scenes) when the Narrator makes it clear who he believes 'done it.' It is crucial to the story that the Pastor responds,

> "You're saying that your pupils, my children included, committed these crimes. Is that right? You realise what you're saying? Do you really know... I assume I'm the first person to hear these monstrosities. If you dare to bother others with this. If you ever accuse respectable families and their children, and denounce them publicly, I'll make sure, take my word for it, that you go to prison" (*The White Ribbon*: 2009).

The Narrator's resolve is tested, his character reproached, and resolution is demanded. Yet, the narrative peters out. We are told of the War and its beginnings; the Narrator's conscription and failure to return to the village. His confrontation with the Pastor–and the latter's failure to acknowledge the culprits–is a finale, a moral test of his fortitude of which he is the sole witness. The telling nature of the Pastor's acrimonious response to the allegations amounts to the second level. The doubt regarding the moral fortitude of his children is notable in his hesitation in awarding Klara the ceremonial gift. He nonetheless perseveres with the consecration. In this, one of the most visually arresting scenes of the film, the Pastor considers rejecting Klara; yet also notably fails to do so.

As with many in *The White Ribbon*, the ceremonial scene is visually ripe. It's as if the angelic Klara, kneeling before her father, withholds her devilish incarnation. Indeed the white cross set against a white background gives to the Pastor's duty a pronounced meaning. It is as if Christianity is embedded in a world of darkness. It is only when failing to entertain the allegation brought before him, as if judging is subservient to duty, the essence of this is felt. The third level is "self-love." If the *"unqualified good pleasure* in oneself" is central to Kantian self-love, the Doctor is an example of this (Kant: 1960; 41). His relationship with Mrs. Wagner and his daughter Anni is a modicum of this. Cutting short his recuperation, prompted by his son found walking to the hospital, the Doctor's first concern is Rudi's wellbeing. He *cares* for his children and Mrs. Wagner (Susanne Lothar), with whom he conducts a secretive and sexual relationship. However, when he ends his liaison with Mrs. Wagner and submits her to a torrent of abuse, he violently derides her physical appearance, and bespokes her bad breath (with a malicious disdain). Mrs. Wagner lets her shackles off and threatens to reveal the paedophilic relationship he has with his daughter Anni. Whether she follows through– and the Doctor's disappearance in the final scene suggests she does–is never clarified. Instead there is little closure to events.

In perhaps the most shocking scene (in a film where monstrous actions are largely left to the audience's imagination), which occurs prior to this, Rudi is shown awakening late at night, then descending the stairs, only to stumble–like the viewer who is positioned in his point-of-view–upon the incestuous primal scene: made to gaze upon his father sexually abusing his sister. It is one of the most disturbing scenes in the film, mainly because of the lack of concern the Doctor shows to his son. However, it is equally disturbing to think what is happening is considered normal by the young girl. His sister doesn't regard Rudi as some kind of saviour. Instead he appears to interrupt the action. Just as "his sensuous nature" (Kant: 1960; 43) appears to triumph, his children victims of perpetual self-love, an age-old expression of monstrousness is found in the Doctor's role; deriving–in Kantian morality at least–from the dictates of self-love (Kant: 1960; 43). The Doctor can care, like the care he shows for Karli as he lies semi-blinded upon his bed but his evil requires the use of others. Committed to pleasure–at the expense of his children–he is empathic towards them.

If the Doctor's pleasure coheres with the facilitation of duty, as a character he is also a fertile distraction from less direct manifestations of evil. All too aware of his crimes, the Doctor–at least–lacks the moralising postures of the Pastor. His incestuous relations with his daughter court moral disdain from an audience as indomitable evil, with Haneke perhaps saying something about abuse having a retrospective rather than present impact. But the question is whether the Doctor is to be considered the sole villain? And are differing types of evil played against each other? The wickedness in acts of self-gratification–in this case incest–based on a recognisable motive is obviously one concern. But an evil spreading virus-like throughout a group is another. Let us assume that the Doctor's self-love is felt at the expense of others. Let us then assume that the children are typical of something else: another evil. Contrasting the on-screen, overtly visible actions attributed to a Doctor is the violation of children with more than purely psychological scars *by* children. These latter crimes are allegedly committed by a group. This is evident in the eyes of the disabled son of Mrs. Wagner, Karli. Up until now, the scars described by the Narrator are simply *said*; without the impact *shown*.

To say rather than to show is uniquely Hanekean as a filmic trope. We find this illustrated around the dead wife of the Farmer Max Felder (Branco Samarovski). Mrs. Felder falls to her death in one of the Baron's factory premises. Asked to work in the loft, the woman–whose face we never see–falls to her death through a rotten timber beam in the roof. The death goes on to spark a series of counter-acts; adding to the unrest and ending with the suicide of Felder. That Mrs. Felder is 'shown' literally faceless makes it difficult to feel empathy towards her. The shot of a decrepit corridor slowly reveals the body and feet of Mrs. Felder. The shot echoes Andrei Tarkovsky's *Stalker* (1979) when the camera pans slowly along the contours of the sleeping couple, Haneke similarly careful not to personalise a victim of this malevolent evil. Later, when the Baron's son, Sigi, is left hanging upside down in the woods–considered an act of vengeance by the Felders against the Baron (Ulrich Tukur)–Sigi's body is never shown, remains off-screen and the true barbarism of the act is left unmediated. Not until the body of Karli appears in the woods are the scars of evil *shown*.

Scenes like these give verse to a systematic type of malice. Far from a specific violation the attacks are part of a ruthless strategy to dehumanise (on which Haneke lays certain emphasis). Because we never 'see' the victims in full (until Karli is attacked at the end); unable to assess them as characters as distinct from types, any such assumption that the children are the perpetrators, like the assumption made by the Schoolteacher (and perhaps the audience is encouraged to make) is dangerous. To come to this conclusion some kind of profound moral collapse must be acknowledged; that of an SS generation. Indeed, the gradual ascent towards the humiliating torture of a Karli, of which the Schoolteacher is a testament witness–both Karla and Martin teasing the semi-blinded disabled child through the window of his room–is accompanied by a rather disturbing realisation: the idea that terror has been reducing the victims of the attack to inconsequential and superfluous types; the focus of Arendt's sustained analysis of modern *radical evil*. On this note, the Doctor's evil contrasts an evil making others, as Arendt states, utterly superfluous as its aim,

> "What radical evil is I really don't know, but it seems to me it somehow has to do with the following phenomenon: making human beings as human beings superfluous (not using them as means to an end, which leaves their essence as untouched and impinges only on their human dignity; rather, making them superfluous as human beings)......And all this in turn arises–or better, goes along with–the delusion of the omnipotence (not simply the lust for power) of an individual man...the omnipotence of an individual man would make men superfluous" (Arendt: 1992; 166).

Omnipotence requires the superfluousness of others. The Schoolteacher's encounter with Martin (Leonard Proxauf) is a case in point. When he stumbles upon Martin fishing in a forest stream, the Schoolteacher stands aghast as the boy walks a beam from the overlooking bridge; the boy oblivious to the danger besetting him. Taken aback, the Schoolteacher awakens the trance-like Martin to the danger he appears oblivious to. Showing him how he could slip, Martin replies that he is endeavouring to test his God's resolve. He says he is instigating divine intervention, "I gave God a chance to kill me. He didn't, so he's pleased with me" (*The White Ribbon*; 2009). If grace is divine intervention (in Augustinian terms), his response is important to the greater scheme of things in that Martin is seemingly wedded to divine omnipotence. The scene fits more generally into the narrative when Karli's body is discovered. Attached to the tree beside Karli's tortured body is a written note, "For I the Lord, your God, am a jealous God, punishing the child for the sins of their parents sins, to the third and fourth generations" (*The White Ribbon*; 2009).

Although a detail, none of the other characters elaborate on this in the film. It takes on significance after the Schoolteacher's encounter with Martin, described above. When Martin asks his God to intervene, we can assume he is involved in Karli's torture; but that Martin subsumes an authority, versed in the omnipotence of a monotheistic God, into his being is equally disturbing. From wire-tripping the Doctor, to attacking Karli (a possible punishment for the sins committed by his mother the mid-wife), a systematically styled evil, making villagers superfluous, gathers in momentum. For there is no other reason why Karli is victimised and blinded like he is, other than the net effect of him being superfluous to others. We must therefore confront the childen. But confronting the children as culprits, means a power over 'the other' significantly different to that wielded by the Doctor, even one who controls the movements of others, must also be confronted. And, for that matter, a Pastor who sees his children as types. If the human attacked as an end in itself is evil, Karli's attack is a fertile expression. The note left is, in this sense, a precise indication of an omnipotent divinity when taking on human expression.

In this context, the attacks can be considered harbingers of a *radical evil* (an institutionalised form of evil where culprits less obvious demonic eschew responsibility less characteristically explicit). But this is in contrast to the evil of the Doctor; whose perversion is that of self-love. In Augustinian terms, the Doctor lacks access to true reality. In addition, as if this wasn't enough, the Pastor's actions reveal the limitations of morality as itself another form of evil. These three types of evil make up a typology, all of which come together in the film, the most significant of which is left to the viewer to decide. The first and second relate to Eichmann, with a sense of the 'institution' behind them. But the Doctor, as I mentioned, is a thoroughly despicable character, yet arguably 'monstrous' in a different way. He is a slave to his passions, and in this way bound by his intractable pleasure principle. The other types of evil seek to keep pleasure at a distance, under the auspice that carrying out duty requires an indifference to the passions.

The Pastor's failure to acknowledge his children as culprits–even though his body language in the confirmation scene serves to evoke doubt and suspicion–is a failure to account for evil. It is a serious failing. It may well be that evil–in its indifference to human suffering–is what exists outside the categorical boundaries of his teachings. Or it may be that failing to see outside the moral system set out by the church he represents is itself the most harrowing evil. Perhaps Haneke's ire is directed at this. That is, directed at the evil of turning away from evil. There is an evil in pretending all is well, worse than the evil committed which it protects. Paul Ricouer, for whom *radical evil* presented a life long challenge, believed the problem with 'evil'–rather than, for example, base immorality– lies in the inability to integrate it into a set of defined moral positions. "Evil," Riceour writes, "is the excess, the disproportion, without being human, that being human cannot fathom" (Riceour; 2007; 11). Similarly, for Emmanuel Levinas, "evil is not only of the non-integratable, it is also the nonintegratability of the non-integratable" (Levinas in Bernstein: 2002; 158). For both, evil reduces its recipients to moral stupour.

In conclusion, it is significant that the Pastor's response to the accusations laid against him by the Schoolteacher is borne of a moral stupor. But, whether this vindicates his actions is pertinent to our inquiry. While tyrannically inculcating the morality for which he reigns over, he withdraws when the system itself becomes the object of scrutiny. Failing to even acknowledge the culprits, hiding behind an institution, is indicative of the fascist 'moral collapse' Arendt explored at such lengths. The Pastor fails to acknowledge his offspring's capacity for evil. Hence the myth of innate goodness in humankind he himself appears to reject, is invariably replenished by his actions. So, given this analysis, we are in a position to conclude. We can now say the Pastor is Haneke's figure of disdain: the Eichmann in our midst. The reason is he knows something is wrong yet hides behind a veil worse than the children, *doli incapax*, he thinks he protects. Theodor Adorno's responses to Arendt are tools to make a final judgment,

> "I would not say that evil is banal, but that banality is evil–banality, that is, as the form of consciousness and mind that adapts itself to the world as it is, which obeys the principle of inertia. And this principle of inertia is what is radically evil" (Adorno: 2001; 115).

In the final instance, the Pastor fails to acknowledge the evil his children have inflicted on others. The 'mind' is now adapted to inertia. For in Adorno's words, the Pastor adapts himself to the principle of inaction, while simply gazing at the evil of others.

The White Ribbon brings Haneke's concern with evil to an interesting conclusion; exploring, in no uncertain, terms a typology of evil and the motivation for it. But the question that really needs to be answered is this: how have Haneke films contributed to the filmic treatment of evil? And, subsequently, what makes Haneke a more important filmmaker to the tradition of 'dangerous' films deliberated on in this book than say, Steven Spielberg (a filmmaker whose oeuvre can also be approached as particularly prominent deliberation on evil)? The answer to this question, as I mentioned earlier, could well instigate a book in itself, such is the concern with violence, cruelty, immoralism, self-love etc., even sadism, in Haneke films. But while the intersection of form and content, and the fact that the formal realisation of the films are rarely removed from the content of them has been well discussed in Haneke studies, it's not my interest to rehearse those claims again here. In other words, I don't want to say that Haneke shifts the burden of deliberation onto his audience and that this is all he does. I would rather say that in Haneke problems rather than answers are set out. Problems are both within the film, asking us to ponder the action, and outside, asking how I should respond. At times we feel compelled to resolve these as spectators, at other times, quick to condemn the film for failing to resolve them itself. If *Benny's Video* is a good example of the former, when as spectators we have to think about what Benny has actually done, before we can respond to the problem of Benny's evil, *The White Ribbon* is a good example of the latter.

In light of the humanism advocated by Spielberg, the viewer can feel comfortably removed from the disturbing issues raised by his film(s), as closure, and the resolution of problems takes precedence. One reason that Spielberg has failed to garner the critical attention his films may well deserve hinges, I believe, on film scholars viewing his films as hermetically sealed, with the distinction between good and evil too readily apparent. If Schindler is the quintessential good Spielbergian hero, his goodness the end product of a will to do good, there is a feeling of a problem resolved in the attention to good overpowering evil. This is not the case with Haneke. For in Haneke, and recall I referred to him as an Augustinian, he is an Augustinian because of his attention to a problem; but also a desire to make others deliberate on this problem themselves. For Augustine, the same is true. Augustine doesn't claim to have resolved the problem of evil. It's rather that he comes to certain conclusions about evil as a way of reaffirming his own commitment to God. I would say that Haneke doesn't claim to resolve the problem either. And that rather than making films about evil to resolve the problem, his efforts expand the debate about the problem itself. This affirms his commitment to exploring problematic situations. And indeed, the spectators of his films need to resolve these themselves.

CONCLUSION

THE "DANGEROUS" FILM

"Humanity pursues two goals–one, the negative, is to preserve life (to avoid death), and the other, the positive, is to increase the intensity of life. These two goals are not contradictory, but their intensity has never increased *without danger*. The intensity desired by the greatest number (or the social body) is subordinated to the care of preserving life and its works... The notion of intensity cannot be reduced to that of pleasure because, as we have seen, the quest for intensity leads us into the realm of unease and then to the limits of consciousness" (Bataille: 1973; 73-4).

"Intensity," Bataille tells us, "has never increased without danger." Death contrasts with the intensity of avoiding it. But is it *always* negative to avoid death, to preserve life, while at the same time positive to increase the intensity Bataille so loosely talks of? And will unease be felt when confronted with, as we've become accustomed so far, a morally dangerous film. If a film is intense, generating anxiety, the behaviour it deals with must in some way conflict with 'common sense' consensus on what certain responses should be. Indeed, in the various discussions, we have seen how unease is rendered, engendering a sense of impending danger in those used to confronting representations of unsavoury behaviour.

Catherine Wheatley's study of Haneke is a comprehensive overview of the ethical strategies Haneke employs to make the spectator uneasy. For Wheatley, Haneke's films are the product of a somewhat boorish attempt to incite (un)pleasure in his viewers; the audience impelled to explore why they feel this way. The *un*pleasure Wheatley talks of, with a nod to the kind of unease Bataille speaks of, is a kind of danger. Danger accrues with, as mentioned earlier, a lack of mastery (set out in the confines of the cinematic auditorium). The spectator, used to feeling at ease with morally challenging behaviour, aesthetically displeasing affects, is at a loss to control their feelings. It is perhaps such a loss that so affronts critics of *The Night Porter*. Cavani, as Kriss Ravetto points out, "counteracts what Lacanian theory exercises as a form of damage control, a conscious repression of desire designed to retard and neutralise what are perceived as *dangerous* imaginary distortions" (Ravetto: 2001; 152). Inappropriate feelings calls for the repression of particular emotion. Danger impels us to pretend emotion doesn't exist. It is in this sense that those who actively campaigned against an elicit danger, leading to criminal charges being brought against Cavani, fail to engage the cathartic elements of the film (Ravetto: 2001; 152). By cathartic I mean the playful feigning, the ritual engagment with evil.

Apter takes emphasis on unease and associated stimuli as his particular point of departure, arguing, as mentioned earlier, that "detachment frames," the feeling of being protected from the impact of displeasurable emotions are crucial if one is to experience a film like *The Night Porter* without immediate distress. A "detachment frame" allows a cinematic audience distance from 'real life' danger; thereby experiencing "parapathic emotions," those emotions contrived "from a situation that both induces the emotion and maintains the protective frame" (Apter: 2007; 74). Yet what makes *The Night Porter* such a dangerous experience, as distinct from a film which makes its audience feel threatened by dangerous content is that in order to experience "parapathic emotions" the audience must first of all identify the "parapathic emotions" of the couple in the throes of the masochistic performance; the contractual relation. Failing to do so, the protective frame shatters, and the distinction between 'real life' and real life dissolves. Cavani's film is a landmark instigation of this process within the terrain of neorealism, considered as a genre of film brushing over the distinction between something set in parenthesis and something not. Hence *The Night Porter* can be considered as an affront to those positioned in the detachment frame, as extreme 'real life' emotions tally with those of real life.

It is interesting then to consider the shattering of the 'real life' illusion that 'dangerous' films, theorised as those which deal explicitly with evil, perform. For this can help distinguish these kind of films from other films concerned with evil. With the shattering of the 'real life' illusion a significant feature, the 'dangerous' film, I assert, aligns the form to the content; the subject matter treated as filmic. Let's consider *The White Ribbon* and how it contrasts with *Schindler's List* to explain this. Both are filmed in monochrome, using a quasi-documentary style; thereby heightening the temporality particular to the period drama. Both concern a male agent, in the face of considerably unannounced evil. And both are impressive in their use of a dazzling camerawork to capture the period style. In addition, in terms of content, both address fascism. Both address evil. Indeed, both address moral responses to evil.

Yet the difference between realism as practiced by Spielberg, and that of Haneke, is crucial if the 'danger' the film elicits as a commentary on evil is to be accounted for. Spielberg doesn't shirk from displaying the absolute horror of the camps, nor does he shirk from illustrating the unnecessary dehumanisation of the victims. Nazism is cruel and violent, even if a mass killing machine generates its mass killing. This is evil, and what Spielberg understands as evil is not difficult to assess. In fact, good and evil are pretty distinctive categories when one involves mass killing of those considered inhuman, and the other the dangerous attempt to stop it. Spielberg is to be applauded for championing moral courage when morality was attacked from the most precarious of positions. One might say for Spielberg the truth unfolds in front of us. Spectators can sit back and comfortably engage the 'real life' situation as it unfolds naturalistically before them. And because Spielberg safely removes the parenthesis at the end of *Schindler's List*, when the real life victims are paired with their 'real life' representatives, the viewer is safely positioned in relation to History.

Now, *The White Ribbon* constructs a past as anything other than sealed off. Indeed, one of the significant features of the film is, as I noted, the voice-over. The Schoolteacher's voice-over commentary brings a subjective element to the film, such that the representation of evil can be considered a representation of a representation. All of what we see is constitutive of memory, however trustworthy it might be. As soon as we are lulled into thinking that Haneke is painting the world objectively, with a real life representation of the past, the voice-over kicks in, recalling the register of the film as a series of memories. It is one thing to make a period drama. It is another to experience the inquiry through the memory of a citizen the essence of whom we know little. What makes *The White Ribbon* a 'dangerous' film is that judgment of what happens in it, and here I am as guilty as any other viewer of the film, is complicated by the fact that the 'story' can be read as a potential fabrication of the past. In this way Haneke calls our attention to the very idea of bearing responsibility. But he also draws attention to the way in which responsibility is passed on from one generation to another. Recall that Haneke informs us over and over again: trust the tale and not the teller. Hence, evil as it becomes meshed in a tale, is inseparable from an evil represented by the teller. Thinking about the problem cinematically is something we are–no doubt–

compelled to do. Is it a surprise critics would miss this? Accusing Haneke of making a film about film. The answer is no: people avoid danger.

It could be that certain types of engagement are dangerous. The paedophile killer of Lang's *M* is a criminal for whom compassion is incited. But one can overlook the danger of *M* if the incited compassion is rejected; and indeed the difficulty in not knowing what happens overlooked. But there is danger also in feeling we should consider what we *consider* to be evil. Like Cavani's anti-heroine, Lang's is not devoid of emotion. Beckert pleads his innocence like a man torn. Yet it is precisely the *depiction* of this plea, as real or *not* real (but appearing to be so), which requires consideration of the courtroom we 'look' upon. If this is a Beckert performing what he feels he should express, acting out what he believes he should 'feel,' should we get our psychology books and start to assess the character before us? Or should we assume his evil comes from elsewhere; making him a pawn in a cosmic struggle between good and evil?

The first concern is whether Beckert is prosecuted on the basis that he is evil. In this sense the court is a 'real' one and it is to be assumed the moral issues at stake in this consideration are as real as in real life. When looked at like this this, Singer's analysis of evil as a conceptual marker tallies with my own consideration of Beckert's real life predicament in the film,

> "The term 'evil' is the worst term of opprobrium that can be applied to a human being. And the concept, in my conception of it, applies primarily to persons and organisations, secondarily to conduct and practices. Evil deeds must flow from evil motives, the volition to do something evil, by which I mean horrendously bad. Through accident or misadventure one can do something wrong or bad, even terrible, but not something evil. So when we say that someone did something evil, we are saying something about that person, that person's motives and consequently about that person's character (I am not saying that someone who did something evil, and who therefore acted on an evil motive or with an evil intention, is necessarily an evil person. The judgment of a person as a whole requires a complicated judgment ranging over a whole life, depends on many complicated factors)" (Singer: 2004; 190).

Singer's point is that to call someone evil is, "the worst kind of opprobrium" possible; just as it is paradoxical in moral terms to do so. Lacking in responsibility, the evil agent is a victim. The alternative position is also contentious. If one is to reject the concept a clear intention, impelling someone like Beckert to act in such a way, is required as an alternative. And yet it is difficult to isolate intention when Beckert claims his will is divided. Thus evil can be sanitised as error; even if, as a conceptual edifice it returns time and again more virile. In other words, no sooner has evil been ridiculed as outmoded than it comes back, resurrected as the most suitable descriptor for a mode of behaviour.

Another way of looking at things is that Beckert is not the killer; 'Beckert' is the fantasy of a man caught by the police. The concern now is with knowing what is real. But like the difficulty in knowing if Beckert is real, a similar difficulty concerns knowing if evil is real: that is, if it exists at all. Earlier I defined this as the Augustinian difficulty. *M* makes of this 'difficulty' a 'discourse on evil.'

Hence differing interpretative strands bleed into each other; the first a 'discourse on evil' concerned with exploring the serial killer and the evil committed from the perspective of responsibility and insanity. The second a discourse concerning the filmic status of a particularly 'probing' inquiry. There is a very distinct possibility that our own outrage at such a murderer, and the sympathy we might then feel towards him is simply the affect of a devious manipulation; so that having to think whether what we 'see' is real tallies with the moral problem of whether evil is real. Filmic content, the problem of evil, tallies with its filmic treatment. Hence whether film, an illusion of light and dark, is actually a platform for moral debate becomes just as central to the inquiry as the existence, substantial nature of evil itself. *M* is one of the cinema's greater masterpieces because it so explicitly bridges the aesthetic, the illusion of form and distillation of light in dark, with content: the possibility that evil is itself an illusion. As much as we would like to use evil as a descriptor for judging others, it is, as Lang demonstrates, morally problematic to do so.

Peter Dews's consideration of 9/11 as a springboard for a renewed turn to evil–for describing acts and persons–across the many disciplines of Western thought (not just among buffoon politicians who use evil to advertently highlight their implicit Good) is a poignant one. *The Idea of Evil* (2008) argues that George W. Bush's phrase 'axis of evil' was coined to designate *rogue* states the considered enemies of America and its prized freedom. For Dews, "the feeling of the American people (was) that they were under some horrendous, unprecedented threat, menaced by a conclave of maleficent powers that already achieved one grievous strike, and might be preparing for more" (Dews: 2008; 2). Dews's point is not that the atrocity could be filed under anything but evil, but that when the other is designated evil (in this case North Korea, Iraq and Afghanistan) feelings of victimhood are reinforced. In other words, the U.S. as, "a superpower fighting global evil in the name of freedom" gathers momentum around the infantile amplification of such projections. But the impulse, under the threat of danger, to revert to fundamentals is something *M* asks us to consider. When a mother of a Beckert victim shouts from the crowd, she sees nature as black and white. Yet in Lorre's display, it is the nature of nature itself which is instrinsically problematic; the authenticity of which the audience must implicitly discern. *M* is far from didactic, but it situates *nature* as more complex and dangerous than we admit. It may be that Beckert is remorseful for what he has done. Or it may be he has learned the way in which remorse is expressed. Either way, the film, in its ethical mode of inquiry, impels us to think of an evil which pertains to being or its lack.

It may be that a consensus as to what black and white mean, regarding the law and its impact on human agency, is the domain of film noir. Noir is the film movement par excellence where danger lies in identifying with the detective the necessary evil of whom contains a critique of the categorical pertaining to everyday life. Dark forces control those who appear most moral, law abiding, honest. In this sense, the consideration of Quinlan's touch of evil in the guise of its being set against the *radical evil* contained in the mandate given Miquel Vargas gives us a platform on which to see *Touch of Evil* as a seductive film, a sobering corrective to the oversimplified good guy/bad guy matrix elicited in genre films; particularly when one degree of evil is said to be opposed to another. If one law impinges upon another, the film shows, transgression is, of course, a necessary evil. Awareness of this is, as Welles informs us, dangerous.

As pointed out earlier, Welles's contribution to a legacy which takes the moral as something which doesn't have direct bearing on the law is substantial. Indeed Welles's contribution to the cinema of evil is noteworthy in its emphasis on the dirty law enforcer whose 'dirtiness' has some explicit link to morality. One of the strange insights of the current research project has been the curious affinity between second-generation Irish cops and films about them upholding the law through immoral means. As an aside, is there something about the Irish historically inventing their moral code in opposition to the imperial British Law which has found its way into crime films the main influence of which is film noir? Maybe, and it's surely a question as an Irishman I would like answers to. Don Siegel's *Dirt Harry* (1971) fits this model. It is perhaps the best example of Welles's legacy. The issue of keeping crime in check with help from the astudious immoral encroaches on the use of evidently and dubious immoral means for enhancing that end. In Machivellian terms, when does the end justify the means? The infamous touch of evil applied by Harry Callahan (Clint Eastwood) in *Dirty Harry* when confronting a killer ostracises him from the police and brings the question of whether catching and removing a killer from society is better than overriding the rules put in place by this society to the fore. The moral is similar in *A Touch of Evil*: when is breaking the law to maintain the moral Law ethically justified?

Interestingly, *Dirty Harry* is used in teaching material in the ethical training of police officers; and the 'dirty harry problem' is the moral problem associated with it; the legacy of Welles's inquiries, and the danger of them readily apparent.

In its attraction to the cinematic spectator, transgression is of course always going to come into question in any study of evil in cinema worth its proverbial salt. And danger, especially in terms of its erstwhile capacity to elicit unease, is a feature of any transgressive practice. The two films taking such practices as their concern, in relation to sadism and masochism respectively are *Saló* and *The Night Porter*. The power of both films lies in the cinematic norms it purposively transgresses; whether representing perpetrators and their victims or using the cinematic apparatus to relay unease back onto the viewer; encouraging a re-evaluation of evil as a problem in itself. For one cannot feel at ease as *Saló* ends. At this point the attempt to experience pleasure becomes the apotheosis of such. We, willing spectators, become accomplices. We support the perpetrators by simply staying to watch. What makes the film dangerous is the aligning of acts presented on screen with the viewer who feels morally immune from these practices, as entertainment and indeed pleasure. The prospective realisation is that thinking film as entertainment (and that its power lies in fulfilling social entertainment quotas) is to overlook its capacity to incite thought; to challenge norms. Only by jilting the spectator, shifting them out of their complacency, can 'thought' replace the banal structures of 'entertainment.'

Equally liable to offend, disgust, the danger involved in a film like *The Night Porter* has already been discussed in relation to the sheer unease it generated in those who watched. Of course, any film that, in taking victimhood as its concern, maps out a psychosexual game between victim and their executioner is liable to run up against the guardians of good taste. But the danger, I argue, a film like *The Night Porter* elicits lies precisely in Cavani's capacity to incite judgment around the victim's need to re-engage with their executioner; propositioning the spectator to consider symbolic power. It is then possible to see that *considering* a micro-historical story with grand historical implications has its own reward. Like Cathar rituals, performative rituals align the moral and aesthetic in opposition to evil. This requires confronting systemic evil through artistic means. We concluded with the somewhat dangerous assertion: Cavani and Pasolini both respond to the legacy of fascism– around their respective understanding of the term–but do so distinguishing fascism as an historical and indeed factional entity from that of a fascist impulse, one at the core of life.

In both cases, the films are set out as challenges to the idea of a true reality; in the sense that they make us 'see' how reality can be said to mask a whole series of 'realities.' The idea that evil is a deviation from a true reality, submergence in a perverted one, is duly challenged. In this sense the films are both abrupt commentaries on evil and abrupt commentaries on reality. In the first, as a product of totalising impulses, the inability to totalise completely, to 'close' what evidentially resists closure is a kind of evil. Something gets in the way, resists it's own capture. Hence when caught in a spiraling terror, the dignitaries remain victims of both language as a perverted entity and 'reality' as defined by language. Objects aren't there to be found; they exist first of all as words. In the second, 'reality' is contested as self-evident experience, something 'seen' as such. Rather, what we find, and *The Night Porter* is an illustration of this, are 'realities' hovering underneath the surface, yet because these aren't the true reality, doesn't make them less important morally. Cavani confronts Augustine head on. For in Lucia and Max, performance helps constitute these 'realities,' and they play a powerful role in resisting the totalising Reality the Nazis want to impose on them.

It is worthwhile considering the projects of Pasolini and Cavani (and their morally complex subject matter) in relation to films which *are* about the factional variant of fascism: one such example being Leni Reifenstahl's *Triumph des Willens* (Triumph of the Will (1934)). Reifenstahl's documentary is based around the Nazi party congress in Nuremberg in 1934, using real footage in its construction. As propaganda for the instated Nazi party, commissioned by Hitler to deify his leadership, *Triumph of the Will* is a morally questionable piece of historical art.

Morality aside, the film has been considered a groundbreaking exercise in filmic development; Reifenstahl a pioneer filmmaker. Of course, valuing the film in this way relies less on its considerably dubious subject matter than the film's aesthetic merit. In other words, factioning off the aesthetic from ethical is required to critically entomb the film, as many film scholars have done, as a veritable masterpiece. Nonetheless, with this in mind, Mary Devereaux believes *Triumph of the Will* is "at once masterful and morally repugnant, this deeply troubling film epitomizes a general problem that arises with art. It is both beautiful and evil" (Devereaux in Levinson (ed): 1998; 227). Devereux's concern is the need to cipher off aesthetically pleasing features while downplaying evil content. Coming to terms with an object both beautiful *and* evil, as Kieran Cashell attests, "means engaging with the moral issue it raises and not ignoring it, setting it aside, suspending or otherwise bracketing it, through the conceptual mechanism of aesthetic distance" (Cashell: 2009; 49).

Situating Pasolini and Cavani, or to be more precise, *Saló* and *The Night Porter,* in this light makes for interesting discussion. Both contest the art cinema's tendency to elevate the 'image' to a position of formal abstraction which requires, for its merit, the screening off of its implicit content. Pasolini wants his audience to confront their complicity in the situation ethically, and to do this he asks us to consider the ethical implications of using the aesthetic defence as a way of disengaging with the troubling ethical content of the film. To look upon the action, as victims are tortured in horrifically brutal acts and see only the compositional beauty of the image requires disengaging with content. And disengaging with content, as Devereux and Cashell inform us, means failing to confront the totality of the experience in question. These are the features which make Cavani's *The Night Porter* such a compelling piece of art. Against the argument that Cavani's art cinema is beautiful in its composition, when bracketing off its morally troublesome subject matter, I have argued that Cavani wants us to confront the manner in which the aesthetic is aligned to morally subversive exercises: one requires the other. It would seem that what happens at a subversive and often subliminal level, most evident in the final scene when Max adorns his SS uniform and Lucia dresses as a little girl, is aesthetic, in that it draws our attention to the Nazi paraphernalia critics such as Giroux saw contribute to a chic abstraction of Nazi style from content, and moral, in that it asks us question whether this act is regressive or progressive, moral or evil.

The films of Michael Haneke emerge from a similar tradition. Dangerously confronting evil at an ethical and meta-ethical level, Haneke's films are morally and aesthetically engaging. Stanley Cavell has said that, "a measure of the quality of a new text is the quality of the texts it arouses" (Cavell: 1979; 5). I take Cavell to mean that the impact of any text can be gauged by the quality of its responses. Responses to Haneke, my own notwithstanding, tend to generate unease about what the proper response should be. I find Haneke's work dangerous precisely because it impels us to respond to one of the last Western taboos: the child murderer. Or to be more precise, *doli incapax*. But Haneke's work is also interesting aesthetically–his manifest formalism (his use of the long take, the digital video image, the rewinds and forward motions)–when a traditional inquest into what constitutes morally dangerous behaviour in morally questionable subjects is considered as an aesthetic component. It is in this context that a prominent concern–around the considerably difficult question of evil and moral responsibility–works itself out in Haneke's films, as moral culpability progesses to the contentious issues of collaboration, on then to the propensity to overlook what lies, seemingly, outside moral measure. *The White Ribbon* is an example. It ends by invoking an evil situated most prominently in the gaze that sees evil. It is therefore unsurprising that Haneke has matched Francis Ford Coppola's two *Palme D'ors* with the recently released *Amour* (Love, (2012)), or that the film is about 'death' as a suppressed reality of modern life. Again the indomitable shadow of the institution hovers. Love turns to hate, as virtues echo their dialectic opposite.

It is my belief that Haneke accounts for evil in an utterly modern guise; and like the Pastor he dwells on, considers evil without measure to be that which induces moral stupor. Dwelling on the cruelty of children and the manner in which the ability to harm others is inculcated, that Haneke is a filmmaker *after* the James Bulger affair has proven to be a fair claim. Like the poet Blake Morrisson, Haneke asks,

> "Another Why, another motive. Why does Why matter so much? Tout comprendre, c'est tout pardoner, that's why. To understand is to forgive. Or maybe not. In the preface to her book The Drama of Being a Child, the psychoanalyst and child abuse expert Alice Miller writes: "My own experience has taught me that the enactment of forgiveness–which, sixteen years ago, I still believed to be right–brings the therapeutic experience to a halt." Her words bring me to a halt. I see what she means: in therapy it's important not to block out feelings of anger. But what kind of a model is this for a whole family? Not forgiveness for parents who abuse, even they themselves were abused. Nor forgiveness for Susan and Neil Venables.....

No forgiveness since they've been judged to be adult murderers–for Robert and Jon" (Morrison: 1998; 239).

Without understanding, a dualist view of the world is all too enticing, comfortable even, as a proposition; a proposition I argued earlier tends to be a familiar safeguard when having to confront horrendous evil. Even the most liberal among us, and Haneke may well be one of these, will retreat into a customary and primitive dualism, when victimised. And so the quest to understand this, which can be read as an epitaph for the present study, compels us to ask Why? Because in the final instance, Why, as I believe Haneke reminds us, and as we will now explore in postcript form, is a starting point for thought. For understanding, as we will see, doesn't always fit the model we expect it to fit.

POSTSCRIPT

A CURIOUS KIND OF ELEPHANT

"In the Scriptures, St. Paul says that all of us in this life see through a glass darkly. So we must walk by faith, not by sight. We cannot lean on our own wisdom. None of this can be fully, satisfactorily explained to any of you, but you cannot lose your faith," Bill Clinton.

"Cinema has missed out on the opportunity it has, new in comparison with literature, to represent reality as a total sensory impression, to develop forms that maintain and even for the first time enable the necessary dialogue between a work of art and its recipient," Michael Haneke.

The initial research for this book began between 1999 and 2002, spurred by significant events on both a political and ethical stage. The first was the Columbine massacre, which made what had become a not so usual happening stateside a major talking point among liberals in Western Europe. Teenage boys, Eric Harris and Dylan Klebold, killed thirteen of their peers, injured twenty-four, and traumatised a nation in an attack, which scarily, *went wrong*. The boys had intended to bomb the school premises before picking off the retreating school kids; the victim count envisaged to reach the hundreds. Both Harris and Klebold had left ample warnings of their intentions on websites, written essays, and were even doing community service for previous crimes. Both believed they were at war; the images of them walking through the library in combat clothing, armed with sawn off shotguns, some of the most harrowing in recent years. In fact, the Columbine massacre, which aired live as soon as news of the initial killings began to break, has been publicly perceived as a failure of the authorities *and* a manifestation of *radical evil*. The nature of an attack in which two teenagers act as *one*, eventually killing themselves, was meticulously planned. This was no kneejerk response.

Media images of the shooters were everywhere. Yet they registered most with those who felt the weaponary allowing the massacre to be carried out in the way it was should never have been accessed. It seemed a no-brainer that behind such colossal acts was 'the system;' a system in which children were enabled in accessing such weapons. This was particularly true when the evidential comparisons between stateside and European gun-crime pointed so firmly in this direction. It wasn't that American schoolchildren were more prone to 'badness,' liberal intellectuals argued, but that laws allowing for the access of 'guns' were markedly slack. The constitutional statute that Americans should be allowed to defend themselves, stoutly defended by people like Charlton Heston, was challenged by liberals who saw in this a terrifying excess: everyone risked attack. But then, everyone was attacked. On September 11, 2001, terror came to America, in an event which, having marked Western political life since has overshadowed Columbine. The second colossal event, 9/11, saw interest in evil re-emerge. With newfound resurgence, it reappeared in everything from reality TV to foreign policy. If morality was needed to put Columbine in a wider societal context, beyond discussion of diminished levels of personal responsibility, 9/11 was a catalyst for it.

The threat of evil would help to shake the post 9/11 generation from the kind of indifference the Columbine shooters were considered representatives of. Suddenly, evil was externalised on a new enemy. For Dews, "the shock of evil is seen as bringing out a depth of commitment and sacrifice in human beings that the pervasive promotion of hedonism by the surrounding culture, and the tranquilizing, trivializing effects of the mass media, positively discourage" (Dews: 2008; 5). The War on Terror, with its call to arms against evil aggressors, came after Columbine. Two strands of debate on the topic of evil emerged from this: *radical evil* as a concept central to understanding state violence, and its counterpart in evangelical castigations of a resurgent evil, mitigated by the failure of personal responsibility.

Cinema and Evil addressed the context in which filmmakers took up these issues. It is therefore of little surprise that both these events had a strong impact on popular consciousness, filmmakers, artists, novelists, in the intervening years. Both events brought a renewed concern with evil into everyday discourse; whether in relation to terrorism set in a uniquely political context or the school shooter in a moral one. Just as the Bulger case had reignited debate about evil regarding young children, Columbine did the same for teenagers; especially as Harris and Klebold both came from relatively privileged middle-class backgrounds. Having set out to investigate filmmakers whose deliberation was also a response to significantly traumatic events (whether the Eichmann case, the U.S. State of Emergency, or James Bulger) it is not surprising the moral problematic of the shooter turns on film again to ask 'why.' Shooter films (the term used Stateside when discussing gun attacks by teenagers against teenagers), two of which will form the basis of the following discussion, constitute a subset if not a genre. In its global reach, the shooter phenomenon can be registered as a particularly abrasive confrontation with the Real; a concept which has been used–in its Lacanian treatment–to account for eruptions in the social fabric; which are, in their totality, irreducible to the symbolic terms on which this fabric rests. Far from an object with substantial or potentially knowable status, the Real, Bowie calls, "the traumatic event proper, which is as extrinsic to signification, as inassimilable to the pursuit of pleasure, as any foreign body encroaching upon the human organism" (Bowie: 1991; 103). Hence, even those predisposed to dismiss evil from a modern liberal position, end up reverting to the term in distress. And even when calling events evil, it is difficult to discern what is meant by evil in this regard. For evil can all too easily cover over the symbolic wound defined as trauma.

Gus Van Sant's *Elephant* (2003) is a case in point. Winner of the *Palme D'or* at Cannes, *Elephant* is a perceived eulogy to Columbine; a timely memorial for the victims of the event. The film is a work of formal innovation–fictionalising in the guise of truth–using (extreme) long takes to personalise the victims last hours. Van Sant's film, set in Watt High School, a fictional school in Portland Oregon, follows the schoolchildren who are the victims of the shooting that day. While Columbine is the obvious reference point, the film is fictional in all but name. *Elephant* is the second installment in Van Sant's 'death trilogy,' a trilogy in which each film deals with a particular American tragedy. Death is explored in particularly tragic terms in *Gerry* (2002), a film about a hiking tragedy that led to one friend murdering another, while *Last Days* (2005), the last film of the trilogy, concerns the days leading to a rock star's suicide; Kurt Cobain the model for the rock star. Like *Elephant*, real life tragedy is explored in fictional, 'real life' terms.

Drawing inspiration from the films of the Hungarian director Béla Tarr, along with Alan Clarke's short masterpiece about the Northern Ireland Troubles, also titled *Elephant* (1989), the film is characterised by its sequential looping affect, in which Van Sant's imagery offers the illusion of temporal progress. Sequences set around a particular character will appear to end, only for the camera to return to renew the trajectory of their day; in an opposing point-of-view. The film takes the form of chapters, each of which are dedicated to a particular character, or couple. Everyday encounters are central to the action. Yet each of these chapters, from which these temporal loops take form, bleed into one another, so that a sense of overlap and communality is felt. The film begins as the school opens and focuses in on a random group of students, ranging from the ordinary to the not so ordinary, from jocks to nerds. These characters are filmed in an unorthodox manner, tracking shots in and out of the school, in a flitting between without any logic as to why this flitting takes place. One of the chapters is given to Alex (Alex Frost) and Eric (Eric Deulen), the teenage shooters; another to Nathan (Nathan Tyson) and Carrie (Carrie Finklea); a romantic couple who are later attacked. No qualified distinction is made between the aggressors and victims and how they are treated. Both are filmed in an everyday, albeit poetic manner. Each is shown at school, going about the regular activities that constitute school life. The showing of *this* life, however, irregularly and aesthetically, differs significantly from other films of this type. If the school corridors constitute the spatial elements of the film's 'real,' the temporal element is felt in the time based there.

In an exploratory examination of cinematic spatio-temporality–in the context of the close-up–a certain coming to terms with, if that's the correct terminology in this instance, with the specificity of Van Sant's innovation can be discerned in Béla Balázs's theoretical writings on film. What Balázs has to say about the close-up is worth recalling,

> "The expression of an isolated face is a whole which is intelligible by itself. We have nothing to add to it by thought, nor have we anything to that which is of space or time. When a face that we have just seen in the middle of a crowd is detached from its surroundings, put into relief, it is as if we were suddenly face to face with it. Or furthermore if we have seen it before in a large room, we will no longer think of this when we scrutinise the face in close-up. For the expression of a face and the signification of this expression have no relation or connection with space. Faced with an isolated face, we do not perceive space. Our sensation of space is abolished" (Balázs: 1979; 59).

Balázs believes the abstracted face is severed from space when its contours take up the whole screen. Over-proximity absolves any notion of space associated with the face. Responding to Balázs, Gilles Deleuze maintains that the contours which take over the whole screen, "retain(s) the same power to tear the image away from spatio-temporal coordinates in order to call forth the pure affect as the expressed" (Deleuze: 1986; 96). The close-up affects by virtue of being abstracted from what comes after.

For this reason the horror genre finds particular value in the close-up. Depersonalisation is the proper word for how the close-up impacts on us. Now, Van Sant's strategy can be confronted as a technical variation of this technique. The looped sequences coalesce and bleed into the shooting scene. It is not that Van Sant wants to abstract his characters from the real, detaching them, but that he wants them embedded so that as victims they are memorialised in a properly ethical fashion. Van Sant doesn't want to diminish reality; he wants to heighten it. Therefore, pointers as to where the action is leading are accompanied by a sense of foreboding: feeling up-close.

Benny (Bennie Dixon), a vigilante who puts himself at risk in order to help others escape the massacre, is just one example. Benny is introduced when leading a girl to safety, helping her through a window but then strangely choosing not to follow. Instead, having turned towards the door of the classroom Benny starts to walk, in a kind of aimless fashion, the corridors, in what appears to be a search for more students. In lurching from corridor to corridor, he simply awaits his fate. He then stumbles upon Eric (Eric Deulen) dressed in army surplus–arguing with the schoolmaster, only to be brutally shot. Benny is profiled in much the same way as the others, with no suggestion given to explain why or how he came to be where he is: time alone is spent with Benny. On his watch, we await Benny's death.

Alex and Eric appear *in* scenes from the present and flash-forwards to the future; anchoring the viewer in the shooting before it unfolds; the loops converging on the massacre. Each victim is named against a black screen, from which singularity is marked significantly as the victims' time. If, in their differentiality, the teenagers are part of an educational structure, it is crucial the attackers are included. Only 'time' differentiates each victim. Michelle (Kristen Hicks), a 'nerd' of sorts struggling to integrate into Phys. Ed., is a pertinent example; her facial grimace a sign of nervousness around others. At no point is it inferred that Michelle has done anything, bullied or bullied others, as a reason for her death. *Elephant* may well be a dangerous film, but this is not because it comments on why victims like Michelle die. Nothing in particular–information wise–differentiates the shooters from the shot; other than perhaps their sexual orientation. If, not unlike *Benny's Video*, a cause is given for why the massacre unfolds, it is the killers' inability to differentiate between non-mediated realities–reality per se–and mediated reality which is most likely it. This 'cause' materialises, if there at all, when Alex plays piano while Eric a video game.

The camera slowly pans the bedroom, as the sound of Beethoven's *Für Elise* plays; leaving it unclear as to whether the origin of the music is diegetic or non-diegetic. As the camera pans left to right, the back of Alex is slowly brought into the frame, as we see his hands move along the piano. If there is certain elegance to the idea of a teenager so taken by one of the great cultural products of Western civilisation, it is given a swift comedown by Eric's vulgar exclamation, "that's awesome" (*Elephant*; 2003). Eric is embroiled in a video game, where shooting victims is the operative aim; as he lies on Alex's bed. Van Sant then cuts to a close-up of the shooter and victim on screen; the on-screen design evoking the later massacre. The key difference between the types that appear on screen, killed by the gamer and the real victims, is that the real victims have been presented up-close to the spectator; each personalised in their daily activities. If Van Sant procures a 'cause' in his explicit reference to gaming, against which the victims are invariably humanised, it is not surprising emotional problems this media generates are emphasised by this,

> "The development of global media, the expansion of the cultural industry and the 'spreading' of the Internet, have not only created new outlets for the discharge of excess energy in, for instance, video and computer games, in chat rooms or web logs, they have changed the perceptive and emotional threshold in the experience of such manifestation" (Mey: 2007; 56-57).

If 'gaming' is a cause, Van Sant would appear to be siding with liberals who position criminals like Alex and Eric as victims of the tragedy they execute; the former intelligent and artistically inclined; the latter subservient to his friend. The fact that 'first person shooter' computer games are used in military training, games such as *Doom* and *Quake*, serves to propel the myth that video games, like those shown in *Elephant*, are directly linked to the rise of school shootings. Part of the 'culture of fear,' the moral panic that accompanies this view was emphasised in Columbine; when the shooters appeared dressed like shooters in a military video game. If video gaming is presented as a possible cause of evil in *Elephant*, the killers can appear more human in contrast; with virtues of communality, loyalty and perhaps even love. The shower scene in which they embrace (after Eric puts away the game), which contrasts the sheer violence of the game, and kiss, is a sign of their humanity. The shower takes place just before the shooter identity is assumed, and is significant in that sexual and emotional expression, lacking in the game, are forwarded to explain the kids behaviour; a crucial factor being that neither adolescent has kissed before. Hence the signifier 'kiss' is pathologically aligned to the signifier 'kill.' It is not that sexual repression is pathological, although Van Sant gives ammunition to those with this conviction, but that these are kids lacking an emotional outlet for their curiosity; the lack of discharge for emotion altering their perception. Peter Bradshaw noted in *The Guardian*, that Alex and Eric act, "without any compunction, remorse, rage, bitterness or obvious emotion of any kind" (Bradshaw: 2003), yet the shower scene, far from depicting two kids unable to empathise, hints at the emotional problems experienced by them; the expression of their desire blocked at its roots. Desire is expressed only when social ties are about to sunder.

To Be (Evil) or Not to Be...

How then does Van Sant depict evil? Or indeed, is evil a category which can help account for Alex and Eric? If the intention was to explore a rampage of unprecedented carnage, it is not always 'clear,' certainly not in the sense that it is expressed in a didactic 'ethical' message, what this commentary entails. The film's 'danger' may well derive from the stance, or possibly lack of, taken on events of Columbine. But, whether a moral stance is taken on the massacre is a question central to understanding the film as an ethical response to Columbine. Are Alex and Eric evil (in a Manichean sense), predisposed to act in the way they do? Or is the film more accurately understood as a depiction of teenagers incapable of moral understanding as a category of human action? For Bradshaw, the answer is yes and no. On the one hand a curiously insensitive inquiry is found, "the idea of Europeans converting, or sponsoring the conversion of one of its most painful tragedies into highbrow fare on film or in print was intolerable. Van Sant's movie certainly declines to signal emotion or indemnify itself against charges of exploitation in the usual way" (Bradshaw; 2004). On the other is an insensitive rendering of tragedy, which, in drawing attention to the 'image,' masks the ethical merit. Taking this ethical view, I will argue that Van Sant's formally inventive film is not so much an aesthetic affront to tragedy, but production in which the ethical component (as response) is intrinsic to its aesthetic value.

So, this second assertion means that the moral and aesthetic, aligned, calls for clarity regarding the nature of this alignment. If a sense of the victims' experience is something Van Sant wants his audience to feel, opposed to the socio-cultural structuring of victims as 'types,' the nature of this sense experience needs to be explored. For it may be that American socio-culture, against which the film is possibly opposed, makes 'types' of victims. With this possibility, I will argue that an aesthetic purpose is felt not in poeticising the disturbing, domesticating the inadmissible Real, but allowing lives to be 'sensed' rather than explained. In other words, Van Sant doesn't explain what happened. Rather he wants us to 'sense' what it is like to be a victim: 'sense' the victim's plight. Even still, certain scenes, such as the one when Alex warns John (John Robinson), as he enters the building to begin the massacre (when bonds which haven't been properly severed are thus foreground) were seen to invest human qualities in the killers, while Alex's and Eric's depiction as boys capable of forgiveness brought charges of bias against Van Sant. Basically, Van Sant was seen to trivialise a national tragedy. Some critics found gestures to gaming..Nazism, 'causes' explored in the FBI report, made in relation to the massacre, yet believed no real answers for why this happened were offered.

Hence, if one was to take an extreme stance on *Elephant*, it is possible to argue that the moral point–that guns and firearms have become so accessible mindless murder is the inevitable result–isn't made at all. In fact, certain scenes set out to mark this point elicit dialectically opposed reactions. For it is very possible, indeed not wholly unlikely, that the evil in the film could be appreciated as a perverse homage to the killers; so that when Alex deliberates on who of Nathan or Carrie to shoot in the final scene, and the camera cuts to a shot of the clouds moving across the sky, it is possible to 'see' this as a metaphor for evil just as easily as a metaphor for irrational behaviour. As one critic remarked,

> "Which brings us back around to the question why? Why has the filmmaker made a film about kids being massacred at school by other kids? To show us it's a horrible thing? We already know it's a horrible thing. To show us what it looks like? We already know what it looks like all too well. I'll be honest: I'm not sure there isn't something unsavory about a picture made for no other purpose than to build suspense and anticipation toward something so monstrous. How much difference is there, after all, between the killers gazing at video images of human beings getting mowed down and a moviegoer buying a ticket, killing 70 minutes and then doing the same thing?" (Kisonak; 2004).

Kisonak echoes Morrison's verdict of the Bulger case in asking why? But the why he poses is not to do with the intentions behind the evil actions performed by Alex and Eric, evoking those of Harris and Klebold right down to the attire, nor is it do to with whether Alex and Eric are corrupted youth, overawed by deep-felt malevolence, but rather that confronting moral queasiness about teenage gun-crimes, the film ends up failing to commit to any particular stance, except immorally accentuating the autonomy in doing evil. Unlike, for example, Michael Moore's *Bowling for Columbine* (2002), in which the director-narrator's moral stance on Columbine requires equating firearm licensing with the shootings, Van Sant fails to push his point; so that Alex and Eric can appear misunderstood, taking revenge against their oppressors. In a massacre which cannot be thought of as anything other than an act of extreme evil, designed and planned, *Elephant*, on these terms, can be seen to glorify the teenagers' attack on their peers. Moral disclaimers for how we should respond to it would be expected. But because they are lacking, for Kisonak, the same strategies the film should critique are evoked: video culture and the mindless violence it exposes teenagers and children to.

Susan Sontag raises a similar point in relation to documentary photographs of extreme violence and their aspiration to be considered as art. "Transforming is what art does," Sontag writes but, "photography that bears witness to the calamitous and the reprehensible is much criticised if it seems "aesthetic;" that is, too much like art" (Sontag: 2003; 76-77). In this light, that Van Sant takes as his subject matter the "reprehensible" horror of Columbine, and re-enacts it to an almost meticulously exact degree, fictionalising the names of the aggressors and victims, and school, can be viewed as a transgressive violation of a common held law, one which Sontag states quite bluntly, "photographs that depict suffering shouldn't be beautiful" (Sontag: 2003; 76-77). When a painful reality is brought to bear in images of a somewhat poetic nature, significant moral issues are raised, such as are we better for seeing these. Or, as Sontag puts it, "do they (the images) actually teach us anything?" (Sontag: 2003; 92). For Kisonak, the answer is no. And the reason the answer is no is because Van Sant doesn't teach us anything about Columbine that the vast amount of documentary footage, the reams of television coverage, hasn't already told us.

Whether Van Sant positions his audience in such a way that they come away thinking, 'these kids are fucked up…but the reason they did what they did is based on x and y' is important; it impacts on another question; whether a clear rationale given for why Alex and Eric do what they do is important to the ethical value of the film. For the depiction of the massacre is repulsive and morally troublesome for the very reason that the students are killed without hesitation. It's as if the killers are compelled. But if repulsed by the callous murders, and indeed the murderers, yet transfixed by our experience of them, should this itself not disturb? Unless, that is, answers are given for why evil of this type exists. If Van Sant's intention, as some have argued, is to offer insight into the minds of the killers, in a way that only film can, this 'insight' can only accrue from us watching them watch TV, make jokes in the company of parents, or practice piano, or other general teenage 'stuff;' added to Alex's assertion, before they begin their killing spree, that the most important thing is to have fun. Because of this the information used to evaluate the state of mind of the killers, is minimum, to say the least. In other words, showing us the killing spree tells us evil exists. But is it enough?

Mary Devereaux's essay 'Beauty and Evil: The Case of Leni Riefenstahl's *Triumph of the Will*' is an intriguing exploration of the way in which beauty and evil coalesce in film and has been discussed in earlier sections of the book. Devereaux's interest, as stated, lies in the aesthetic classification of *Triumph of the Will* as a masterpiece given its disturbing content. The specifics of what makes Devereaux's a compelling argument have already been addressed, but suffice it to say that she sets out to reject the downplaying of Riefenstahl's disturbing 'vision' when attention alone to form is paid. Here, an exploration of what constitutes a documentary defined as propaganda is involved,

> "If *Triumph of the Will* shows that the Platonic tradition is wrong to identify beauty and goodness, it also provides support for the idea that the *unity* of beauty and goodness is a standard by which art should be measured. If good art must not only please the senses, but also engage and satisfy us intellectually and emotionally, then we are, I suggest, justified in criticizing *Triumph of the Will* for rendering something evil beautiful" (Devereaux in Levinson (ed): 1998; 250).

Devereaux believes *Triumph of the Will* is disturbing because it deifies Hitler, making him out to be an heroic figure with an organically procured value system; the natural outgrowth of progressive modernity. The events depicted in the film procure this vision. All the elements which documentarians point to as groundbreaking features of Riefenstahl's film are devised to present something we know to be historically evil as something which is divine. Now *Elephant* is not a documentary. Nor could it be argued *Elephant* is propaganda. As a film it fictionalises an evil event. Van Sant uses real people to re-imagine Columbine; the action of which takes place in a narrative building towards a crescendo of extreme evil. Yet if Van Sant uses mesmerising cinematography so that the viewer can experience the brutality of the shooting at the end, it cannot offer a significant reason for why this happens. Under the terms Devereaux employs, it is suspect for the precise reason that it is morally neutral on the events it depicts (and their closeness to real events). This is indeed objectionable. The film's characterisation–Van Sant refers to the teenagers as archetypes–fails to intellectually satisfy; that is, point to the reasons for such evil, in the way Devereaux speaks. As mentioned, cinematography is used to maximum effect, yet scant information about the lives it records is given. Elias, a wannabee photographer, flits on the margins; Nathan is a jock with the qualities of an archetype; Benny, at the end, is the archetypal hero who dies to save others. The psychological nature of the characterisation contrasts with mainstream film. In fact, the characterisation of a TV series like *The Sopranos* is an interesting contrast.

The series is built around a mafia don, Tony Soprano (James Goldolfini), striving to protect his biological-mafiosa family from harm: from endemic problems of post-industrial life. Identification is encouraged from the outset, whether through the psychiatric therapy Tony takes up in the first series with Doctor Melfi (Lorraine Bracco), or the family problems he endeavours to solve. Identifying with a morally complex character encourages the viewer to become emotionally involved, swayed by an essentially troubling subject. And as the characters, as critics have noted, can appear 'good' while caught in an 'evil' network, even though we know the network is evil we can end up rooting for the person ruling over it: Tony. In light of this, Emily Nussbaum's reference to the saving of Tony from his life of crime, which the series promises but never delivers, as 'the long con' is poignant. Redemption is itself deconstructed in incisions into the Tony-Melfi axis; doomed to moral failure. Melfi's ex-husband Richard (Richard Romanus) is penetrative in this, "man's a criminal Jennifer. And after a while, finally, you're going to get beyond psychotherapy, with its cheesy moral relativism, finally you're going to get to good and evil. And he's evil" (Chase; 2000-2006); his judgment one of many.

In *The Sopranos and Philosophy* (2004) dangerous fiction and the morality of identifying with characters like Tony is sufficiently explored. James Harold makes the point,

> "The problem with this sympathetic identification is that sometimes the character with whom we identify has thoughts and feelings that are morally reprehensible, and identifying with that character we risk being

infected by these vicious sentiments" (Harold in Greene and Vernezze (eds): 2004; 141).

Indeed, if sympathy for reprehensible characters is incited, this is most likely the case because the action isn't meant to harm for the sake of harm alone. Tony is a 'dangerous' character in that he shares virtues held as virtues by his TV audience; loyalty, a desire to see his kids well educated, generosity to the poor. As much as we want to believe these will save him, it is increasingly apparent as the show develops that therapy, the saving device, makes Tony more ruthless in execution. Tony's is a more pronounced evil the greater his therapy advances. Like Fritzl, Tony believes what he does is for the betterment of his family. But if believing this morally compromises our position, it could be the show elicits the dubious moral investments made by 'us' even in the realm of popular culture.

Now, given that we are in a position not to know enough about the characters to answer why they do what they do, is it morally suspect to call *Elephant* beautiful, in a simplistically formalist context, while, at the same time saying it is morally neutral. That is, the properties Kisonak finds morally objectionable in the film are explicitly aligned to the rendering of morally repulsive behaviour in aesthetically pleasing images; morally troubling events presented in a non-judgmental, spectacularised form. I will argue against this objection. But to do so, I reference the ideas explored when beginning this postscript. To not so audaciously argue that a morally neutral stance on Columbine is taken by Van Sant, I am taking account of the fact that the film can be 'seen,' irrespective of the director's intention, to memorialise victims in a way that could be perceived as a homage to the killers. Considering then, as some have done, the one-dimensional characterisation, lacking in depth, and generally subservient to a dazzling formal display of cinematography, it is important to remember that the film can be 'seen' in this way. Thus, rather than equate a shot of a teenage couple killed in cold blood with the aimless irrationality of cloud movement, as Van Sant's concluding montage encourages, the opposite is equally possible: evil is a cloud, and the good the sun which shines through.

It is possible that *Elephant* incites a morally ambiguous response. But if a moral defence is needed, I believe it can begin with the following claim: the value of *Elephant* lies in victim and victimiser, good and evil being equated with certain categories. In other words, what makes *Elephant* such a successful film morally, a key commentary on Columbine, is the reduction of aggressor and victim to the category of 'teenager' using significantly expansive and formal means. The 'teenager' is a differential rather than homogenous entity. Singularity distinguishes the characters. Van Sant has referred to the archetype: the jock, the nerd, the cheerleader, and the arty type, to differentiate teenagers. The 'jock' Nathan wears a lifeguard hoody, even though he is about to die. Elias is the quirky arty type who makes portrait photographs of his classmates; he captures life in process of dying. For Van Sant, these characters are part of a schema of archetypes which constitute the spectrum of teenage identities he remembers from his schooldays. While little information is given to form an opinion on them, little expression, this, coupled with the fact that amateur actors are used to play the part is crucial. Tracking shots bring us up-close to the characters, to reveal the archetypal teenagers in *their* fundamental difference. Van Sant positions us so as to empathise with the victim. In other words, Van Sant wants us to 'sense' the immanence of death from a nominal position: the position of the victim.

The film opens with John (John Robertson), a friend of Alex, as his drunken father drives him to school; a figure that reappears when the first bomb has exploded and the school is in flames. The camera cuts intermittently to John, walking through the school, disciplined by his teachers for being late, or a girlfriend inquiring into his wellbeing. Notably uncomfortable, he becomes significantly more distanced from his problems as he integrates into the daily life of the school. What makes him so teenagerly in his actions, nonetheless, is his difficulty expressing himself: his inability to explain how he feels. Time is the significant feature, the looping nature of which is the significant element of the film. It's not that Van Sant wants us to know his characters, invest in their problems, although this is not overlooked, it's that he wants his audience to invest in the story of what happened, all the more to 'sense' the gravity of the tragedy. For example, the chapter dedicated to John sees the popular student walking the grounds outside and then into the corridors, before he encounters Elias. Elias asks him if he can take his photograph. The moment is significant in that John then poses for a snap just as the point-of-view changes, almost imperceptibly back to Elias again. Later, Elias as 'character' is returned to as we find him leaving the dark room, before stumbling upon John again on the corridors. Elias's encounter with John is thus repeated. The same scene is now repeated from another point-of-view. In the zone and maze-like prism of the school, the 'sense' of being can be felt from the point-of-view of the victims. Hence, 'sensing' the victims' plight from their point-of-view allows the gravity of death to be felt.

Elephant was criticised for its failure to add to the debate as extending into all areas of American public life. Van Sant, his critics argued, failed to respond to the question of why the killers killed. In response, Van Sant has remarked, "I know it's in our interest to identify the reason why (Columbine happened) so we can feel safe..and feel we're not a part of it, that it's demonized, identified and controlled" (Van Sant: 2003). Hence, if focusing–in a very precise manner–on the massacre were all the film offered, the film would become more of an investigative documentary than the documentary artwork that it is. Rather than investigate evil on these terms, *Elephant*, I argue, memorialises the victims: and this, alarmingly, includes the perpetrators themselves. As *Elephant* ends, Eric has died, and Alex is deciding which of Nathan and Carrie to shoot first. It is only in drawing a parallel with Columbine, and there is no doubt we are encouraged to do so, can it be assumed Alex will also die. But with this assumption, we are left in the knowledge that nearly every teenager, will die. That is, almost every teenager we are experientially exposed to will die.

Van Sant has been attacked for failing to outline a cause for why this happens. Failing to take a clearly defined moral position on the murders, could, however paradoxical, be the moral position itself. That failing to explain why Columbine or murders like it happens is part of the ethical merit of *Elephant*. Perhaps the same title as the film which served as an inspiration for *Elephant*, Alan Clarke's 1989 exploration of the Northern Ireland Troubles, was used for this reason. In titling his film *Elephant*, Clarke was asserting that 'violence,' the subject matter for his film, was 'the elephant in the room,' the topic brushed over regarding the Troubles. Sectarianism, hatred, discrimination, the unnecessary use of violence, were talking points, but the question why people resort to violence at all was, for Clarke, the real issue. Now, if the moral purpose of *Elephant* is to memorialise the victims of Columbine, it is much more likely 'elephant' is a reference to elephants remembering traumas years after their passing. For critics like Sontag, who consider the efficacy of projects like Van Sant's, when images are closely modelled on real life trauma, the question of aestheticising such trauma is of pertinent moral concern. In other words, Sontag's concern is whether images like those in *Elephant* can actually hinder the emotional response necessary for working through the trauma on which those images are based; the film, in this case, aestheticising trauma. This is an important concern. For as I have sought to emphasise here, the memorialising properties of *Elephant* can be considered to be its *ethical* component; and the fact that *Elephant* has cathartic value as a work of art lies in the fact it memorialises the victims in a non-judgmental way. What I mean is that images have aesthetic value *because* of their ethical impact.

We can then finally assert that the film is a testament to memory; a testament to remembering as defined by healing. For it would be wrong to assert that the film is an inquest; the FBI had already conducted a relatively (un)successful one of these; and right to say it is a memorial to tragic death.

The Evil of Banality

Adorno's comments on banality and evil were quoted in the concluding chapter of *Cinema and Evil*. Arendt's commentary on the banality of evil was contrasted with Adorno's exploration of banality itself as a kind of evil; mediocrity, normality as a breeding ground for evil. A consciousness that adapts to 'the world as it is' is a consciousness conducive to evil. And so, the inertia identified with *things as they are*, is experientially impervious to difference. In the context of Van Sant's film, such an analysis rings loudly. If *Elephant* aesthetically consolidates the experiences of the victims to ethically counter the evil impacting upon them at the end, it has ethical merit.

Lionel Shriver's *We Need To Talk About Kevin* (2003) (and its film adaptation by Lynne Ramsay) can be confronted as a response to the problem of evil. In both a character/narrator, Eva Khatchadourian, reflects back on the past in the aftermath of her son's incarceration for a school massacre (akin to that of Columbine). This takes the form of letters to her murdered husband Franklin in the novel; Eva exploring their decision to procreate, and then the raising of their child: Kevin. In this sense at least, the book deliberates on nurture–nurturing a cold-blooded killer–and nature: beings genetically programmed as coldblooded psychopaths. Indeed, parallels with Shelley's *Frankenstein* are found in both style and content; Shriver exploring the birth of a monster; albeit in a child seemingly destined to become a criminal. The form is also similar to that pioneered by Shelley, in that written correspondences to Eva's husband, each of which address a specific instance before and after the massacre make up the content of the novel. Although the letters appear to be cathartic attempts to blame Kevin, with Eva's husband Franklin the addressee, the novel concludes with the formally unrepentant Kevin demonstrating a degree of humanity previously withheld. A degree of aspersion can then be cast on the content of letters; that is, the letters considered as truthful renditions of the past. The novel therefore draws our attention to what is true and what is not. There is a strong likelihood we will forget we are reading letters taken from Eva's point of view: not a factual rendering of the truth. Hence, we have to take events as *events as they are.*

The exploration of grief in *We Need To Talk About Kevin* complicates the attribution of blame in any concrete fashion. Just as Augustine set out to refute the idea that evil is a substance, Shriver's narrator could be said to do the same. Eva's attempt to make sense of a 'son' she never even wanted, is marred by a predilection to harm others she perceives in him from an early age. Kevin is blamed for all sorts of things in the letters, reading as a kind of Damian figure. The symbolic practice of writing therefore has Cathartic resonance; each letter a defence against the evil that has invaded Eva's life. Like a Perfect mumbling prayer, her letters help to stave off the evil of the world represented to her by her son. Yet, at the same time, Eva's blame is brushed over by Franklin as a paranoid projection. On the one hand is a son, who, prior to entering adulthood locks a group of schoolchildren in a school gym before picking them off with a bow and arrow. Kevin then reveals himself to the police, convinced of having committed his massacre with precision. Later, in his correction centre, he boasts of his massacre's success, specifically in relation to the perceived failure of the Columbine massacre. On the other hand is a mother, whose mothering skills, as she admits herself, are indeed morally questionable. Eva is a mother who 'finds'–according to the letters–in a meticulous devotion to the 'average' a teenager using evil to rise above it. Eva's letters are insightful and literary, probing and exacting. She looks at the history of the family with a precise need for understanding. She exacts moments with precision, and gets under the skin of her relationship with Franklin. Yet at the same, Eva is a mother doubting her son's moral fibre from an early age, doing little to confront it by way of intervention. If the concern expressed in the letters is truthful, why was Kevin not assessed in some form? After all, Eva and Franklin are middle-class, and professionals.

The problem of evil re-emerges as a significant concern of Western literature, from Milton to Dostoevsky, in *We Need To Talk About Kevin.*

Yet far from Kevin displaying powers and intelligence beyond the normal, which of course he does, the evil Eva identifes in Kevin is masked by all-prevailing mediocrity: a mask, no doubt, for his imperious wickedness. As if this wasn't enough to tweak our interest, the novel is also a profound exploration of grief. The truth of a grieving mother's testimony must be given some consideration. For it is possible the penning of letters to a dead husband allows Eva–in the process of course–to construct a mask for her guilt in cradling her son. The letters, with their sceptical tone, change course dramatically at the end. It is for this reason that the truth content of the letters is suddenly thrown into question. It is as if the 'present' suddenly intrudes on a past grief has distorted beyond recognition.

At the novel's end then, Eva writes about Kevin and his doubt as to why he killed. The memory of prior events is now muddied, and an ethical re-evaluation called for. Eva propositions Kevin "you killed eleven people. My husband. My daughter. Look me in the eye and tell me why?" and, surprisingly, her son responds with a display of emotion,

> "Unlike the day he turned to me through the police car window, pupils glinting, Kevin met my gaze this afternoon… "I used to think I knew," he said, glumly. "Now I'm not so sure"…… Without thinking I extended my hand across the table and clasped his. Does my gratitude seem odd? In fact, I'd harboured no preconception of what answer I wanted. I certainly had no interest in an explanation that reduced the ineffable enormity of what he had done to a pat sociological aphorism about "alienation" out of *Time* magazine or a cheap psychological construct like "attachment disorder" that his counsellors were always retailing at Claverack. So I was astonished to discover that his answer was word-perfect. For Kevin, progress was deconstruction. He would only begin to plumb his own depths by first finding himself unfathomable" (Shriver: 2003; 464).

Resisting the claims of his elders, Kevin is unsure why he killed. Yet, it's not that Eva's wounds are healed by not knowing. It's rather Kevin elicits an emotional response when saying this. And when he says this, the truth content of the letters, the pictures they've painted of Kevin, are cast in doubt. The letters had, as grief-ridden documents, considered all sorts of reasons for the massacre. Yet they had reached fever pitch when Eva writes of Kevin's teacher suggesting he rebels in doing what he's told. Eva responds in stating he has a privileged background, only to be told,

> ""Maybe that's what he's angry about….Maybe he's mad that this is as good as it gets. Your big house. His good school. I think it's very difficult for kids these days, in a way. The country's very prosperity has become a burden, a dead end. Everything works, doesn't it? At least if you're white

and middle class. So it must often seem to young people that they're not needed. In a sense, it's as if there's nothing more to do"'" (Shriver; 2003: 391).

In Eva's letters, a certain image of 'Kevin' emerges; that of a teenage boy distinctly average at whatever he turns his attention to. Yet this masks that he is something other than average. Concrete issues are raised in the letters, around school shootings; reasons deliberated on as such. If a nation's intellectuals–Francis Fukuyama an obvious reference point–are heralding the 'end of history,' is it a surprise that an experience of vacuity, of nothing left to strive for is the dominant one. Hence 'alienation,' far from a suitable means for understanding the shooter, actually appears as a diversion from it. These kids are over-integrated. In his analysis of the Columbine massacre, Paul Cullen helps contextualise moral debates about the shooter (in relation to Eva's memory). A reporter at the time of the massacre Cullen went on to spend ten years researching the event. His study, addressing the tragedy in multiple contexts, debunks the myth that the shooters, Klebold and Harris, were 'alienated' from their peers. Indeed, Cullen emphasises the killers' wide circle of friends, and their participating in regular activities. As with Cullen, one could argue the shooters, in essence, weren't alienated at all; exposed to less affluent others. Like Kevin's teacher says, they hated the very thing enabling their comfort living. In other words, they came to hate the banality of their surroundings.

In Eva's judgment, Kevin's distinction is defined by banality; a considered mask for devilish intent. He is average if well-integrated at school; nothing suggests that he is an 'outsider.' His all-round mediocrity is what disturbs. Eva remembers a teenager planning his attack with precision, right down to using an archery kit instead of a gun, and talks about Kevin's disturbing desire to dispel the argument, in advance, that the shooter problem can be discerned as the perverse effect of perverse gun-licensing laws. In Eva's opinion, in planning his massacre, Kevin wages war on banality he has to adjust to. It is crucial within the context of the letters, until the end changes things dramatically, that 'Kevin' talks incessantly about not wanting to be classified a teenager who was able to access weapons; rather he wants to be classified as evil. A teenager emerges in the letters who wants to rise above the banal; wants to insert himself into history. This 'incision' will disable reasons–other than evil–to explain his behaviour. The specialists, who rationalise on his behaviour in uniquely psychological terms, have their conceptualisations negated in advance. Only evil can suffice. Yet, all of this is put into question at the end: the tone of the letters change dramatically. As the letters advance,

Eva writes about meeting Kevin, and we are suddenly faced with the fact that as much as would like to blame Kevin, call him evil, this is the easy thing to do. The difficult thing to do is to see the humanity in Kevin.

Scottish filmmaker Lynne Ramsay's adaptation of Shriver's novel is a highly original interpretation of the novel's 'vision,' altering the focus yet remaining true to the pivotal concerns of the novel. Ramsay's stated influences lie in the European art-house tradition of Bergman, Fassbinder, Bresson etc., with an affinity for the realism of independent British cinema. From her early shorts, to her award-winning debut feature *Ratcatcher* (1999), to *Kevin* (2011), a significant style of filmmaking has been forged by the starkly independent Scot. *Ratcatcher* is a particular example of this. Much of the genre traits of Social Realism–poverty, the working classes, the marginalised city spaces–are rendered afresh; while a signature style, considered by the guardians of realism to run counter to realism itself, is evident.

Advancing the intricacies of the moving image as a form of art, while delving into a Social Realist tradition in which film is considered utterly removed from art, Ramsay's offering has an era-defining status; exploring the possibilities of the moving image. *Morvern Callar* (2002) is an interesting follow up; an adaptation of Alan Warner's novel of the same name. When the working class Callar (Samantha Morton) finds her boyfriend dead on Christmas morning, having left behind an unpublished novel, rather than call the authorities, she presents the novel as her own and sends it to a publisher, before doing away with the body of her boyfriend. Callar's strange decision to do what she does is never deliberated on in the film, and there is no psychological explanation given. Instead, the film serves as a journey, a kind of movement between trauma and the reaction to it. Susan Sontag said of Robert Bresson, that his films replace the psychology of action with the physiology of movement, and Ramsay takes this difference as a starting point. Callar intrigues, not because she has multiple reasons to explain her behaviour but because, and the style of the film–its long dialogue free passages, the physiology and languid expressions, the semiotics of emotion–calls on the imagination of the spectator to rationalise Callar's acts. On the face of it, her reaction to her boyfriend's death smacks of immoralism, cashing in on the death of her lover; using death for financial gain. Yet there is something about this verdict which doesn't quite fit; and in not fitting we are asked to consider why. For in moments, like when Callar momentarily lies with the body, as the Xmas lights flash, the complexity of human existence, and the fact that decisions don't always make sense, comes crashing home. We might not come to 'know' Callar, or what makes her tick. But this is not important. What is important, irrespective of the moral decision we make, is the realisation that grief, like the place where Callar receives her advance, is a foreign country; a point of correspondence between Ramsay's interest here and in *Kevin*.

After a number of years working on an adaptation of Alice Sebold's bestselling novel *The Lovely Bones* (2002), Ramsay returned with aplomb with another, *We Need to Talk About Kevin*. Ramsay's *Kevin* has, in its contortion of bright colour, the forebodingness of a William Eggleston photograph. But is also has the characteristic emptiness of a Wes Anderson comedy. Yet the film maintains a pictorial quality found in few films of its kind. It is, however, as much about family dysfunction as it is the school shooter phenomenon. Like the novel, the charades families perform concealing their dysfunction is explored regarding Eva's (Tilda Swinton) specific recollection of events, "I actually wanted to call the film 'Performance.' That's what it's essentially about–façade and performance. The dad is looking away, the mum is not quite there, and the son is playing them against each other. It's the essential family drama taken to terrible extremes" (Ramsay in O'Hagan: 2011). In Ramsay's adaptation of the novel the problematic nature of memory is foreground. Objective memory, the idea of remembering things as they actually happened, is set in contrast to the subjective, remembering things 'our' way. Rich imagery is therefore crucial. The possibility Eva's grievance subtly distorts the past is set against the possibility the signs of psychopathology in her son are recalled. Ramsay's Eva is a narrator like Haneke's in *The White Ribbon*, fixated on a 'past.'

In Ramsay's *Kevin* the structural features are altered, the letter writing hardly noticeable, but what underpins them is maintained: memory. 'Visions' intrude on Eva's present. From one instrusive vision to the next, a traumatic memory unfolds in its furious impact. The opening sequence of the film is an example of this. It begins with an overhead shot of a semi-naked crowd during a Spanish tomato festival, before a crowd knee-deep in tomato juice can be discerned. In what gradually emerges as a kind of dream displacement for the 'bloodbath' she was witness to, Eva is lifted above the head of the crowd, closing her eyes, as (the hue of) the colour red assumes a hypnotic presence. The all-prevailing 'blood' on the screen cuts to a curtain, intimating that Eva has just awoken. Her dream of being lifted above the tomato juice is an unconscious response to the bloodbath her son is responsible for.

Though emphasis on writing is such a strong feature of the novel, the obvious lack of dialogue in the first twenty minutes of the film is significant. This is a very different aesthetic experience. In addition, the remembering process takes the form of the letters to Franklin (John C. O'Reilly) in the novel, while composite images of Kevin's youth are central to the film; from his time as a child intent on exposing his mother's fraudulence, to his adolescence when no attempt is made to conceal his masturbation from her–enticing her even–to a Robin Hood fixation which enables him to kill his family and school peers. In the midst of the massacre, for example, Kevin is shown walking around the locked gymnasium. He then takes a bow from the stage: the massacre performed in the precise manner he envisaged. If the scene is considered as a 'set of images,' their truth status is nonetheless problematic. Kevin's being alone in the gymnasium (with his victims) is important. It means Eva couldn't have been present; couldn't have remembered it. It is likely such 'images' are generated by an Eva wanting 'to see' things. For Eva is a woman with a 'past.'

Kevin is not just a film about evil. It is also a commentary on imagery. It explores memory as imagery. With subjective images *seemingly* and *perhaps* retrospectively projected onto Kevin, it is distinctly possible the monster Eva wants to find is fashioned: her memories are tainted by grief. What we have to realise, and this is integral to the film, is that Eva is crippled emotionally, shocked to the point that when a sexual advance is made at a work party she is unable to process it: her ability to connect emotionally with other human beings has been completely eroded. Hence, if Eva remembers 'objective' instants, those which might have warned her, the tension between both forms of memory is felt. In a particular instance of this, and a suitable example of the tension concerned, Kevin sits at the breakfast table. He asks Celia (Ashley Gerasimovich) for a root beer before teasing her with a vacuum cleaner he calls a 'vacuum monster.' There is no doubt Kevin frightens his sister, but Eva's gaze towards her son, is clearly at odds with the severity of his actions. It is indicative of her difficulty around children but also a moment when she 'sees' or wants to 'see' the badness in Kevin. The camera cuts to Eva outside a bathroom, listening to grunting, before intruding on Kevin masturbating. Instead of ceasing, Kevin quickens his actions. He stares at his mother; enticing her judgment.

Assessing these scenes, as objective content, requires a child no amount of nurture could alter for the better being confronted. Hence Eva attributes blame to him. Kevin, in this respect, is evil, punishing his mother for bringing him into the world. The androgynous Ezra Miller, smiling in his tight fitting t-shirts, cranks up the challenge to semiotically decode the images he appears in. It is interesting then that Ramsay researched the area of psychopathology, considering the lack of empathy Kevin 'appears' to have, for it is generally held that psychopathic traits can be identified in children from an early age. Dave Cullen has addressed the issue in relation to Columbine,

> "Symptoms appear so early, and so often in stable homes, so that the condition seems to be inborn. Most parents report having been aware of disturbing signs before the child entered kindergarten…a five-year-old girl repeatedly attempting to flush her kitten down the toilet. "I caught her just as she was about to try again," the mother said… when the woman told her husband, the girl calmly denied the whole thing. Shame did not register; neither did fear. Psychopaths are not individuals losing touch with their emotions. They never developed them from the start" (Cullen: 2009; 241-242).

Cullen's is an interesting insight into retrospective diagnoses of Columbine murderer Eric Harris as a textbook aggressive psychopath, hell-bent on destroying those he felt markedly superior to. Like Kevin, Harris came from a white middle-class background, although two years older when he committed his crimes. The fact that he had been criminally profiled, and left a list of clues of what he was going to do, sent shockwaves to the U.S. public. Here was a young adult, like Kevin, who had a criminal record, openly stating on his website that he wanted to commit mass murder. The event saw hysteria grip the U.S. public. Not only were the police seen to be incapable of reigning in juvenile psychopaths, schools were considered breeding grounds for evil. Harris's psychological profile suggested his actions were in some ways determined by evil: that he was destined to become a killer. For the FBI, along with a team of America's most high-profile psychologists, Harris was a textbook psychopath: committed to killing those believed to be inferior. If Harris went to war with banality, not unlike Kevin, it wasn't because he believed it was evil, but believed himself so. With this, the debate about psychopathological evil, or the absolute personality trait of the psychopath, reigned. The idea that humans are hard-wired biologically, that is neurologically, to commit horrendous evil acts cuts right into the debate about psychopathology as manifesting evil. In this light, many of the concepts discussed so far, from the banality of evil found, to the self-love elicited by the paedophiliac Doctor in *The*

White Ribbon, can be discerned in the infamous checklist devised by Canadian criminiologist Robert Hare, to ascertain whether a criminal is a psychopath.

We Need to Talk About Kevin leaves it open as to whether Eva is identifying the psychopathological in her selected memories of her son. Yet, what makes the film so crucially ambiguous, challenging even, is the inconclusive nature of the flashbacks. Looking back in anger, Eva may well find what she needs to find. This is the subjective position. Yet, why she doesn't bring her son to a specialist to alleviate doubt accrues in the mind of the viewer as an objective one; doubts also arising as to why Kevin warrants such suspicion from Eva yet little from Franklin. It may be that Eva sees her son as evil: past incidents pointing to an inherent badness: Kevin blinding his sister, taunting his mother by masturbating in front of her examples of this; yet this remains definitively inconclusive. It is important to note, given the tension between the subjective and objective viewpoint, that Kevin taunts his mother on her visits to his detention centre in the novel, when he justifies his crime in relation to Columbine, but appears incarcerated for the first time at the end of Ramsay's film. Little room is given to Kevin (in the present) until this final scene. The film differs by withholding Kevin's presence in the present until the end. While Eva talks about Kevin's incarceration, and specifically comments on Kevin after the massacre in the novel, Ramsay's 'vision' alters this by ending in the present. Hence, Ramsay's adaption, as I will argue in conclusion, is filmic in its method. It uses the visual, in this case the dramatics and semiotics of the face, as its primary ethical tool. Eva, of course, is crucial to this 'vision.' When she visits Kevin for the first time in the film he is in the process of being transferred to adult prison. Like in the novel, she simply asks why.

The piecing together of fragments either remembered correctly or fabricated to enable the grieving process to be resolved is required to get to this point. If the reasons Eva stays in the area are unclear, we are never given an indication why. Her moral support for her son is hinted at. Eva's support, unlike the expression of this in the novel, is withheld. Reasons for why she remains in the community where the massacre took place remain unanswered. For, it is now two years since Eva drove to the crime scene only to return home and find her husband and daughter dead. As the film concludes, and she is seen visiting Kevin for the first time, she propositions him to answer 'why.' At this point, however, as she gazes intently, he fails to return her gaze. She then teases him about moving to 'big school;'

referring to adult prison; and in doing so attempts to elicit a response from a boy the film has encouraged us to suspect will show little remorse. Crucially, however, Eva sits at the table and stares, asking "want you to tell me why?" Kevin is hesitant and trembles for over ten seconds in silence. He then responds, "I used to think I knew....now I'm not so sure." The camera cuts to Eva. Just as Kevin qualifies his remark, he is told his time is up, and stands up. His mother does so also, and embraces him. Shriver's Kevin's behaviour is set out in a series of reflections; consistent with the psychopathological tendencies Eva recalls to her husband regarding his youth (his collection of computer viruses just one example of these tendencies); but Kevin appears *present* only at the end of the film. With his visibly shaken demeanour, he is less abrasive than we are led to believe. The real, if this is what the end unveils, jars with the real of memory.

Ramsay has made numerous references to the influence Robert Bresson's *Notes of the Cinematographer* (1975), the aphoristic reflections he made on his practice as a filmmaker, have had on how she films. In the section 'On Automatism' from the text Bresson reflected, "a sigh, a silence, a word, a sentence, a din, a hand, the whole of your model, his face, in repose, in movement, in profile, full face, an immense view, a restricted space....Each thing exactly in its place" (Bresson: 1975; 36). In the 'restricted space,' in this case the jail–like the jail at the end of Bresson's *Pickpocket*–Kevin's face can assume such an 'immense' status, one which, when coupled with a sentence, leaves a lasting impression. The "sigh," the "silence," the "sentence" fall into place, leaving the face of a criminal to linger "in profile."

The face is ethically procured for a reason. It relates to the judgment on evil; that is, considering Kevin as evil. It might be said that Eva nourishes this judgment. But now Eva has failed to make this judgment herself. Her expression changes as she looks upon her son. Indeed, the son's face, with its sorrowful gaze and tilted head, is marked by newfound humility. Like the ethical demand Emmanuel Levinas finds in the 'face to face' encounter with an Other, *quo* Van Sant's profiling of teenagerly faces, the ethical *quo* Other, as 'sensed' by Eva is sensed in the face of a 'man,'

> "There is here a relation not with a very great resistance, but with something absolutely *other*: the resistance of what has no resistance–the ethical resistance. The epiphany of the face brings forth the possibility of gauging the infinity of the temptation to murder, not only as a temptation to total destruction, but also to the purely ethical impossibility of this

temptation and attempt.....The epiphany of the face is ethical" (Levinas: 2000; 199).

We are now able to consider the ending in more pertinent ethical terms. Kevin stares at his mother, and his mother returns his gaze. The camera cuts from one face to the other, the scene ending as both embrace. Two faces come together under the watching gaze of the officer. The absolute destruction of others, as envisaged by the shooter, is structurally *impossible*, with the face the signal for this. As Levinas states, the infinite power of ethics is dialectically opposed to a "murder" marked by that which "paralyses the very power of power" (Levinas: 2000; 198). Murder's impact has all but squashed Eva's will; torn by the horror that preceded her grief. But now the words "I'm not so sure" issue from her son's trembling mouth, the camera fixed on facial gesture. A mouth stuttering, "I'm not so sure" (*We Need To Talk About Kevin*; 2011) illustrates the resistance Levinas speaks of and the face in which it resides. This is a Kevin who thought he had planned the perfect crime, yet its *impossibility,* fundamental to ethics, has become apparent to him.

Ramsay's ending lacks dramatic intent. There is no revelation of truth: we cannot know if Kevin really changes. Yet the face is a *sign* of potential drama and change. It may well be that Kevin's rehabiliation is hinted at in this seductive ending, and that the image encourages a forgiveness previously unthinkable; a moral position also taken by Simon Baron-Cohen, a leading researcher on human empathy. Baron-Cohen's expressed views tally with an ending encouraging forgiveness. When discussing the rehabilitation of those who partake in an extreme evil, Baron-Cohen notes,

> "My own view is that we should do this–no matter how bad their crime. It is the only way we can establish that we are showing empathy to the perpetrator, not just repeating the crime of turning the perpetator into an object, and thus dehumanising them. To do that renders us no better than the person we punish" (Baron-Cohen: 2012; 125).

Eva's impulse in writing such a frenzy of letters, may have its origins in the need to objectify Kevin, an object she can then distance herself from. Yet she fails in doing so. As Baron-Cohen says, this would make her position no less morally questionable than the person she seeks to objectify. By not doing this, emphasised in the face and the hug, significant Western tropes, Eva eventually finds a subject where she would have found an object. As such, Kevin is removed from her grasp as a man.

We can now end this postscript by stating that responses to Columbine *Elephant* and *We Need To Talk About Kevin* insist on bringing us up-close to the subject; the faces of whom serve as the quintessential point of reference. The manner in which both films achieves this differs in ways the current postscript has merely delved into; but in both cases the aesthetic heightens the ethical issue it depicts, the first by serving as a kind of fictional memory of the victims and their time, a moving image testimony to those who died, the second taking the problematic status of a memory and making it subservient to the primordial ethical relation as the ethical. Suffice it to say that the trauma of Columbine, and indeed, the bind it has on us, is uniquely deliberated on; to the extent that as viewers the problem of evil is felt to be everybody's problem.

BIBLIOGRAPHY

Adams, Jeffrey. 2002. Orson Welles's *The Trial*: film noir and the Kafkaesque. *College Literature* 29 (3) (2002): 140-157.

Adorno, T.W. Else Frenkel-Brunswik, Daniel J. Levinson and R. Nevitt Sanford. *The Authoritarian Personality* (New York: Norton Library, 1950).

Adorno, Theodore and Max Horkheimer, trans. John Cumming. *Dialectic of Enlightenment*, (New York: Seabury Press, 1972).

Alighieri, Dante, *Cantica I: Hell (L'Inferno)*, ed. Dorothy L. Sayers, (London: Penguin Books, 1949).

Allen, Beverly, ed. *Pier Paolo Pasolini: The Poetics of Heresy* (Georgia: Amni Libra, 1993).

Allen, Graham. *Intertextuality*, (London: Routledge, 2000).

Allison, Henry. E. *Idealism and Freedom*, (London: Cambridge University Press, 1996).

Andrew, Geoff. Michael Haneke: *The White Ribbon* interview. *Sight and Sound*, 244 (2009).

Apter, Michael. *Danger: Our Quest for Excitement*, (Glasgow: One World Publications, 2007)

Aquinas, Thomas. *Selected Writings*, ed. Ralph McInerney, (Harmondsworth: Penguin, 1998).

Arendt, Hannah. 'Nightmare and Flight:' *Essays in Understanding, 1930-1954*, ed. J. Kohn, (New York: Harcourt Brace, 1994).

—. "Eichmann in Jerusalem: An Exchange of Letters between Gershom Sholem and Hannah Arendt" in The Jew as Pariah, ed. R.H Feldman, (New York: Grove Press, 1978).

—. Eichmann in Jerusalem: A Report on the Banality of Evi,l (New York: Viking Press, 1964).

—. *Hannah Arendt/ Karl Jaspers. Correspondence 1926-1969*, ed. Lotte Kohler and Hans Saner, (New York: Harcourt Brace Jovanovich, 1992).

—. *The Human Condition*, (Chicago: University of Chicago Press, 1958).

—. *The Origins of Totalitarianism*, (London: Harvest\ HBJ, 1973).

Augustine. *City of God,* trans. Henry Bettenston, (Harmondsworth: Penguin, 1984).

—. *Confessions,* trans. R.S. Pine-Coffin, (Harmondsworth: Penguin, 1961).

—. *On Free Choice of the Will*, trans. Thomas Williams, (London: Hackett Publishing, 1993).

—. *Patrologia Latina*, (J.P. Maguire: Paris, 1844-64).

Badiou, Alain. *St. Paul: The Foundation of Universalism*, trans. Ray Brassier, (California: Standford University Press, 2003).

Baker, Houston A., Manthia Diawara and Ruth H. Lindeborg, eds. *Black British Cultural Studies: A Reader*, (Chicago: University of Chicago, 1996).

Balázs, Béla. *Le Cinéma: nature et evolution d'un art noveau*, trans. Jacques Chav, (Paris: Payot, 1979).

Barber, Malcolm. *The Cathars: Dualist Heretics in Languedoc in the High Middle Ages*, (London: Longman, 2000).

Barber, Stephen. *Projected Cities: Cinema and Urban Space*, (London: Reaktion Books, 2002).

Baron-Cohen, Simon. *Zero Degrees of Empathy: A New Theory of Human Cruelty and Kindness*, (London: Penguin, 2012).

Bataille, Georges. *Literature and Evil*, trans. Alastair Hamilton, (London: Marion Boyars Publishing Ltd, 1973).

—. *The Accursed Share Vol. 2*, trans. Robert Hurley, (New York: Zone Books, 1991).

—. *Visions of Excess: Selected Writings, 1927-1939*, trans. by Alan Stoekl, (Minneapolis: University of Minnesota Press, 1985).

Bazin, André. "Fellini's Voyage to the End of Neorealism" in *What is Cinema? Vol. 2*, trans. Hugh Gray, (London: University of California Press, 1967).

—. *Orson Welles: A Critical Review*, (London: Elm Tree Books, 1978).

—. *What is Cinema? Vol. I*, trans. Hugh Gray, (London: University of California Press, 1967).

Benjamin, Walter. *Illuminations*, ed. Hannah Arendt and trans. Harry Zorn, (London: Pimlico, 1999).

—. *The Origin of German Tragic Drama*, trans. John Osbourne, (London: Verso, 1977).

Bernstein, Richard J. *Radical Evil: A Philosophical Interrogation,* (London: Polity Press, 2002).

Bhabha, Homi. The other question: the stereotype and colonial discourse. *Screen* Vol. 24 (1) (1983): 7-32.

Blanchot, Maurice. *The Infinite Conversation*, trans. Susan Hanson, (Minneapolis: University of Minnesota Press, 1993).

Bondanella, Peter. *Italian Cinema: From Neo-Realism to the Present*, (New York: Frederick Ungar, 1983).

Borde, Raymond and Étienne Chaumeton. *Panorama du Film Noir Américain*, (Paris: Flammarion, 1955).

Bowie, Malcolm. *Lacan*, (London: Fontana Press, 1991).

Bradshaw, Peter. "Elephant: Review" in *The Guardian*, 2004, Friday 30.

Brady, Frank. *Citizen Welles: A Biography of Orson Welles*, (New York: Charles Scribners Sons, 1989).

Bresson, Robert. *Notes on the Cinematographer*, trans. Jonathan Griffin, (Los Angeles: Green Integer Books, 1997).

Brooker, Peter, ed. *Modernism/ Postmodernism*, (London & New York: Longman, 1992).

Brooks, Peter. *The Melodramatic Imagination: Balzac, Henry James, Melodrama and the Mode of Excess*, (New York: Columbia University Press, 1985).

Brown, Norman O. *Of Life Against Death*, (Connecticut: Wesleyan University Press, 1969).

Brunette, Peter. *Michael Haneke*, (Urbana and Chicago: University of Illinois Press, 2010).

—. *Roberto Rossellini*, (New York: Oxford University Press, 1987).

Butler, Judith. *Bodies that Matter: On the Discursive Limits of "Sex,"* (London: Routledge, 1993).

—. *Gender Trouble: Feminism and the Subversion of Identity*, (London: Routledge 1997).

—. *Subjects of Desire: Hegelian Reflections in Twentieth-Century France*, (New York: Columbia University Press, 1999).

Caputo, John D. *Against Ethics: A Contribution to a Poetics of Obligation with Constant Reference to Deconstruction*, (Indiana: Indiana University Press, 1993).

Cartwright, Lisa. "Emergencies of survival:" moral spectatorship and the 'new vision of the child' in postwar child psychoanalysis. *Journal of Visual Culture*, Vol. 3 (1) (2004): 35-49.

Cashell, Kieran. *Aftershock: The Ethics of Contemporary Transgressive Art,* (London: IB Tauris, 2009).

Cavell, Stanley. *Must We Mean What We Say?: A Book of Essays*, (London: Cambridge University Press, 1979).

—. *Philosophy the Day After Tomorrow*, (Boston: Harvard University Press, 2005).

Chesterton, Gilbert Keith. *Orthodoxy*, (Ignatius Press: San Francisco, 1995).

Coates, Paul. *The Gorgon's Gaze: German Cinema, Expressionism, and the Image of Horror*, (Cambridge: Cambridge University Press, 1991).

Cohn, Norman. *Europe's Inner Demons*, (Granada: Sussex University Press, 1976).

Conrad, Peter. *Modern Times, Modern Places*: *How Life and Art Were Transformed in a Century of Revolution, Innovation and Radical Change*, (London: Thames and Hudson, 1998).

Copjec, Joan, ed. *Shades of Noir*, (London: Verso, 1993).

Copjec, Joan, ed. "Sex and the Euthanasia of Reason" in *Supposing the Subject*, (New York: Verso, 1994a).

Copjec, Joan, ed. *Radical Evil*, (New York: Verso, 1999).

Copjec, Joan. *Imagine There's No Woman: Ethics and Sublimation*, (Boston: MIT Press, 2002).

—. *Read My Desire: Lacan Against the Historicists,* (Boston: MIT Press, 1994b).

Crary, Alice. *Beyond Moral Judgment*, (London: Harvard University Press, 2006).

Critchley, Simon. Das Ding: Lacan and Levinas. *Research in Phenomenology*, 28 (1998): 72-90.

Cullen, Paul. *Columbine*, (New York: Hatchett Book Group, 2009).

Dadoun, Roger. *Metropolis: mother-city-mittler-Hitler*, trans. Arthur Goldhammer. *Camera Obscura* 15 (1986): 137-163.

De Lauretis, Teresa. Cavani's 'Night Porter': a woman's film. *Film Quarterly* 30, (1976): 35-38.

—. Language, representation, practice: rereading Pasolini's essays on cinema. *Italian Quarterly* 20-21 (1981): 81-125.

Deleuze, Giles and Felix Guattari. *Anti-Oedipus: Capitalism and Schizophenia Vol. 1*, trans. R. Hurley (London: Athlone Press, 1984).

Deleuze, Gilles, 1986. *Cinema 1: The Movement Image*, trans. Hugh Tomlinson and Barbara Habberjam, (London: Athlone).

—. *Francis Bacon: The Logic of Sensation*, trans. Daniel W. Smith, (London: Continuum Press, 2004).

—. *Kant's Critical Philosophy: The Doctrine of the Faculties*, trans. Hugh Tomlinson and Barbara, (Habberjam London: The Athlone Press, 1995).

—. *Masochism: Coldness and Cruelty*, trans. Jean McNeil, (New York: Zone Books, 1989).

Derrida, Jacques. *Aporias*, trans. Thomas Dutoit, (Stanford: Stanford University Press, 1993).

—. *Mémoires: for Paul de Man*, trans. Cecile Lindsay, Jonathan Cutter and Eduardo Cadava, (New York: Columbia University Press, 1986).

Dews, Peter. *The Idea of Evil*, (London: Blackwell Publishers, 2008).

Dimendberg, Edward. From Berlin to bunker hill: urban space, late modernity and film noir in Fritz Lang and Joseph Losey's *M. Wide Angle* 9(4) (1997): 62-93.

Dobranski, Stephen B. and John P. Rumrich, eds. *Milton and Heresy*, (Cambridge: Cambridge University Press, 1998).

Docherty, Thomas, ed. *Postmodernism: A Reader*, (London: Harvester Wheatsheaf, 1993).

Eagleton, Terry. *The Eagleton Reader*, ed. Stephen Regan, (London: Blackwell Press, 1997).

Ebert, Robert. "The Gospel According to St. Mathew" in *The Sun Times*. 2004.

—. "The Night Porter" in *The Sun Times*. 1975.

Edwards, Karen and Keith Reader. *The Papin Sisters*, (Oxford: Oxford University Press, 2001).

Elsaesser, Thomas. "Tales of Sound and Fury: Observations on the Family Melodrama," in eds. Gerald Mast, Marshal Cohen and Leo Braudy, *Film Theory and Criticism*, 512-35, (New York: Oxford University, 1992).

—. *New German Cinema: A History*, (London: Palgrave Macmillan, 1989).

Emily Nussbaum. "The Long Con" in *New Yorker*. 2007, July 14.

Ezra, Elizabeth and Jane Sillars. *Hidden* in plain sight: bringing terror home. *Screen* 48 (2) (2007): 215-221.

Farrel, James T. The problem of public sensibility: a review of the film, *The Open, City. October* 128 (2009): 69-83.

Fellini, Federico. *Fellini on Fellini*, trans. Isabel Quigley, (New York: De Capo Press, 1996).

Fish, Stanley. *Surprised by Sin*, (London: Macmillan, 1997).

Forsyth, Neil. *The Old Enemy: Satan & The Combat Myth*, (Oxford: Princeton University Press: 1986).

—. *The Satanic Epic*, (Oxford: Princeton University Press, 2003).

Foster, R. J. *Yeats: The Arch-Poet 1915-1939*, (Oxford: Oxford University Press: 2003).

Foucault, Michel. *Discipline and Punishment: The Birth of the Prison*, trans. Alan Sheridan, (London: Routledge, 1977).

Frielānder, Saul. *Reflections on Nazism: An Essay on Kitsch and Death*, (New York: Harper and Row, 1984).

Gallagher, Brianne. Policing Paris: private publics and architectural media in Michael Haneke's *Caché. Journal for Cultural Research*, 12:1 (2008): 20-36.

Garcia, Ernesto, 2002. A Kantian theory of evil. *The Monist* 85 (2002): 194-209.

Goldhagen, Daniel. *Hitler's Willing Executioners: Ordinary Germans and the Holocaust*, (New York: Abacus, 1997).

Gordon, Robert S.C. *Pasolini: Forms of Subjectivity*, (Oxford: Oxford University Press, 1996).

Gramsci, Antonio. *Prison Notebooks: A Selection*, ed. Quintin Hoare and trans. Geoffrey Nowell-Smith, (New York: International Publishers, 1971).

Greene, Naomi. Fascism in recent Italian films. *Film Criticism* 6 (1) (1981): 31-42.

—. *Pier Paolo Pasolini: Cinema as Heresy*, (Princeton: Princeton University Press, 1990).

Greene, Richard and Peter Vernezze, eds. *The Sopranos and Philosophy*, (Chicago: Open Court Publishing, 2004).

Grossman, David and Gloria deGaetanno. *Stop Teaching Our Kids to Kill*, (New York: Random House, 1999).

Gunning, Tom. *The Films of Fritz Lang: Allegories of Vision and Modernity*, (London: BFI Publishing, 2000).

Hall, Allan. *Monster*, (London: Penguin, 2008).

Haneke, Michael. "*71 Fragments of a Chronology of Chance*: Notes to the Film (1994)" in *After Postmodernism: Austrian Film and Literature in Transition*, ed. Willy Reimar, 171-5, (Riverside, CA: Ariadne Press, 2000).

Harrison, Carol. *Christian Truth and Fractured Humanity*, (Oxford: Oxford University Press, 2000).

Heath, Stephen. Film and system, terms of analysis. *Screen* 16 (1-2) (1975): 1-77.

Heidegger, Martin. *Being and Time*, trans. Joan Stambaugh, (Albany: State University of New York Press, 1996).

Heston, Charlton. *In the Arena: An Autobiography*, (New York: Simon and Schuster, 1995).

Hick, John. *Evil and the God of Love*, (New York: Harper San Francisco 1977).

Highsmith, Patricia. *Ripley's Game*, (London: Chancellor Press, 1974).

Hoffheimer, Michael H. Artistic convention and natural law: didactic treatment of justice and authority in works of Fielding, Hawthorne, and Fritz Lang. *Temple Law Review* 63 (3) (1990).

Holmes, Ronald and James de Burger. *Serial Murder*, (California: Sage, 1988).

Humphries, Reynold. *Fritz Lang: Genre and Representation in his American Films*, (London: John Hopkins University, 2003).

Indiana, Gary. *Saló*, (London: BFI, 2000).

Irwin, Jones. Augustine and the impossibility of moral action. *Minerva - An Internet Journal of Philosophy* 6 (2002): 162-177.

Jancovich, Mark, ed. *Horror: The Film Reader*, (London: Routledge, 2002).

Jenkins, Henry, ed. *The Children's Culture Reader*, (New York: New York University Press, 1998).

Jenkins, Stephen, ed. *Fritz Lang: The Image and the Look*, (London: BFI Publishing, 1981).

Jonas, Hans. *The Gnostic Religion: The Message of the Alien God and the Beginnings of Christianity*, (Boston: Beacon Press, 1970).

Kaes, Anton. *M*, (London: BFI, 2000).

Kafka, Franz. *The Trial*, trans. Idris Parry, (Harmondsworth: Penguin. 2004).

Kant, Immanuel. *Critique of Practical Reason*, (New York: Macmillan, 1993).

—. *Groundwork for the Metaphysics of Morals*, trans. Mary Gregor, (Cambridge: Cambridge University Press, 1996).

—. *Religion Within the Limits of Reason Alone*, ed. and trans. Theodore Green and Hoyt H. Hudson, (New York: Harper & Row, 1960).

—. *The Essential Kant*, trans. Arnulf Zweig, (New York: New American Library, 1970).

Kearney, Richard. *Strangers, Gods, and Monsters: Interpreting Otherness*, (London: Routledge, 2003).

Kerrigan, John. *Revenge: Aeschylus to Armageddon*, (Oxford: Clarendon Press, 1996).

Kierkegaard, Søren. *Either/ Or: Fragments of a Life*, trans. Alistair Hannay, (London: Penguin, 2004).

Kisonak, Rick. "Elephant: A Review" in *Film Threat*. 2003.

Kolker, Robert. *The Altering Eye: Contemporary International Cinema*, (London: Oxford University Press, 1983).

Kristeva, Julia. *Black Sun: Depression and Melancholia*, trans. Leon S. Roudiez, (New York: Columbia University Press, 1989).

Lacan Jacques. *Television: A Challenge to the Psychoanalytic Establishment,* eds. Joan Copjec & trans. Dennis Holier, Rosalind Krauss and Annette Michelson, (New York: W.W. Norton, 1993).

—. Kant and Sade, trans. James B. Svenson Jnr. *October* 162 (1989): 55-75.

—. *Seminar IV: The Ethics of Psychoanalysis*, ed. & trans. Jacques-Alain Miller, (London: Routledge. 1993).

—. *The Seminar of Jacques Lacan Book VII: The Ethics of Psychoanalysis,* ed. Jacques-Alain Miller and trans. Denis Porter, (London: Routledge, 1992).

Laclau, Ernesto and Chantal Mouffe. *Hegemony and Socialist Strategy: Towards a Radical Democratic Politics*, (London: Verso, 1985).

Lacoue-Labarthe, Philipe and Jean-Luc Nancy. The Nazi myth. *Critical Inquiry* 16 (1990): 291-312.

Lambert, Malcolm. *Medieval Heresy: Popular Movements From the Gregorian Reform to the Reforma*, (Oxford: Blackwell Publishers, 1992).

—. *The Cathars*, (London: Blackwell Publishers, 1998).

Lara, María Pía, ed. *Rethinking Evil: Contemporary Perspectives*, (Berkeley: California University Press, 1999).

Larrimore, Mark. ed. *The Problem of Evil*, (London: Blackwell Publisher, 2000).

Laurance, Jeremy. "Born bad or made bad? The is reignited" in *The Independent*, 2010. July 24.

Leprohon, Pierre. *The Italian Cinema*, (London: Secker and Warburg, 1972).

Lever, Maurice. *Marquis de Sade*, trans. Arthur Goldhammer, (London: Flamingo, 1995).

Levi, Primo. *The Drowned and the Saved*, trans. Ramond Rosenthal, (London : Abacus books, 1988).

Levinas, Emmanuel. *Difficult Freedom: Essays on Judaism*, trans. Seán Hand, (London: The Athlone Press, 1990).

—. *Totality and Infinity: An Essay on Exteriority*, trans. Alphonso Lingis, (Pittsburgh: Duquense University Press, 2000).

Levinson, Jerrold, ed. *Aesthetics and Ethics: Essays and Intersection*, (Cambridge: Cambridge University Press, 1998).

Lewalski, Barbra K. 'Federico Fellini's Purgatorio,' in ed. Peter Bondanella, *Federico Fellini: Essays in Criticism*, New York: Oxford University Press, 1978).

Lewis, C.S, 1967. *A Preface to Paradise Lost*, London: Oxford University Press.

Lieberman, Joseph. 'On the issues': Senator Joseph Lieberman on Children and Families, www.issues2000.org/2004/Joseph_Lieberman_Families_=Children.htm. 2006.

Loughlin, Gerard. *Alien Sex: The Body and Desire in Cinema and Theology*, (London: Blackwell Publishing, 2004).

Lukes, H.N. Is the rectum *Das Ding?* Lacan, Bersini and the ethics of perversion. *Oxford Literary Review* 20 (1998): 103-142.

Lyotard, Jean-François and Jean-Loup Thébaud. *Just Gaming*, trans. Wlad Godzich, (Manchester: Manchester University Press, 1985).

Lyotard, Jean-François. *The Lyotard Reader*, ed. Andrew Benjamin, (Oxford: Blackwell, 1989).

MacCabe, Colin and Laura Mulvey. *Godard: Images, Sounds, Politics*, (London: Macmillan, 1980).

MacCabe, Colin. *Godard: A Portrait of the Artist at 70*, (London: Bloomsbury Publishing Plc., 2003).

—. *Performance*, (London: BFI Publishing, 1998).

Marcus, Milicent. *Italian Film in the Light of Neo-Realism*, (Princeton: Princeton University Press, 1986).

Marques, Gabriel Garcia. *Love in the Time of Cholera*, trans. Eidth Gorssman, (Penguin: London, 2003).

Marrone, Gaetonne. *The Gaze and the Labyrinth: The Cinema of Liliana Cavani*, (Princeton: Princeton University Press, 2000).

Marx, Karl. *Selected Writings*, ed. Lawrence H. Simon, (Indianapolis: Hackett Publishing Company, 1994).

Masterson, Whit. *Badge of Evil*, (London: Corgi Books, 1957).

Mathewes, Charles T. *Evil and the Augustinian Tradition*, (New York: Cambridge University Press, 2001).

May, Larry and Jerome Khon, eds. *Hannah Arendt: Twenty Years Later*, (London: MIT Press, 1997).

McCannell, Juliet Flower. *Figuring Lacan: Criticism and the Cultural Unconscious*, (Lincoln: University of Nebraska Press, 1986).

McMahon, Jeff. *The Ethics of Killing: Killing at the Margins of Life*, (Oxford: Oxford University Press, 2002).

Mellencamp, Patricia, ed. *Logics of Television: Essays in Cultural Criticism (Theories of the Contemporary)*, (London: BFI Publishing, 1990).

Mey, Kersten. *Art and Obscenity*, (London: I.B. Tauris, 2007).

Milton, John. *Selected Poems*, (Wordsworth: Cambridge, 1967).

—. *The Collected Poems of John Milton*, (Hertfordshire: Wordworth Editions, 1994).

—. *The Prose of John Milton*, ed. Max Patrick, (New York: DoubleDay Anchor, 1988).

Mizejewski, Linda. *Divine Decadence: Fascism, Female Spectacle, and the Making of Sally Bowles*, (Princeton: Princeton University Press, 1992).

Molloy, Séan. Escaping the politics of the irredeemable earth - anarchy and transcendence in the novels of Thomas Pynchon,' *Theory and Event*, Vol. 13.3 (2010).

Morrison, Blake. *As If*, (London: Granta Books, 1998).

Murphet, Juliet. Film noir and the racial unconscious. *Screen* 34 (1) (1998): 1-30.

Nadeau, Chantal. "Girls on a Wired Screen: Cavani's Cinema and Lesbian S/M" in *The Strange Carnalities of Feminism*, 211-230, eds. Elizabeth Grosz and Elspeth Probyn, (London: Routledge, 1995).

Naussbaum, Charles. Aesthetics and the problem of evil. *Metaphilosophy* 33.3 (2003): 251-282.

Neale, Stephen. *Genre*, (London: BFI Publishing, 1980).

Nietzsche, Frederic. *On the Genealogy of Morals: A Polemic*, trans. Douglas Smith, (Oxford: Oxford University Press, 1996).

—. *The Gay Science: With a Prelude in German Rhymes and an Appendix of Song*, ed. Bernard Williams trans. Adrienne Caro and Josephine Nauckhoff, (Cambridge: Cambridge University Press, 2001).

Nietzsche, Friedrich, *The Antichrist*, trans. Anthony M. Ludovici, (New York: Prometheus Books, 2000).

Nowell-Smith, Geoffrey. Minnelli and Melodrama. *Screen* 18:2 (1977): 113-119.

Nussbaum, Martha C. *Hiding from Humanity: Disgust, Shame and the Law*, (Oxford: Princeton University Press, 2004).

O'Hagan, Séan. "Lynne Ramsay: Just Talk to Me Straight" in *The Observer*, 2011, October 2.

O'Neil, Onera. *Constructions of Reason: Explorations of Kant's Practical Philosophy*, (Cambridge: Cambridge University Press, 1990).

Parkin, David, ed. *The Anthropology of Evil*, (Basil Blackwell: Oxford, 1985).

Pasolini, Pier Paolo. "Le ceneri di Gramsci (*Gramsci's Ashes*)" in *Pier Paolo Pasolini Poems*, trans. Norman MacAffee, (New York: Vintage, 1982).

—. *Heretical Empiricism*, trans. Ben Lawton and Kate L. Barnett, (Bloomington: Indiana University Press, 1972).

—. *Scritti Corsari*, (Milano: Garzanti, 1975).

Pease, Donald E. Borderline Justice/ States of Emergency: Orson Welles' *Touch of Evil*. *The New Centennial Review* 1 (2001): 75-105.

Peucker, Brigitte. Effects of the real: Michael Haneke's *Benny's Video* (1994). *KinoEye* 4 (2004).

Poe, Edgar Allan. "The Purloined Letter" in *Selected Tales*, (London: Penguin Group, 1994).

Price, Brian and John David Rhodes, eds. *On Michael Haneke*, (Detroit: Wayne University Press, 2010).

Quandt, James, ed. *(revised) Robert Bresson*, (Indiana: Indiana University Press, 2011).

Rabaté, Jean-Michel, ed. *The Cambridge Companion to Lacan*, (Cambridge: Cambridge University Press, 2003).

Rappaport, Mark. The autobiography of Pier Paolo Pasolini. *Film Quarterly* 56 (2002): 2-8.

Ravetto, Kriss. *The Unmaking of Fascist Aesthetics*, (Minnesotta: University of Minnesotta Press, 2001).

Reader, Keith. *Robert Bresson*, (Manchester: Manchester University Press, 2000).

Restivo, Angelo. *The Cinema of Economic Miracles: Visuality and Modernization in the Italian Art Film*, (London: Duke University Press, 2002).

Rhodes, John David. *Stupendous Miserable City: Pasolini's Rome*, (Minnesota: Minnesota University Press, 2007).

Rhodie, Sam. *The Passion of Pier Paolo Pasolini*, (London: BFI Publishing, 1995).

Ricoeur, Paul. *Evil: A Challenge to Philosophy and Theology*, trans. John Bowden, (New York: Continuum, 2007).

Ritzenhoff, Karen. Visual competence and reading the recorded past: the paradigm shift from analogue to digital video in Michael Haneke's *Caché. Visual Studies* 23: 2 (2008): 137-145.

Ronson, Jon. *The Psychopathic Test: A Journey Through the Madness Industry*, (London: Picador, 2011).

Roudinescou, Elisabeth. *Lacan & Co.: A History of Psychoanalysis in France 1925-85*, trans. Jeffrey Mehlman, (Chicago: Chicago University Press, 1990).

Rowlands, Mark. *The Philosopher at the End of the Universe: Philosophy Explained Through Science Fiction Films*, (London: Ebury, 2005).

Sartre, Jean Paul. *Being and Nothingness,* trans. Hazel E. Barnes, (England: Routledge, 1954).

Schmitt, Carl. *The Concept of the Political*, trans. Georges Schwabb, (London: University of Chicago Press. 1996).

Scott, A.O. "A Vicious Attack On Innocent People, On the Screen and In the Theatre" in *The New York Times*, 2008, March 14.

—. "Wholesome hamlet's horror sends a jolt to the system," in *The New York Times*, 2008, Dec. 30.

Sebold, Alice. *The Lovely Bones*, (London: Pan MacMillan, 2002).

Shoaf, R. A. *Milton: Poet of Duality*, (New Haven: Yale University Press, 1993).

Shriver, Lionel. *We Need To Talk About Kevin*, (New York: Perseus Books Group, 2003).

Silver, Alain and James Ursini, eds. *A Film Noir Reader*, (New York: Proscenium Publishers, 1996).

Silverman, Katja. *The Acoustic Mirror: The Female Voice in Psychoanalysis and Cinema*, (Bloomington: Indiana University Press, 1988).

Silverman, Max. The empire looks back. *Screen* 48 (2) (2007): 245-24.

Singer, Marcus G. The concept of evil. *Philosophy* 79 (2004): 185-214.

Sitney, P. Adams. *Vital Crises in Italian Cinema: Iconography, Stylistics, Politics*, (Austin: University of Texas Press. 1995).

Sitwell, Osbert. *The Scarlet Tree*, (London: Macmillan, 1946).

Skall, David. *A Cultural History of Horror*, (London: Plexus, 1993).

Smith, David (with Carol Anne Lee). *Witness: The Story of David Smith, Chief Prosecution Witness in the Moors Murders Case*, (Edinburgh: Mainstream Publishing Company, 2011).

Sontag, Susan. *Regarding the Pain of Others*, (New York: Penguin, 2003).

Speck, Oliver C. *Funny Frames: The Filmic Concepts of Michael Haneke*, (New York: Continuum, 2010).

Spicer, Andrew. *Film Noir*, (Harlow: Pearson Education, 2002).

Stack, Oswald. *Pasolini*, (Bloomington: Indiana University Press, 1969).

Steele, Carlos. Avicennca and Thomas Acquinas on evil. *Ancient and Medieval Philosophy Series* 28 (2001): 171-196.

Stoller, Robert. *Presentations of Gender*, (New York: Yale University Press, 1985).

Surya, Michel. *Georges Bataille: An Intellectual Biography*, trans. Krzystof Fijalowski and Michael Richardson, (London: Verso, 2002).

Tatar, Maria. *Lustmord: Sexual Murder in Weimar Germany*, (Princeton: Princeton University Press, 1995).

Thomson, David. *Rosebud: The Story of Orson Welles*, (New York: Abacus Books, 1996).

Trend, David. *The Myth of Media Violence: A Critical Introduction*, (London: Blackwell Publishers, 2007).

Turkle, Shirley. *Psychoanalytic Politics*, (Burnette Books: Andre Deutsch, 1979).

Vache, Dalle. *The Body in the Mirror: Shapes of History in Italian Cinema*, (Princeton: Princeton University Press. 1992).

Viano, Maurizio. *A Certain Realism: Making Use of Pasolini's Film Theory and Practice*, (New York: University of California Press, 1993).

Victoria, Brian. *Zen at War*, (London: Weatherhill Publishers, 1998).

Villa, Dana R. *Politics, Philosophy, Terror: Essays on the Thought of Hannah Arendt*, (West Sussex: Princeton University Press, 1999).

Vlasov, Eduard. Overcoming the threshold: Bahktin, Eisenstein and the cinema of German expressionism. *Canadian Review of Comparative Literature*, 23 (1996).

Waller, Marquirite. "Signifying the Holocaust: Liliana Cavani's *Portiere di notte,*" in eds. Laura Petropaolo and Ada Tagliaferri, *Feminisms in the Cinema*, (Bloomington: Indiana Press, 1995).

Weis, René. *The Yellow Cross: The Story of the Last Cathars 1290-1329*, (Harmondsworth: Penguin, 2000).

Wheatley, Catherine. *Michael Haneke's Cinema: The Ethic of the Image*, (Oxford: Berghahn Books, 2009).

Willett, Ralph. *Hard-Boiled Detective Fiction*, (Staffordshire: British Association for American Studies, 1992).

Williams, Bernard. *Morality: An Introduction to Ethics*, (London: Cambridge University Press, 1993).

Wills, Garry. *Saint Augustine*, (London: Weidenfeld & Nicholson, 1999).

Wilson, David, ed. *Cahiers du Cinéma Vol. 4: 1973-1978*, (London: Routledge, 2000).

Wilson, Emma. *Memory and Survival: The French Cinema of Krzysztof Kieślowski,* (Oxford: Legenda, 2000).

Wittgenstein, Ludwig. *Philosophical Investigations*, trans. G.E.M. Anscombe, (Oxford: Blackwell Publishing, 2009).

Wood, Robin. "Hidden in Plain Sight" in *Artforum*, 2006, Jan.

—. *Hollywood from Vietnam to Reagan*, (New York: Columbia University Press, 1986).

Žižek, Slavoj, ed. *Everything You Always Wanted to Know About Lacan (But Were Afraid to Ask Hitchcock)*, (London: Verso, 1992).

Žižek, Slavoj. *For They Know Not What They Do: Enjoyment as a Political Factor*, (London: Verso, 1993).

—. *In Defense of Lost Causes*, (London: Verso, 2008).

—. *On Belief*, (London: Routledge, 2001).

—. *Organs without Bodies: On Deleuze and Consequences*, (London: Routledge, 2004).

—. *Tarrying with the Negative: Kant, Hegel and the Critique of Ideology*, (Durham: Duke University Press, 1993).

—. *The Fright of Real Tears: Krzysztof Kieślowski between Theory and Post-Theory*, (London: BFI Publishing, 2001).

—. *The Plaque of Fantasies*, (London: Verso, 1997).

—. *The Puppet and the Dwarf: The Perverse Core of Christianity*, (Massachusetts: MIT Press, 2003).

—. *The Sublime Object of Ideology*, (London: Verso 1989).

—. *The Ticklish Subject: The Absent Centre of Political Ontology*, (London: Verso, 1999).

Zupančič, Alenka. *Ethics of the Real: Kant, Lacan*, (London: Verso, 2000).

—. *The Odd One In: On Comedy*, (London: Verso, 2008).

—. *The Shortest Shadow: Nietzsche's Philosophy of the Two,* (London: The MIT Press, 2003).

FILMOGRAPHY
(ENGLISH TITLES)

71 Fragments of a Chronology of Chance (dir. Michael Haneke, Austria, 1994)

8½ (dir. Federico Fellini, Italy-France, 1963)

Accatone (dir. Pier Paolo Pasolini, Italy, 1961)

Arabian Nights (dir. Pier Paolo Pasolini, Italy-France, 1974)

Arlington Road (dir. Mark Pellington, USA, 1999)

Assembly of Love (dir. Pier Paolo Pasolini, Italy, 1965)

Bad Lieutenant: Port of Call - New Orleans (dir. Werner Herzog, USA, 2009)

Benny's Video (dir. Michael Haneke, Austria-Switzerland, 1992)

Beyond Good and Evil (dir. Lilianna Cavani, Italy-France, 1977)

Bicycle Thieves (dir. Vittoria de Sica, Italy, 1948)

Blue (dir. Kryzysztof Kieślowski, France, 1993)

Bowling for Columbine (dir. Michael Moore, USA, 2002)

Canterbury Tales (dir. Pier Paolo Pasolini, France-Italy, 1971)

Child's Play 3 (dir. Tom Holland, USA, 1998)

Citizen Kane (dir. Orson Welles, USA, 1941)

City of God (dir. Fernando Meirelles, Brazil, 2003)

Decameron (dir. Pier Paolo Pasolini, West-Germany-France-Italy, 1970)

Deliver Us From Evil (dir. Amy Berg, USA, 2007)

Dirty Harry (dir. Don Siegel, USA, 1971)

Double Indemnity (dir. Billy Wilder, USA, 1943)

Elephant (dir. Alan Clarke, UK, 1989)

Elephant (dir. Gus Van Sant, USA, 2003)

Francis of Assisi (dir. Liliana Cavani, Italy, 1960)

Funny Games (dir. Michael Haneke, Austria/USA, 1997/2007)

Gerry (dir. Gus Vant Sant, USA, 2002)

Hawks and Sparrows (dir. Pier Paolo Pasolini, Italy, 1966)

Hidden (dir. Michael Haneke, France, 2007)

Kes (dir. Ken Loach, UK, 1973)

Kiss Me Deadly (dir. Robert Aldrich, USA, 1955)

Last Days (dir. Gus Van Sant, USA, 2005)

Lord of the Rings: The Fellowship of the Ring (dir. Peter Jackson, New Zealand-UK-USA, 2001)

Lost Highway (dir. David Lynch, USA, 1996)

Love (dir. Michael Haneke, France-Austria-Germany, 2012)

M (dir. Fritz Lang, Germany, 1931)

Mamma Roma (dir. Pier Paolo Pasolini, Italy, 1962)

Minority Report (dir. Steven Spielberg, USA, 2002)

Morvern Callar (dir. Lynne Ramsay, UK, 2002)

No Country for Old Men (dir. Coen Bros, USA, 2007)

Obsession (dir. Luchino Visconti, Italy, 1943)

Pickpocket (dir. Robert Bresson, 1959)

Pigsty (dir. Pier Paolo Pasolini, Italy-France, 1969)

Pyscho (dir. Alfred Hitchcok, 1960)

Ratcatcher (dir. Lynne Ramsay, UK, 1999).

Ripley's Game (dir. Liliana Cavani, Italy-UK-US, 2002)

Roma (dir. Federico Fellini, Italy-France, 1972)

Rome, Open City (dir. Roberto Rossellini, Italy, 1945)

Saló, or The 120 Days of Sodom (dir. Pier Paolo Pasolini, Italy, 1975)

Satan's Tango (dir. Béla Tarr, Hungary, 1995)

Schindler's List (dir. Steven Spielberg, USA, 1993)

Silence of the Lambs (dir. Jonathan Demme, USA, 1991)

Stalker (dir. Andrei Tarkovsky, USSR, 1979)

The Andalusian Dog (dir. Luis Buñuel and Salvidor Dali, Spain, 1928).

The Berlin Affair (dir. Liliana Cavani, Italy-West Germany, 1985)

The Cannibals (dir. Liliana Cavani Italy, 1970)

The Devil, Probably (dir. Robert Bresson, France, 1977)

The Flowers of St. Francis (dir. Robert Rossellini, Italy, 1950)

The Gospel according to St. Matthew (dir. Pier Paolo Pasolini, Italy-France, 1964)

The Lady of Shanghai (dir. Orson Welles, USA, 1947)

The Lives of Others (dir. Florian Henkel von Donnersmarck, Germany, 2007)

The Night Porter (dir. Liliana Cavani, Italy-USA, 1973)

The Omen (dir. Richard Donner, USA, 1976)

The Piano Teacher (dir. Michael Haneke, France-Austria, 2001)

The Seventh Continent (dir. Michael Haneke, Austria, 1989)

The Silence of the Lambs (dir. Jonathan Demme, USA, 1991)

The Son (dir. Jean-Pierre Dardenne, Belgium-France, 2002)

The Sweet Life (dir. Federico Fellini, Italy-France, 1960)

The Usual Suspects (dir. Bryan Singer, 1995)

The White Ribbon (dir. Michael Haneke, France-Germany, 2009)

The Woman in the Window (dir. Fritz Lang, USA, 1945)
Theorem (dir. Pier Paolo Pasolini, Italy, 1968)
Touch of Evil (dir. Orson Welles, USA, 1958)
We Need To Talk About Kevin (dir. Lynne Ramsay, UK-USA, 2011)
Weekend (dir. Jean-Luc Godard, Italy-France, 1967)
Whoever Says the Truth Shall Die (dir. Philo Bregstein, Netherlands, 1981)

011215392 (MH)